Thinking Skills Instruction:
Concepts and Techniques

Thinking Skills Instruction:
Concepts and Techniques

Marcia Heiman
Joshua Slomianko
Editors

nea PROFESSIONAL LIBRARY
National Education Association
Washington, D.C.

Note

The opinions expressed in this publication should not be construed as representing the policy or position of the National Education Association. Materials published as part of the Building Students' Thinking Skills series are intended to be
discussion documents for teachers who are concerned with specialized interests
of the profession.

Library of Congress Cataloging-in-Publication Data

Thinking skills instruction.
    (Building students' thinking skills)
    1. Thought and thinking.   2. Reasoning.   3. Thought
and thinking—Study and teaching.   I. Heiman, Marcia.
II. Slomianko, Joshua.   III. Series.
LB1590.3.T47   1987   370.15'24   86–3322
ISBN 0–8106–0229–6
ISBN 0–8106–0201–6 (pbk.)

CONTENTS

The Editors

Marcia Heiman is Director, Learning to Learn Program, Boston College, Chestnut Hill, Massachusetts.

Joshua Slomianko is Co-Director, Learning Skills Consultants, Cambridge Massachusetts.

INTRODUCTION

by Marcia Heiman and Joshua Slomianko, Editors

Harold Anderson begins this anthology with an inventive and whimsical tale of what happens when thinking instruction is introduced into a school—how do teachers react when thinking is suddenly part of the explicit curriculum? What problems arise, and how are they resolved?

Next, chapters by Arthur L. Costa, James J. McTighe, and Barbara Z. Presseisen explore some of the issues raised by integrating thinking skills into the classroom. All three feel that thinking skills instruction has arrived at a time when it is badly needed—when facts are instantly obsolescent, and we need to teach children the *how*, not just the *what*, of things. Presseisen suggests that the thinking skills movement makes new demands on teachers, and wonders if teachers and administrators will have the "courage to respond positively."

Robert H. Ennis, David N. Perkins, and Alma M. Swartz discuss different aspects of the transfer question. Ennis maintains that there are thinking skills that transfer across disciplines, although much research is needed to understand and facilitate this process; Perkins argues that thinking skills are best taught within specific domains, since transfer is problematic; Swartz suggests that good critical thinking *attitudes* are necessary preconditions for the transfer of thinking skills.

Then, a cross-section of chapters presents a variety of approaches to integrating thinking skills into content classrooms. Diane F. Halpern defines some of the conditions and practices needed for teaching thinking skills in content areas. Barry K. Beyer provides two models for introducing thinking skills in the classroom, both of which emphasize modeling and student awareness of their own thinking processes. Marcia Heiman describes a program that has been effective in improving students' academic performance in courses across the curriculum. Joel Rudinow and Richard Paul discuss the importance of reflective self-criticism in developing mature critical thinking in students, and Joseph S. Karmos and Ann H. Karmos suggest ways to help students become more active problem solvers. Robert J. Swartz illustrates how curricular material can be reshaped to allow for classroom teaching of critical thinking skills. Finally, Lynn Langer Meeks discusses using peer response groups to improve elementary school students' writing.

Several selections illustrate classroom applications of Bloom's taxonomy of thinking skills. Norma J. Hoelzel uses the taxonomy to develop students' question-generating skills; Natalee C. Yeager uses it to teach literature; Patsy A. Jaynes uses it to teach basic skills in a modified English as a Second Language classroom; and Ronald E. Charlton shows how the taxonomy can be combined with Beyer's teaching framework to improve the analytic skills of students in a variety of areas.

Arthur Whimbey's work is examined next. Whimbey discusses the nature of thinking and how students can improve their thinking with structured practice, especially by working together in pairs. Kendall Didsbury discusses using Whimbey's work to improve students' writing; and Jack Lochhead applies paired-problem-solving methods in science instruction. Then, William A. Sadler, Jr., who shares Whimbey's view of intelligence as a series of identifiable behaviors, describes a holistic approach to improving thinking skills.

This is followed by chapters from theorists and practitioners who believe that thinking skills are best taught outside subject-matter areas. Reuven Feuerstein and colleagues argue that effective intervention requires content-free exercises incorporated into a structured mediated learning experience. Ernestine W. Roberts suggests that vocabulary development—much of which transcends specific academic disciplines—can be used to facilitate students' higher-order thinking. Maintaining that conventional thinking skills programs do not teach the skills needed in later life, Robert J. Sternberg suggests a content-free thinking skills program that has no ''right'' answers, and that improves students' real-life decision-making skills. Edward de Bono shares Sternberg's criticism of most thinking skills programs. His CoRT system, also content-free, concentrates on improving divergent and creative thinking. Like de Bono and Sternberg, Ronald Lee Rubin teaches thinking skills that foster divergent thinking and promote improved decision making. Unlike others in this group, however, Rubin incorporates such instruction into content-area teaching.

The last group of chapters deals with the application of thinking skills in a variety of content areas. Douglas E. Reahm shows how thinking skills can be incorporated into a music rehearsal class, while Nancy A. Watts illustrates their use in a home economics class. Maria Tymoczko, Paula K. Flemming, and Ronald Levitsky suggest ways to integrate thinking skills instruction into the study of literature, composition, and history, respectively. John M. Feeser provides an entire instructional unit that incorporates thinking skills into the study of American Indian history. And Delores Gallo provides a unit on teaching the metric system that illustrates how both critical and creative thinking can be incorporated into subject-matter instruction. The last chapter, by Erling Skorpen, illustrates the use of thinking skills in philosophy. Using one of Socrates' dialogues as his text, Skorpen describes the process of instruction in analytical reasoning.

ENCOUNTER WITH THINKING

by Harold S. Anderson

Harold S. Anderson's story of the arrival of thinking skills instruction in a mythical (but typical) school is amusing and instructive. We follow his main character through reluctantly attended Task Force meetings on the new thinking skills curriculum (where he plans to sabotage the idea before it takes hold), watch him wade through stacks of material on thinking skills, and attend a much-awaited PTA meeting with him (which he anticipates as the final blow to the new program). Slowly, we see Anderson's character become involved in the idea of teaching students to think—against his better judgment, he finds himself and his students increasingly excited by the possibilities of the new program.

The author is Professor of Education and Head, Division of Human Services, College of Great Falls, Montana.

To tell the truth, I didn't think much of the idea when Ames announced it. Every principal in the system sells the party line. But Ames outdoes the others, bucking for favor with central administration.

We teach a fairly standard curriculum here and our kids learn to think in all the different subjects. Most of our pupils score average or better on national tests. Of course, the tests mostly measure recall of factual knowledge and basic skills, perhaps a few principles.

Principal Ames didn't sell our teachers easily on the new thinking emphasis. With all the paper shuffling and record keeping they have to do now, they don't get enough time to teach all the basics. Most of us carry home an armload of papers to grade and lesson plans to complete.

I wasn't convinced that "thinking at higher levels," as he called it, was really fair. Kids feel responsible for knowing the facts in their subjects, such as social studies and science, and they can make sense of mastering the rules in arithmetic, and spelling, and punctuation. But these other thinking things seem like mental gymnastics, almost magic, inside secrets that are not quite fair for marking and grading.

My hand went up to object at just the wrong time (I know better than to volunteer for more thankless committee work) and I got put on the Teaching Thinking Task Force. I cringed at the prospect of hours and hours wasted in endless arguing. By the time the staff meeting finished, I had jotted down a paragraph, the gist of my memo to decline membership.

During the week before the first meeting, two other members mentioned how pleased they were that I was on the Task Force. They would rely on me to bring the group to early closure so we wouldn't waste our time for the whole school year. I forgot to finish my memo. We met at the worst time, on Friday afternoon.

Shelley Weeks had no agenda for the meeting. The discussion drifted in all directions. If Ames hadn't showed up, I would have offered a motion to adjourn. To get off dead center, I suggested we all agree to do some research, individually, before our next meeting. Each teacher should try to bring in one or two journal articles or other items about thinking. Principal Ames offered to spring for duplication of copies for everyone. We should all think about how much it will cost, however, if we all pick long articles.

Purely wishful thinking—that no would find any articles and with nothing to work on, we could dismiss and go home. But I wasn't prepared for the volume of stuff they found. Twice in that last week the copier in the principal's office went down from overuse and on Thursday we ran out of paper.

As I looked at the piles of material they had brought, I hoped no one else remembered who had suggested this. We could all hope that everyone had found the same articles. They hadn't.

Each member explained briefly each item and handed copies around. They must have all looked in different places; only two people had found two things alike. I groaned silently. Enough here to discuss every week until Christmas.

I left the meeting carrying a lot more than I had brought in. But not before I had exacted a promise from Shelley to postpone any more meetings for at least three weeks to give us time to look through all this stuff.

I couldn't believe the excitement at the next meeting. Normally sensible, stable, sober teachers grew wide-eyed with exhuberance for teaching their kids to think in some new wild way. Flory, who teaches a fourth grade down the hall from me, started it. She said, "I'd like to try that comprehension exercise, reversing the hands on the clock. My old wall clock has hands." Can you imagine Elsie sitting beside her with sad eyes because her newer model flashed lighted digits?

Before long, Elsie jumped in with her own project for science class. She would challenge her kids to compare two things that were alike in some way, such as "rock and ice" or "bicycle and boat" to expand their comprehension.

With all the digressions and disruptions holding up the discussion, it took two more meetings to finish all the articles. Before the third meeting was over, someone suggested each of us find a good book on thinking and review it for discussion.

Well, you guessed it. At the next meeting, everyone named a book, author and title, to be reviewed. Most were recent editions but some were old, from the 20s and 30s. They ranged from huge tomes to modest paperbacks. I volunteered to order one recently announced by NEA, *Critical Thinking Skills* by Marcia Heiman and Joshua Slomianko. I didn't mention that I had picked it for size, under 50 pages. It turned out to have a lot packed into a small space.

Enthusiasm for teaching of thinking spread from task force members to other teachers. What could I do?

It came to me one morning driving to school. The parents should be informed, before we take this any further. As concerned as our conservative parents are for mastering the basics, they'll put the kibosh on this idea before it slides the whole school curriculum off into a swamp. When I moved the suggestion, all members of the task force, innocent, and distracted by their enthusiasm, voted for it. Ames, visiting again that meeting, said he would arrange it with the PTA president.

Just wait until the parents hear that we're going to grade their kids on how well they can build plastic straw bridges and how quickly they can get the fox and the goose and the bucket of corn across the river. They'll have such a collective fit that Ames will have to scratch the whole project.

Not only were teachers frittering away their own teaching time, but they began to intrude on my time. Fred needed help hauling eight quarts of water back from the barrel, given two buckets that held seven quarts and five quarts. He couldn't just admit in front of his kids that he was stuck by the puzzle. Wilma couldn't figure out how to move the coins on her balance to detect the counterfeit coin. I burned a few cords of mental stove wood on that one, too, before I worked out the best sequence for her.

I got to thinking about teachers' thinking. Where do teachers learn to think? Certainly not in their study of college subjects. Successful college study calls for mastery of factual knowledge and faithful recall on demand. Neither in their general studies, nor in their major and minor, nor in the professional sequence do they practice thinking, beyond perhaps knowledge and comprehension levels. Not in selection, or training, or certification is there any assurance that teachers can think in the ways of Bloom's taxonomy of the cognitive domain details.

Ames reported to the Task Force that the agenda was jammed and the discussion of thinking at the PTA (which would expose the whole scheme to parents) had been postponed to a future meeting. I firmed my resolve to risk the wrath of my colleagues. But I lost the opportunity to throw their own deficiencies in thinking ability at them when we tangled with the term critical thinking. Everyone wanted to define it differently. And each teacher had some source to cite in defense of his/her definition. Not limited to criticism, certainly. It covered analysis and synthesis, too. And evaluation. And problem solving. Even creating. A marvelously flexible, all-purpose term, apparently. We ran out of time without ever getting close to an agreed definition.

With Thinking on the agenda of the PTA meeting three weeks away, Shelley asked the Task Force to convene again on Friday afternoon, the 13th. I'm not superstitious but things went badly from the beginning. I wanted to present the picture upfront and honest. We had looked at the possibility of teaching thinking and found it not feasible. I even volunteered to make the presentation for the Task Force. Ames, ever present, pointed out that Shelley should make the presentation as is customary and proper for a chairperson.

Our school is not widely known for PTA attendance. Typically, more seats remain empty than are filled. Having to carry in folding chairs for the overflow crowd furnished some hope. If, among a lot of irate folks, there are just a few bold souls to speak their minds, they might set this thinking thing to rest.

Task Force members sat together in the front row. As Shelley introduced us, we had to stand up and turn around. I thought I would see more serious, frowning faces in that whole audience. Still, they may just be expressing friendliness to their children's hard-working teachers.

Shelley recounted the deliberations of the Task Force, maintaining a neutral stance with care. She could have stopped short of the possibility for practicing thinking and planning to proceed with it next year but she threw that in, too.

When questions and comments were invited, I couldn't believe my ears. A young woman claimed that her two children had shown more enthusiasm for school than ever before. An older man explained that he lives with his son and daughter-in-law and his grandson. He enjoyed coping with the thinking challenges the boy brought home from school. He had gained not only more admiration for his grandson but also new zest for life. Another mother of two reported that their dinner table conversation sparkled when her children shared thinking experiences. The comments continued, all warmly colored by approval.

Shelley Weeks, anticipating a snag somewhere ahead, raised the issue of grading students on their thinking abilities. The responses from parents and patrons surprised me. It's as fair to grade on all kinds of thinking as on just recall. Better to grade on students' use of information than on the size of their storage; encyclopedias contain facts for the thumbing.

As we partook of cookies and caffeine following the meeting, I avoided clusters with teachers. I joined my friend, Tom, who was talking with two women. He's a single parent of a girl in my class. He had found some neat thinking challenges in several of his magazines. He'd be willing to send me photocopies if I wanted to use them. When I asked which magazines, he grinned and looked at the wall and said he couldn't remember. Another parent, Mavis Summers, offered me a booklet of thinking exercises produced by Reader's Digest. I thanked them, trying to make my expression of appreciation sound genuine.

Other friends and parents have been sending me thinking things, too. In the two months since the PTA meeting, the faculty has been working every Friday afternoon. We let the kids go a little early for extra time. We have a consultant coming in to furnish advice. But most of the work is done by our teachers. They take turns presenting thinking tasks that fit the different categories in Bloom's taxonomy. I don't let on to the other teachers, but I get a kick out of some of the puzzles and games. I can sort out the solution to a lot of them, in fact, faster than most of the others.

Two weeks from Friday will be my turn. Actually I get a short section of the previous meeting to get them started. I'm going to challenge them to build a better candy bar. The category is creative thinking, but they'll get involved in other kinds of thinking, too. The name and form and advertising material will demand creativity, of course. But choosing the ingredients will require judgment (they'll pick stuff they like to chew on) as well as analysis, in discerning the cost, and synthesis in deciding the price per unit.

I invented a sample for them, called the Partitioned Pinnacle Piñata (Three-P, for short). You fill a sugar cone with marshmallow creme one dollop at a time, push smoked almonds into the creme, and then seal off that section with melted chocolate. When you've filled three compartments like that, the cone is full and you coat the outside all over with chocolate and stand it on its wide end. Some folks find they suffer a strange inhibition biting into the point, but almost everyone with a sweet-tooth for candy enjoys the Three-P. I'll bet my students will love it. Which reminds me, I'll have to check with all the parents to see if their kids can eat sweets, but I can do that next fall.

THINKING SKILLS:
NEITHER AN ADD-ON NOR A QUICK FIX

By Arthur L. Costa

Arthur L. Costa discusses the emergence of thinking skills instruction in the classroom. He notes that many educators have come to view thinking skills as perhaps the most basic of the basic skills—they are skills that facilitate the acquisition of all other learning. Schools have moved away from the concept of intelligence as fixed and invariant; instead, they focus on thinking skills that range across the curriculum and into the non-academic world—encompassing "what human beings do when they behave intelligently." Thinking skills instruction is not viewed as an add-on, but rather as an integral part of all learning—in the physics laboratory as well as in driver training. Further, there is a recognition that students need time to acquire these new skills—both learner and the curriculum must be informed by "reflective, rational, and reasoned decision making."

The author is Professor of Education, California State University, Sacramento.

The educational reform movement of the 80's is stressing the development of students' thinking abilities in preparing them for the information age of the future. In the tradition of past reform movements, many educators were quick to jump on bandwagons making politically expedient and financially parsimonious decisions. Recent experiences with many school districts' efforts to install THINKING as a goal of education, however, have turned my head around.

Happily, what is being witnessed is a dedication to incorporate the EDUCATION OF THE INTELLECT neither as an add-on nor a quick fix. Rather, cognitive curriculum is serving as the basis for reconsideration of our theoretical foundations, a realistic view of what is basic for all learners, and a thoughtful dedication to long-range planning and development. What follows are some joyful observations of these new directions and an invitation to compare them with your own progress.

WHAT'S BASIC

Recent research, while not yet sufficient to confirm, tends to indicate that when thinking skills become an integral part of the curriculum and instructional practice, test scores in academic areas increase (Whimbey, 1985). It seems that the ability to perform certain cognitive processes is basic to success in school subjects. Hierarchical thinking, for example, when taught prior to or along with the skill of outlining produces better results than if taught without that cognitive prerequisite. When reading is taught as a strategy of thinking, students seem to increase their comprehension (Andre, 1979). When teachers take the time to teach comparative behavior, for example, students are better able to contrast the differing points of view of the North and the South during the Civil War using a consistent set of attributes (Beyer, 1985).

As a result, many educators are forming a new understanding of what is a basic skill. We are realizing that there is a prerequisite to the ''basics''—the ability to think.

THINKING IS FOR ALL STUDENTS

For many years we thought that thinking skills programs were intended to challenge the intellectually gifted. Indeed, some thought that any child whose I.Q. fell below a certain static score was forever doomed to remedial or compensatory drill and practice.

Gaining wide acceptance, four fundamental and refreshing concepts underly modern cognitive curriculum and instructional practices. They are the Theory of Cognitive Modifiability (Feuerstein, 1980), the Theory of Multiple Intelligences (Gardner, 1983), the faith that Intelligence Can Be Taught (Whimbey, 1985), and Sternberg's thesis that traditional I.Q. scores have very little to do with success in dealing with the problems encountered in daily life (Hammer, 1985; McKean, 1985).

These theoretical concepts equip us with the realization that ALL human beings are both retarded in certain problem solving skills and gifted in others (Link, as quoted in Makler, 1980). They provide us the faith that ALL human beings can continue to develop their intelligent behavior throughout a lifetime. Indeed, much research with hydrocephalic, Down's Syndrome, senile, and brain-damaged persons demonstrates that over time and with proper intervention, they can continue to make amazing growth in problem solving abilities. Until recently, we would have given them up as hopeless.

Furthermore, and perhaps most reassuring, we are demonstrating that increasing the effectiveness of instruction produces a corresponding increase in learning. Teachers CAN grow intelligence.

LANGUAGE AND THOUGHT IN LOCO PARENTIS

We are increasingly aware of the close connection and interaction between language and thought processes. Vygotsky and Piaget taught us this long ago. Perhaps we never realized it so fully, however, until it was made apparent through recent sociological upheavals.

17

We know that most cognitive structures are built in the child's mind within the first few years of life—long before they come to school—and that these schema are the result of (along with other nutritional, genetic, and environmental factors) interactions with significant adults in the child's environment.

With the transition of the traditional family in our culture, with an increasing number of "latchkey kids," with an increasing number of children giving birth to children, and with a dramatic increase in passive television watching, there has been a corresponding decrease in the amount of verbal interaction between parents and children in the home. Indeed, some students come to school parentally deprived.

Correlations have been found between the complexity of language used in the home, the mental development of the child, and the family's affluence or educational level. Sternberg and Caruso (1985) report increasing complexity of language and questioning tendencies in families at higher socioeconomic levels.

Realizing that thinking is basic, and that children's early language (and therefore cognitive) development may be lacking, we are witnessing a new direction for classroom instruction: INCREASING VERBAL IN-TERACTION. Teaching and learning are invigorated with increased opportunities for dialogue: developing listening skills, cooperative learning, pair problem solving, thought-provoking inquiry discussions, dialogical reasoning, collaborative planning, and brainstorming. Teachers are finding renewed power as they stimulate students' thought processes by using challenging questions and probing. They search for increases in diversity and creativity of students' responses as they provide a safe, nonjudgmental classroom environment in which students can risk verbalizing innovative ideas (Costa, 1985).

EXPANDING DEFINITIONS: FROM THINKING SKILLS TO INTELLIGENT BEHAVIOR

As schools begin the process of infusing "thinking skills" into their curriculum and instructional practices, they often start with the task of defining what it means—just what are thinking skills? This search seems to begin with a rather narrow list of cognitive skills—classifying, inferring, categorizing, hypothesizing, etc. Soon, however, some perplexing questions arise: How are these skills applied in a wide variety of subject areas and problem-solving situations? How are they transferred from situations in which they were learned to life situations outside the school? Should creativity, social skills, and ethical/moral reasoning be included in the definition? Resolving these concerns seems to cause an expansion of the concept of thinking from narrow definitions and lists of discrete

18

skills to a more generalized, all-encompassing set of descriptors of what human beings do when they behave intelligently (Glatthorn and Baron, 1985).

From research on what "good thinkers" do when they solve problems, the definition of thinking skills is being enlarged to include such generic behaviors as persistence, flexibility, striving for precision and accuracy, reducing impulsivity, considering others' points of view, supporting conclusions with evidence, risk taking, metacognition, and empathy.

PERVASIVE—NOT AN ADD-ON

Refocusing on this larger picture seems to encourage the acceptance and applicability of teaching thinking to a wider range of teachers' interests, subject matter, grade levels, and learning activities.

All teachers can agree that such cognitive skills as following directions, striving for precision, checking for accuracy, perseverance, listening to others' points of view, and creativity are basic to their discipline. ORGANIZATIONAL SKILLS are as basic to the auto shop as they are to the physics laboratory. PLANNING AHEAD is as much a requirement in the home economics curriculum as it is in written composition. BEING ALERT TO CUES is a survival skill applicable in driver training and in preparation for marriage and family life.

As a result of this wider acceptance, thinking skills are NOT being viewed as mere additions to an already overcrowded, time-squeezed, cemeterial compendium of scopes and sequences. Rather, teachers are finding comfort, agreement, and rededication in some common goals—that process is as important as product; that thoughtful and reflective teaching (rather than coverage) is acceptable once again; and that students' PRODUCTION of knowledge is as important as their REPRODUCTION of knowledge.

GIVE IT TIME

Unlike many other educational innovations and experiments, educational planners are viewing the infusion of thinking skills as a three- to five-year process. They are realizing that such a change cannot be a quick fix. Rather, it requires altering instructional strategies, communicating with community and parents, reevaluating class schedules, reorganizing curriculum materials and evaluation techniques, and rededicating the basic value system and norms of entire faculties.

They are realizing that the process of change must be consistent with the product of that change. If teachers are expected to teach reflectiveness, rationality, and reason to students, then the processes of curriculum

19

development and educational improvement must also involve reflective, rational, and reasoned decision making (Bellanca, 1985).

Taking precious classroom time to teach thinking is gaining acceptance. We've known that the amount of time on task affects student learning. This relationship is as true for academic achievement as it is for acquiring thinking skills. When thinking becomes a goal of instruction, teachers and administrators place greater value on allocating classroom time for learning activities intended to stimulate, practice, and discuss cognitive processes.

SCHOOLS AS INTELLECTUALLY STIMULATING PLACES

Perhaps it is a happy combination of applying school effectiveness research, improving the professionalism of education, and the emphasis on cognitive education. John Goodlad's (1983) generalized description of schools in our country as being intellectually depressing places is giving way to the stimulation of teachers' intellectual processes. It is hypothesized that teachers will not teach for thinking unless they are in an intellectually stimulating environment themselves.

As a result, teachers are feeling a great sense of efficacy—gaining more control of and becoming involved in those school and district level decisions that affect them most. This trend is in sharp contrast to the recent view of the teacher's role as being accountable for implementing decisions being mandated from "above."

Teachers' thinking, decision making, and problem solving are being enhanced because they are viewing the act of teaching as a creative, experimental, problem-solving, decision-making process rather than a recipe to follow. (Indeed, teaching by the number is equally as creative as painting by the number.) Renewed interest is being exhibited in developing the teacher's repertoire of teaching strategies (Joyce, 1985) rather than in training a narrow range of instructional behaviors. Teachers are jointly planning lessons, teaching strategies, and curriculum, and then are opening their classroom doors and inviting their colleagues and supervisors to observe their interaction, to gain feedback about the thinking skills students display, and to search for ways of enhancing cognition.

It is with renewed excitement, therefore, that participation in the educational profession is intellectually growth-producing for ALL its constituents (Sprinthall and Theis-Sprinthall, 1983).

EVALUATION—A PARADIGM SHIFT

Usually when we think of gathering evidence of pupil achievement, we think of tests—norm referenced, paper and pencil, multiple choice.

Several states (California, Vermont, Pennsylvania, New Jersey, and Connecticut) are revising test items to include critical thinking in their assessment programs (Kneedler, 1985; Baron and Kallick, 1985).

With the need to assess growth in thinking skills, we are finding, however, that some of our traditional assessment techniques are inadequate. One reason is that performance on a test is overt; but thinking is a covert process and thus not directly observable and measurable in our traditional behavioristic ways (Winocur, 1985).

Another reason is that tests usually seek to determine how many answers a student knows. Rather, we are witnessing a refocus of assessment practices on how the student behaves when the answer is NOT known—how they behave in everyday, problem-solving situations. Thus, the focus on learning OF objectives is being replaced by learning FROM objectives (Andre, 1979).

We are finding renewed interest in longitudinal growth studies—child study teams, collecting anecdotal records and portfolios of students' work which may reflect cognitive development over time. Teachers are becoming alert to the clues, found in everyday classroom problem solving, which indicate growth in intelligent behaviors (Baron and Kallick, 1985).

NOT JUST EDUCATORS—PARENTS AND INDUSTRY, TOO

Free enterprise, entrepreneurship, innovation, problem solving, creativity—industrial leaders are telling educators about their needs for the Twenty-first Century. The information age is well upon us. The work force of the future needs skills in collaborative problem solving, being alert to problems as they arise, handling massive amounts of information, and finding innovative ways to deliver a product more quickly, efficiently, and economically (Education Commission of the States, 1982).

By some estimates it is predicted that workers of the future will be changing jobs five to six times during their careers. Flexibility, continuing to learn how to learn, and dealing with ambiguity and change seem to be the paramount survival skills of the future.

Because of this need, industry is realizing education as the lifeblood of their future. New alliances and partnerships are being formed among schools, communities, and businesses in an effort to learn from each other about the need for and development of intelligent and creative behavior (Dageforde, 1985).

MODELING

With the understanding that imitation is the most basic form of learning, teachers, parents, and administrators are realizing the importance of their display of desirable intelligent behaviors in the presence of children. Thus, in the day-to-day events and when problems arise in schools, and classrooms, and homes, students must see adults employing the same types of behaviors that the new curriculum demands.

Without this consistency, there is likely to be a credibility gap. As Emerson is often quoted, "What you do speaks so loudly they can't hear what you say."

From the cumulative effects of these efforts we are finding that all the members of the educational enterprise—teachers, administrators, trustees, parents, and students—are profiting. All are becoming more rational, thoughtful, and creative in the process. Indeed, thinking about thinking is producing more thinking.

REFERENCES

Andre, T. "Does Answering Higher-Level Questions While Reading Facilitate Productive Learning?" *Review of Educational Research* 49, no. 2 (Spring 1979): 280–318.

Baron, J., and Kallick, B. "What Are We Looking For and How Can We Find It?" In *Developing Minds: A Resource Book for Teaching Thinking*, edited by A. Costa. Alexandria, Va.: Association for Supervision and Curriculum Development, 1985.

Bellanca, J. "A Call for Staff Development." In *Developing Minds: A Resource Book for Teaching Thinking*, edited by A. Costa. Alexandria, Va.: Association for Supervision and Curriculum Development, 1985.

Beyer, B. "Critical Thinking: What Is It?" *Social Education* 40 (April 1985): 271–76.

Costa, A. "Teacher Behaviors That Enhance Thinking." In *Developing Minds: A Resource Book for Teaching Thinking*, edited by A. Costa. Alexandria, Va.: Association for Supervision and Curriculum Development, 1985.

Dageforde, L. "Partnerships in Industry and Education." Presentation at the Project IMPACT Leadership Training, Orange County Superintendent of Schools Office, Costa Mesa, California, August 27, 1985.

Education Commission of the States. Denver, 1982.

Ennis, R. "Critical Thinking: A Definition." In *Developing Minds: A Resource Book for Teaching Thinking*, edited by A. Costa. Alexandria, Va.: Association for Supervision and Curriculum Development, 1985.

Feuerstein, R. *Instrumental Enrichment.* Baltimore: University Park Press, 1980.

Gardner, H. *Frames of Mind: The Theory of Multiple Intelligences.* New York: Basic Books, 1983.

Glatthorn, A., and Baron, J. "The Good Thinker. In *Developing Minds: A Resource Book for Teaching Thinking*, edited by A. Costa. Alexandria, Va.: Association for Supervision and Curriculum Development, 1985.

Goodlad, J. *A Place Called School: Prospects for the Future.* New York: McGraw-Hill, 1983.

Hammer, S. "Stalking Intelligence." *Science Digest* 93 (June 6, 1985): 30–38.

Joyce, B. "Models for Teaching Thinking." *Educational Leadership* 42, no. 8 (May 1985): 4–9.

Kneedler, P. "California Assesses Critical Thinking." In *Developing Minds: A Resource Book for Teaching Thinking*, edited by A. Costa. Alexandria, Va.: Association for Supervision and Curriculum Development, 1985.

Makler, S. "Instrumental Enrichment: A Conversation with Francis Link." *Educational Leadership* (April 1980).

McKean, K. "The Assault on IQ." *Discover* 6, no. 10 (October 1985): 25–41.

Sprinthall, N., and Theis-Sprinthall, L. "The Teacher as an Adult Learner: A Cognitive Development View." In *Staff Development*, edited by G. Griffin. Eighty-second Yearbook of the National Society for the Study of Education. Chicago: University of Chicago Press, 1983.

Sternberg, R., and Caruso, D. "Practical Modes of Knowing." In *Learning and Teaching the Ways of Knowing*, edited by E. Eisner. Eighty-fourth Yearbook of the National Society for the Study of Education, Part II. Chicago: University of Chicago Press, 1985.

Whimbey, A. "The Consequences of Teaching Thinking." In *Developing Minds: A Resource Book for Teaching Thinking*, edited by A. Costa. Alexandria, Va.: Association for Supervision and Curriculum Development, 1985.

Whimbey, A. and Whimbey, L. *Intelligence Can Be Taught*. New York: Bantam Books, 1976.

Winocur, S.L. "Developing Lesson Plans with Cognitive Objectives." In *Developing Minds: A Resource Book for Teaching Thinking*, edited by A. Costa. Alexandria, Va.: Association for Supervision and Curriculum Development, 1985.

TEACHING FOR THINKING, OF THINKING, AND ABOUT THINKING

by James J. McTighe

James J. McTighe maintains that teaching for thinking has long been part of many teachers' goals. Teachers ask questions that elicit different levels of thinking, from definitional through evaluative; they promote interpretive reading and discussion, debates, and simulations as part of the teaching for thinking process. However, these techniques may not be enough to ensure the "systematic development and improvement of student thinking." A more direct approach involves the explicit teaching of thinking. McTighe notes that a third approach to thinking development is teaching about thinking—that is, helping students think aloud, thereby becoming their own thinking strategies. This approach makes students more systematic and reflective in their learning; it is especially helpful to students whose thinking habits are impulsive and chaotic, who pay little attention to details and fail to check the common sense of their answers.

This chapter is adapted from School 33 *(June 1985): 1–6; Maryland State Department of Education, Baltimore.*

The author is an Education Specialist with the Thinking Improvement Program of the Maryland State Department of Education, Baltimore.

Helping students become more effective thinkers is an ancient educational goal that today is receiving renewed attention. Socrates questioned the youth of Athens and engaged in elaborate dialogue with them "to bring forth from within" the reasoning and ideas that only needed prompting to develop and clarify. John Dewey saw the development of "reflective thinking" in students as a major goal of education. For years many of the best teachers have emphasized students' thinking along with the development of the skills and knowledge of the disciplines.

An explicit focus on thinking as an educational goal has received varying degrees of national attention during the last several decades. The 1957 launch of Sputnik prompted, in particular, an urgent call to upgrade education. Out of the resulting curriculum reform movement of the 1960s came classroom materials that stressed concept development, reasoning, and problem solving. Discovery and inquiry teaching methods were encouraged.

While many teachers continue to value and utilize these approaches, several recent educational movements have emphasized other priorities. The most recent movement, often referred to as "back to basics," was prompted by the serious concern that students were not mastering the most fundamental skills. Much attention has been devoted to correcting this problem, and these intensive efforts are now being rewarded by consistently improving student performance in basic skills as measured by standardized achievement and competency skills tests.

While these tests affirm gains in basic skill development, they also point to areas needing attention. Specifically, students are having difficulty on those tasks that require the thoughtful application of basic skills and factual knowledge. The National Commission on Excellence in Education expressed its concern that "many 17-year-olds do not possess the higher order intellectual skills we should expect from them. Nearly 40 percent cannot draw inferences from written material; only one-fifth can write a persuasive essay; and only one-third can solve a mathematics problem requiring several steps."

Similarly, the National Assessment of Reading and Literature, after testing students nationwide, found that "students seem satisfied with their initial interpretations of what they have read and seem genuinely puzzled at requests to explain or defend their points of view. Few students could provide more than superficial responses to such tasks, and even the better responses showed little evidence of well-developed problem-solving strategies or critical thinking skills."

Such findings point to the need to strike a better balance between basic skills and thinking skills. A balanced approach does not view the goals of basic skills development and thinking skills development as incompatible, one prospering at the expense of the other. Rather, it acknowledges that thinking is fundamental to the acquisition of knowledge, concepts, and skills required by all school subjects and, further, that skills and knowledge are incomplete without the capability for thoughtful application.

FOR THINKING

In what ways might we develop and improve students' thinking abilities? Three distinct yet complementary approaches have been recognized as effective: teaching *for* thinking, teaching *of* thinking, and teaching *about* thinking.

Teaching for thinking includes those teaching strategies, student activities, and curriculum materials that engage students in thinking. This approach provides students with opportunities to practice and "exercise" their thinking. The most natural way teachers invite thought is by asking questions.

As every teacher knows, different types of questions encourage differ-

25

ent types or levels of thinking. Some questions call for basic recall of information previously given: Who are the current United States senators from your state? What is the chemical symbol for mercury? When was the National Anthem written? Other questions call for interpretation: What do you think is the editorial writer's stand on gun control? Or comparison: How are the two songs about "old friends" alike and different? Or judgment: Should the number of hours in the school day be extended? Or hypothesizing: What might happen if gasoline prices doubled in the next six months? Or analogical reasoning: How is an exothermic reaction like an argument?

In addition to the question itself, other techniques influence the quality of thinking that goes into the answer. For example, employing the technique of "wait time" (waiting several seconds after asking a question) is likely to encourage more careful thinking by more students. The thinking originally evoked by a good question can also be maintained and extended by such followup questions as, Tell me more. . . Why?. . .Do you agree?. . .Can you elaborate?. . .Can you explain or defend your idea? . . . What do you think about what Susan has just said?

Calling on students randomly, and not always choosing the hand-raisers, also helps to involve a greater number of students in the thinking process. The teacher interested in improving students' thinking should seek to elicit more thought from more students through such questioning and response strategies.

A number of researchers have described what seems to be a common pattern of interaction in many classrooms. The pattern consists of a teacher question, followed by a student response, followed by teacher elaboration. The teacher does most of the talking while student involvement is minimal. Teachers interested in modifying this pattern to increase student participation have successfully employed a variety of classroom grouping structures. By utilizing cooperative problem-solving teams, peer response groups, and "think-pair-share" periods, the degree of student participation and interaction can be markedly increased.

In addition to questioning and grouping techniques, other *teaching for thinking* activities are especially effective in engaging students in thought. Interpretive reading and discussion, writing, laboratory experiments, problem solving, debates, simulations, design activities—these and related methods have been used for years by teachers who value thinking in their classrooms.

Are these methods sufficient to ensure the systematic development and improvement of student thinking? Increasingly, experts are questioning whether teaching for thinking, by itself, is sufficient. Thinking, they contend, cannot be assumed to develop automatically as a result of activities of the kind previously mentioned. These activities provide opportunities to practice thinking (just as spending time in the water provides an opportunity to increase one's swimming ability). But they do not *teach* thinking. A more direct approach, which complements those previously mentioned techniques, seems to be required.

OF THINKING

Advocates for the explicit *teaching of thinking* maintain that thinking involves sets of skills and processes that can be identified and systematically developed. This approach utilizes a direct teaching strategy whereby a specific thinking skill, such as comparing, becomes the content of a lesson.

Consider a social studies class in which the teacher wants the students to explore the similarities and differences between the American Revolution and the Civil War.

The teacher defines the skill: to compare is to examine two or more ideas, or objects of study, to see their relationship; in particular, to determine ways in which the ideas or objects are similar and different. The class then discusses when comparing is used: when you want to see how two or more things relate in terms of their similarities and differences.

The steps of comparing are then developed as follows:

1. Present the objects (ideas) to be compared.
2. Have the students observe and describe them one at a time.
3. Compare the objects and make a list of their similarities.
4. Repeat the process, making a list of differences.
5. Identify the criteria used in making the comparisons.
6. Summarize the significant similarities and differences.

The teacher would then have the students apply the skill to a new example and provide feedback on their performance.

Notice that this lesson focuses on the thinking skill and not the subject matter. It has been found that thinking skills taught in this direct manner are more readily understood when the objects or ideas that are used in the teaching example are familiar to the students. Content-relevant material may be used if students have an adequate knowledge base. As an alternative, teachers may capitalize on the common experiences of students in designing thinking skill "focus" lessons. In the lesson on comparing, for example, two different brands of automobiles could be used as the objects of comparison. Once the students demonstrate an understanding of the skill of comparing, the skill can be applied, as intended, to the American Revolution and the Civil War. Once learned, the skill can be applied to other social studies topics, and in other subject areas, throughout the year.

According to this approach, the most efficient and effective means of developing any skill, including thinking, is through direct teaching. Direct teaching of thinking promotes explicit understanding by not assuming that thinking automatically improves as a by-product of other activities. This method has been used to teach and develop fundamental thinking skills, such as classifying, comparing, hypothesizing, judging, paraphrasing, sequencing, and summarizing. It may also be applied to more complex mental processes, such as critical thinking and problem solving. For example, the component skills involved in critical thinking, such as detecting bias, can be explicitly identified, directly taught, and then applied as appropriate to the content area.

Direct instruction in thinking skills can also follow a more inductive approach. An inductive thinking skill lesson would be sequenced as follows:

Step 1. Students introduce and operationally define the identified thinking skill.

Step 2. Students use the thinking skill.

Step 3. Students reflect on the thinking process involved in using the skill.

Step 4. Students apply the thinking skill to new material within the content area.

Step 5. Students review the steps or procedures involved in using the thinking skill.

Step 6. Students discuss how the thinking skill may be transferred to new situations (in other subjects as well as outside of school).

Strategies for generating new ideas such as brainstorming and synectics are also effectively developed through direct instruction.

To assist in the direct teaching of thinking, an increasing number of teachers are discovering the power of graphic organizers. A graphic organizer provides a visual representation which assists students in organizing and integrating information. These organizers also provide a holistic, visual portrayal of elements of the thinking process. In the case of comparison, for example, a teacher might use a Venn diagram to depict the areas of commonality and difference. Other examples of graphic organizers include story maps, matrices, sequence chains, criteria grids, and decision-making flow charts. The commonly used technique of webbing illustrates the use of a graphic organizer to generate thought and to elaborate on and relate ideas. As one student remarked, graphic organizers "give shape to thought."

ABOUT THINKING

A third approach to thinking development has generated considerable interest recently. Referred to as *teaching about thinking,* this approach focuses on helping students become more aware of their own thinking processes. Research has shown that effective learners and thinkers monitor their own learning and thinking. They are aware of what they know, what they don't know, and what they need to know in order to solve a problem or comprehend a difficult concept. Many of these capable reasoners engage in "self-talk" during which they ask questions ("What is the main idea here?"), maintain concentration ("You're daydreaming. Go back and re-read that last paragraph."), try new problem-solving strategies ("Maybe if I draw a picture . . . ."), and check performance ("What is the next step?"). Poor thinkers are less likely to engage in this inner dialogue, are generally unable to describe their learning and reasoning strategies, and hesitate to "shift gears" when a particular strategy is not working.

Teaching about thinking includes several strategies for improving these "metacognitive" abilities. One of these strategies is known as the "think aloud" technique, in which students are asked to describe their reasoning process when tackling a problem, writing an essay, or struggling to grasp a new concept.

One effective application of the "think aloud" technique has been in paired problem solving. One member of the pair serves as the listener and is responsible for listening to and recording the strategies used by the problem solver, who reads aloud. Roles are reversed for the next problem. The problem-solving process is then discussed in pairs and/or as a class. In cases where students have difficulty thinking aloud, the teacher can model the technique and provide a "window to the mind" by sharing his or her reasoning verbally with the class.

While "think aloud" techniques stress immediate verbalization, another method asks students to examine their reasoning after the fact. This "process reflection" can take the form of a discussion among an entire class or a small group such as a writing response group, or it can be done individually through "thought tracing" in a journal.

Activities such as thinking aloud, process reflection, and journal writing serve as vehicles for illuminating the invisible process of thinking.

EXPLORING COGNITIVE HABITS

Teaching about thinking also explores the cognitive habits and attitudes of students. Considerable research has been conducted to determine how the habits and attitudes of effective thinkers differ from those of less capable reasoners. The results from studies of preschool children through graduate students are remarkably consistent. For example, the poorer thinkers often exhibit a high degree of impulsivity. This impulsive behavior may be seen in those primary children who enthusiastically raise their hands to answer a question before it is completed. ("Who can tell me . . . ?"—hands already waving!) In older students impulsive tendencies may be manifested by a failure to attend to details, a tendency to rush through directions, and an interest in obtaining "the answer" quickly.

A characteristic related to impulsivity has been termed "one shot" thinking. Poor problem solvers of all ages are inclined to make superficial, sporadic attempts at a solution. Often the attempt is little more than a guess. Carelessness abounds and accuracy suffers.

Effective problem solvers, in contrast, view problems as challenges and are persistent in seeking solutions. If a particular strategy is unsuccessful, they take a different approach. Other attitudes and habits of effective thinking are well known: open-mindedness, flexibility, ability to defer immediate judgment, attention to detail. Teaching about thinking gives conscious attention to qualities, such as these, which we seek to cultivate in our students.

Success in improving students' thinking skills will require long-term commitment and a continuing emphasis on those proven teaching methods and activities that engage students in thinking, that explicitly focus on specific thinking skills, and that help students become more aware of their own thought processes.

Instruction in thinking skills will have lasting benefits—students better able to acquire new information, to examine complex issues critically, and to solve new problems. In a world of rapid change and increasing complexity, it is difficult to imagine skills that are more fundamental. Like the ability to fish in the Chinese proverb, the ability to think lasts a lifetime.

Give me a fish and I'll eat today.
Teach me to fish and I'll eat for a lifetime.

THINKING AND CURRICULUM: CRITICAL CROSSROADS FOR EDUCATIONAL CHANGE

by Barbara Z. Presseisen

Barbara Z. Presseisen finds new opportunities in the thinking skills movement. The idea that "some essential cognitive processes. . . underlie good thinking" and that these processes can be acquired through guided practice has sparked a "redefinition of what it means to be an educated person facing the 21st century." Presseisen suggests that a curriculum emphasizing thinking skills makes new demands on teachers: they must examine the skills involved in thinking in their subject areas, work collaboratively with others to identify practices that will reinforce these skills, and take time to study and understand the new thinking skills programs. Further, a focus on thinking skills changes the role of the teacher from "fount of all wisdom" to "mediator, questioner, critic, inspirer, enabler, coach."

The author is Director, National Networking, Research for Better Schools, Inc., Philadelphia, Pennsylvania.

American education is at an unusual point in its development. It is under criticism for being mediocre and inefficient while, at the same time, there are claims that educators have never been so knowledgeable about how to improve schooling or how to provide academic motivation for young minds. Much focuses on the desire to have students *achieve*, which frequently is characterized as scoring high on the Scholastic Aptitude Test (SAT) or the National Assessment of Educational Progress (NAEP).

THE CHALLENGE TO CLARIFY PURPOSE

For teachers and administrators in the schools, the real question is "Achieve what?" There is a problem of confused goals and a need to clarify purpose in schooling. Such issues not only touch on teaching and testing, but also center on program and learning, teacher preparation and continued development, long-range planning, and resource allocation. At the heart is the redefinition of what it means to be an educated person facing the 21st century, the measure of the citizen in a high tech world and a global economy. The danger is that many educators may not

31

realize that a critical opportunity is at their doorstep and they may miss the chance to debate the great issues of the day.

What mission should direct American schooling? Current arguments about excellence and equity fill the reform literature (1). Obviously, the greatest democracy in the world must accomplish both, but that is no simple task. "The challenge," says one of the recent reports (2), "is not simply to better educate our elite, but to raise both the floor and ceiling of achievement in America." Underlying each of the objectives of excellence and equity is the assumption that the country's youngsters—*all* of them—need to become accomplished thinkers. That is the major challenge of current schooling. It is rooted in a new appreciation that just having information is not sufficient; one must be able to do something with it. Even more importantly, the learner must be in control of his or her learning and be able to adjust his or her thinking as changing conditions require it (3). These circumstances generate the focus of this article: thinking and curriculum. In the interplay between these two aspects of schooling lie the most critical relationships of education today.

A formidable new movement is emerging in American education. Actually, it is not new; it has a long history associated with the various fields allied to cognitive research. The current phase is known as thinking skills development and much literature—both theoretical and practical—is being generated in its name (4). Like the period of the early 1960s which preceded it, the thinking skills movement today holds much promise for informing and improving classroom instruction. To improve that instruction requires an understanding of thinking skills and an examination of what they mean to the curriculum of the school.

THE CURRENT MOVEMENT FOCUSED ON THINKING

There is no academic discipline called "Thinking skills." The movement draws from a number of research areas based in human development: cognitive and developmental psychology (5), cognitive science (6), educational practice (7), and child development (8). One of the most notable characteristics of the current movement is its changing view of human intelligence and the nature of the school's program in terms of that view.

The classic orientation of intelligence as an immutable, quantifiable, and genetically determined quality has been challenged by current research and theory (9). The possibility that various capabilities can be developed or modified in youngsters and that instruction and school organization can significantly influence student performance are viable positions developed in recent literature (10). Some theorists contend that thinking and intelligence can actually be taught (11) and that how we teach is as powerful as—or perhaps even more powerful than—what we teach. Other researchers maintain it is most significant that particular bodies of knowledge or courses of study be examined in terms of their relationship to cognitive processes (12). This is especially so in the so-called higher order processes of critical thinking, decision making, problem solving, and creative thinking.

There is in the thinking skills position an understanding that there are some essential cognitive processes, both basic and complex, that underlie good thinking, that these processes can be learned and taught—in fact, good coaching does just that—and that being aware of how one masters these processes is the key to good learning. Metacognition, the consciousness of how one learns and how one works with difficult problems, including failure, is one of the hallmarks of the current concern for cognitive improvement compared to the era of the 1960s (13). The development of aspects of metacognition such as intuitive and heuristic capabilities for problem solving is central to the movement of the 80s. The spatial-visual abilities of video technology and microprocessor-based information systems have also influenced an instructional base that incorporates interactive student responses into the classroom (14).

A CURRICULUM FOR THINKING

What does the thinking skills movement mean to the traditional curriculum, the school's planned program and the core of common learning? Lochhead suggests education is no longer "a process of passing facts from those who had them to those who didn't, and pedagogy . . . the art or science of packaging these facts" (15). A curriculum that is responsive to an information-rich world must concentrate on how knowledge is created and disseminated, how experts perform their capabilities, and how new problems are addressed and resolved. Such a curriculum reveals a new functionalism as the major overriding concern of teaching and learning in the current era. Educators are encouraged to use the findings of more than thirty years of cognitive research and turn them into realities in the classroom that lead to greater productivity and creativity. The curriculum of the industrial economy, geared to pre-existing jobs and the use of static knowledge and known information, says Mulkeen, is outmoded (16).

A curriculum focused on thinking skills then requires that the cognitive processes imbedded in a body of learning be explicated and made obvious. That does not mean one throws out the disciplines of language, history, science, the arts, or mathematics. It does say that teachers ought to examine what it means to think in a particular area and be concerned with what is required to develop the skills of an accomplished scholar. It also suggests one needs to look for the metacognitive skills often hidden in the learning of a particular content and teach those explicitly to students. There is, then, an assumption that the persons responsible for delivering classroom instruction ought to (1) know their own subject area at some depth and (2) work collaboratively with their colleagues to determine what the content of instruction should be and what kinds of activities are most appropriate for learning by the student population who will use the curriculum. This does not suggest that all curriculum efforts are individual and idiosyncratic. School personnel would be well advised to examine existing published programs in thinking skills like *Philosophy for Children* developed by Matthew Lipman and *Instrumental Enrichment* developed by Reuven Feuerstein (17), or particular thinking skill programs developed by school districts such as Baltimore, Maryland, and Shoreham-Wading River, New York (18). These exemplary efforts may help identify the processes associated with good thinking and the variety of activities that can be developed to teach thinking skills throughout the curriculum. But educators should be alert to the primary need which is to identify the appropriate thinking skills intervention for the population they teach. These needs should be determined by regular curriculum assessment procedures and ongoing diagnosis of student achievement (19).

A curriculum focused on thinking skills also requires that the instructional strategy inherent in the curriculum emphasize the model of learning that most encourages the development of intellectual autonomy on the part of the student. The student as the constructor of his or her own learning is the cornerstone of many thinking skills approaches and reflects the Piagetian roots of the current thinking skills movement (20). Obviously, the role of the teacher in the classroom dramatically shifts with this conceptualization. The teacher as mediator, questioner, critic, inspirer, enabler, coach, but *not* fount of all wisdom, dominates. The teacher as a model of thoughtful processing, as the gadfly of knowledge in particular contents, may then become valued in the school community. Ideally, thinking ought to be valued in that community, too, not just as a standard to be measured by higher test results, but as a reality to be realized in the performance of all students educated by that curriculum. Such an education is much more than the sum of a school's testing; hopefully, it is the foundation for the learning society envisioned by the current reform reports and the nation's educational leaders (21).

AN OPPORTUNITY FOR CHANGE

The historic juncture of thinking and curriculum in this period of educational reform can be played out in various ways. Let's explore the possibilities. The thinking skills movement can be treated as a fad, an ephemeral idea that's momentarily interesting, which generates a great number of journal articles, and then withers away when the next bandwagon idea comes along and captures educators' attention. Thinking skills could also be received as a new subject matter. Some schools or school districts could actually allocate instructional time for its instruction and seek special materials for these special classes. American schools have an extensive history of purchasing instant, "plug-in" programs, often imposed upon the classroom teacher by administrative decree.

Unfortunately, research shows both these approaches are long-range curricular failures (22). "Teacher-proof" programs of the 1960 vintage are not an ideal model for introducing thinking skills to American educators. The already heavily burdened school program does not need additional courses; indeed, anything that could streamline the program is probably desirable.

In order to build a sound thinking skills program, there is need for teacher involvement as well as teacher acceptance in planning the program. Matched to support from administrative leaders in a systemwide effort, these are the ingredients of a curricular change that is expected to last.

Perhaps the most convincing argument for thinking skills development is that there must be professional commitment to teaching. There is a great deal of discussion today about teachers being valued and considered professional. Thinking skills are important to that characterization. If the central purpose of schooling is to help students think and learn better, and the primary agents of that instruction or mediation are teachers, thinking is the important raison d'être of a teacher's competence. Thinking skills is a rare topic of discussion that cuts across all subject matters of the school's curriculum and reaches to the university community as well. How students learn to think in a particular subject area or what are the most appropriate ways to present a specific lesson are no less problems of a primary teacher than of a college professor. Curriculum is the link between the processes of cognition and the larger instructional design which drives schooling (see Figure 1). To see this relationship is to be able to address the needs of educational change today in American education. To ignore this relationship, in Cornbleth's words, is to continue with curriculum not as active inquiry but as "passive acceptance of tradition, authority, or 'common sense' " (23).

There are some critical steps to be taken if the possibilities of the current historical juncture are to be realized. If we want to enable students to be critical thinkers and capable of higher order cognitive skills, we must make it possible for teachers to act as professionals in the determination and instruction of those skills. We cannot expect that teachers must serve as heroes or heroines to introduce thinking skills into their

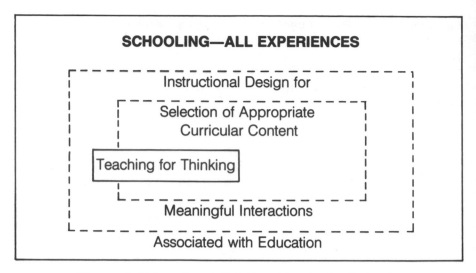

Figure 1: Educational Relationships in the School

Source: *Thinking Skills Throughout the Curriculum: A Conceptual Design* by Barbara
Z. Presseisen (Philadelphia: Research for Better Schools, 1985), 14.

classrooms. Corbett and D'Amico suggest four major conditions that are
necessary to support such a program of change:

- Make local resources available.
- Provide a grace period at the onset of effort.
- Encourage implementation and reward accomplishment.
- Incorporate the change into regular procedures (24).

Teachers need time to study the current thinking skills programs and
the related literature. They need time to talk among themselves about
what this movement means to their own subject areas and to the larger
curricular concerns of their district. They probably will want to try some
of the existing materials or talk with educators who have had direct experience with published programs. Some effort should be made to relate
this examination to the needs of a school's current population and the
data that exist about the achievement of that population, particularly as
related to the development of thinking. Obviously, teachers and administrators in a district need to communicate with the policy makers of the
district, too.

It is important to recognize that thinking skills development—no less
than curriculum development—is not a quick-fix repair job in schooling.
Improvement takes time and patience, as well as funding, and innovative projects that are worthwhile need to be supported, particularly in
their initial phase. At the same time, implementation needs to be en-

couraged not by making thinking skills an add-on to the curriculum, but by making it a bona fide part of the regular school program. This means that course work and regular subject matter across the school's program must be involved in such an implementation and all teaching personnel need to be encouraged to take the effort seriously. Results of the implementation ought to be shared with these persons on a regular schedule.

In the current thinking skills movement a possibility has been offered to redirect the course of American education. Particularly in the area of curriculum, a new focus for schooling has been proposed amidst a hectic reform period. Will America's educators have the courage to respond positively? Can they afford not to? These are questions worthy of serious thinking.

REFERENCES

1. Barbara Z. Presseisen, *Unlearned Lessons: Current and Past Reforms for School Improvement* (Philadelphia and London: Falmer Press, Taylor and Francis Group, 1985).
2. Task Force on Education for Economic Growth, *Action for Excellence: A Comprehensive Plan to Improve Our Nation's Schools* (Washington, D.C.: Education Commission of the States, 1983), 7.
3. Barbara Z. Presseisen, "Thinking Skills: Meanings, Models, and Materials," in *Developing Minds: A Resource Book for Teaching Thinking*, ed. Arthur L. Costa (Washington, D.C.: Association for Supervision and Curriculum Development, 1985).
4. See, for example, Judith W. Segal, Susan F. Chipman, and Robert Glaser, eds., *Thinking and Learning Skills*, vols. 1 and 2 (Hillsdale, N.J.: Lawrence Erlbaum Associates, 1985); *Educational Leadership*, September and November 1984, and May 1985; George R. Kaplan, *Items for an Agenda: Educational Research and the Reports on Excellence* (Washington, D.C.: American Educational Research Association, 1985).
5. See, for example, Robert J. Sternberg, "Intelligence as Thinking and Learning Skills," *Educational Leadership* (October 1981): 18–20; Harry Beilin, "The Psychology of Mathematics Learning," *Education and Urban Society* (August 1985): 377–85; Jerome Bruner, "Models of the Learner," *Educational Researcher* (June/July 1985): 5–8.
6. See, for example, Lauren B. Resnick, "Introduction: Changing Conceptions of Intelligence," in *The Nature of Intelligence*, edited by Lauren B. Resnick (New York: 1976), 1–10; Alan H. Schoenfeld, "Teaching Problem Solving Skills," Lawrence Erlbaum Associates, *The American Mathematical Monthly* (December 1980): 794–805.
7. See, for example, Barry K. Beyer, "Improving Thinking Skills—Defining the Problem," *Phi Delta Kappan* (March 1984): 486–90; Barry K. Beyer, "Teaching Thinking Skills: How the Principal Can Know They Are Being

Taught," *NASSP Bulletin* (January 1985): 70-83; Arthur L. Costa, "Mediating the Metacognitive," *Educational Leadership* (November 1984): 57–62.

8. See, for example, Jean Piaget, "Piaget's Theory," in *Carmichael's Manual of Child Psychology*, vol. 1, ed. Paul H. Mussen (New York: John Wiley, 1970), 703–32; John R. Berrueta-Clement and others, *Changed Lives: The Effects of the Perry Preschool Program on Youths Through Age 19* (Ypsilanti, Mich.: The High/Scope Press, 1984).

9. See, for example, Robert J. Sternberg, "The Nature of Mental Abilities," *American Psychologist* (March 1979): 214–30; Robert J. Sternberg, "Testing Intelligence Without I.Q. Tests," *Phi Delta Kappan* (June 1984): 694–98; Howard Gardner, *Frames of Mind* (New York: Basic Books, 1983); Kevin McKean, "Intelligence: New Ways to Measure the Wisdom of Man," *Discover* (October 1985): 25–41.

10. See, for example, Reuven Feuerstein, Mogens Reimer Jenson, Mildred B. Hoffman, and Yaacov Rand, "Instrumental Enrichment, An Intervention Program for Structural Cognitive Modifiability: Theory and Practice," in Segal, Chipman, and Glaser, *Thinking and Learning Skills*, vol. 1, 43–82; Jack Lochhead, "Introduction to Section 1—New Horizons in Educational Development," in *Review of Research in Education*, vol. 12, ed. Edmund W. Gordon (Washington, D.C.: American Educational Research Association, 1985), 3–9; Stewart C. Purkey and Susan Degen, "Beyond Effective Schools to Good Schools: Some First Steps," *R & D Perspectives* (Eugene, Ore.: Center for Educational Policy and Management, 1985), 1–8.

11. See, for example, Arthur Whimbey and Linda Shaw Whimbey, *Intelligence Can Be Taught* (New York: E.P. Dutton, 1975); Schoenfeld, "Teaching Problem Solving Skills."

12. See, for example, Catherine Cornbleth, "Critical Thinking and Cognitive Process," in *Review of Research in Social Studies Education 1976–1983*, ed. William B. Stanley and others (Boulder, Colo.: ERIC Clearinghouse for Social Studies/Social Science Education, Bulletin 75, 1985), 11–63; James G. Greeno, "Forms for Understanding Mathematical Problem Solving," in *Learning and Motivation in the Classroom*, ed. Scott G. Paris, Gary M. Olson, and Harold W. Stevenson (Hillsdale, N.J.: Lawrence Erlbaum, 1983), 83–111.

13. See, for example, Ann L. Brown, "Knowing When, Where, and How to Remember: A Problem of Metacognition," in *Advances in Instructional Psychology*, vol. 1, ed. Robert Glasser, (Hillsdale, N.J.: Lawrence Erlbaum, 1978), 77–165; Ann L. Brown, *Teaching Students to Think as They Read: Implications for Curriculum Reform* (Washington, D.C.: American Educational Research Association, 1984); Arthur L. Costa, "Mediating the Metacognitive," *Educational Leadership* (November 1984): 57–62.

14. John Seely Brown, "Idea Amplifiers—New Kinds of Electronic Learning Environments," *Educational Horizons* (Spring 1985): 108–12.

15. Lochhead, "Introduction to Section 1," 3–4.
16. Thomas A. Mulkeen, "Introduction," *Education and Urban Society* (August 1985): 371–76.
17. See, for example, Matthew Lipman, Ann Margaret Sharp, and Frederick S. Oscanyan, *Philosophy in the Classroom* (Philadelphia: Temple University Press, 1980); Reuven Feuerstein, *Instrumental Enrichment* (Baltimore: University Park Press, 1980).
18. The Baltimore City Schools Thinking Skills Project is in its third year of development under Dr. Robin B. Hobbs. The Shoreham–Wading River Central Schools have developed a program known as the Cognitive Levels Matching Project. Dr. Martin G. Brooks and Jacqueline Grennon are co-directors of the project.
19. For a discussion of thinking skills program development in the context of regular curriculum planning and assessment, see Barbara Z. Presseisen, *Thinking Skills Throughout the Curriculum: A Conceptual Design* (Philadelphia: Research for Better Schools, 1985).
20. These roots are discussed in Connie Kamii, "Autonomy: The Aim of Education Envisioned by Piaget," *Phi Delta Kappan* (February 1984): 410–15. Also see Jerome Bruner, "Models of the Learner" for a further discussion of Piaget's constructivism.
21. The phrase "learning society" appears in the National Commission on Excellence in Education, *A Nation at Risk: The Imperative for Educational Reform* (Washington, D.C.: Government Printing Office, 1983), 16. It is, in spirit, a notion related to John Dewey's concept of lifelong learning and Thomas Jefferson's view of an enlightened electorate.
22. See, for example, Marvin Lazerson, Judith Block McLaughlin, and Bruce McPherson, "New Curriculum, Old Issues," *Teachers College Record* (Winter 1984): 299–319; Michael W. Kirst and Gail R. Meister, "Turbulence in American Secondary Schools: What Reforms Last?" *Curriculum Inquiry* (Summer 1985).
23. Cornbleth, "Critical Thinking and Cognitive Process," 13.
24. H. Dickson Corbett and Joseph J. D'Amico, *No More Heroes: Creating Systems to Support Change* (Philadelphia: Research for Better Schools, 1985).

CRITICAL THINKING AND THE CURRICULUM

by Robert H. Ennis

Robert H. Ennis finds fault with the idea that thinking is subject-specific, and therefore must be taught within academic disciplines. He argues that there are general principles of thinking that bridge disciplines, and gives several examples of principles that appear to apply to all areas of activity. He suggests practices that can increase the transfer of these skills; they include using many different examples; being receptive to students' questions; asking students to clarify their statements, focus their thoughts, and supply reasons for their ideas; and helping students be aware of and think about their thinking processes. Ennis concedes that this advice is vague, but notes that sufficient research has not yet been done on the transfer question to arrive at definitive solutions to the problem.

This chapter is reprinted with permission from National Forum: The Phi Kappa Phi Journal, *vol. 65, no. 1 (Winter 1985): 28–31.*

The author is Professor of Philosophy of Education at the University of Illinois and Director of the Illinois Critical Thinking Project.

Suddenly, it seems, critical thinking is truly popular. Perhaps starting with the 1980 recommendation by the Rockefeller Commission on the Humanities that the U.S. Office of Education include critical thinking in its definition of the basic skills, concrete interest has rapidly expanded. Prior to this, critical thinking often appeared on lists of goals of education, but not much was done about it. In 1961, for example, the Educational Policies Commission held that the central purpose of American education was the development of the ability to think, but public and professional interest moved in other directions.

Since 1980, however, much has happened. As of the fall of 1983, all students in the California State University System are required to study critical thinking in order to graduate. The Community College Humanities Association in 1983-84 had critical thinking as the topic of the presession workshops that preceded its annual meetings in Hartford, St. Louis, and San Francisco. Programs leading to the master's degree in the teaching of critical thinking have been set up at Sonoma State University and at the University of Massachusetts in Boston. The College Board (sponsor of the Scholastic Aptitude Test—the SAT) through its Project

EQuality has identified reasoning (defined roughly as I would define critical thinking) as one of the six basic skills needed for college (1983). A task force of the Education Commission of the States did a similar thing (1983). The states of California and Connecticut are incorporating critical thinking in their statewide testing programs for 1984–85. Sales of the leading critical thinking tests, the Cornell critical thinking tests and the Watson-Glaser test, have increased greatly in the past year. And those of us who are working in the field are now deluged by requests for help in establishing and appraising curricula and instruction aimed at critical thinking.

Though gratified by this real interest, I am concerned by the large number of problems facing teachers, school systems, colleges, and universities trying to do something about critical thinking instruction. There is much that we do not know about the capabilities for critical thinking of students of various sorts at various levels. Teaching materials and tests need to be developed. Teachers need to be retrained. And there is disagreement about what critical thinking is and how it can be included in the curriculum. One controversial question about inclusion of critical thinking courses in the curriculum is, Should critical thinking be taught as a separate course, or be included in the instruction in existing courses, or both? A topic that always arises in discussing this last question is the subject specificity of critical thinking, my first topic because it is current, crucial, and inadequately conceptualized in discussions I have seen, and because it is a good starting point for discussion and investigation of other critical thinking problems.

DISCIPLINE SPECIFICITY VS. TOPIC SPECIFICITY

One immediate tangle arises from different interpretations attached to the term "subject." Sometimes "subject" is meant to refer to a discipline, a standard body of subject matter in accord with which schools, colleges, and universities are often organized. Sometimes the word "subject" means the topic under consideration in a given context, the latter being a much broader interpretation, because it can refer to the topics of the disciplines as well as to whatever the topic might be in a context.

When I served on a jury recently, we were faced with the question of whether the defendant lied about whether the deceased threatened her life before she stabbed him. Deciding whether a defendant has lied about such things was not part of one of the standard disciplines in accord with which my education was organized. Yet such decisions and the evidence sifting on which they are based are a very important kind of activity for all of us, and judging whether others have lied is a subject

41

about which we all have acquired considerable knowledge. It is an important *subject* calling for critical thinking. But it is not part of one of the standard *disciplines* that I studied in my general education.

Another example is the case of the airline traveler that Robert Glaser drew from the National Academy of Science's *Outlook for Science and Technology: The Next Five Years:* "At the security gate, the airline passenger presented his briefcase. It contained metallic objects. His departure was delayed." Glaser, a specificity advocate, observes, "To understand this commonplace incident, an individual must have a good deal of prior knowledge of air terminals." Knowledge of air terminals is subject knowledge in the broad sense of the term "subject," but not in the more restricted sense used to refer to the standard disciplines.

These two examples give you the idea. Perry Weddle in his delightful way mentions many more:

> This week the Typical Educated Person had to find a new mechanic, listen to the broker, advise a friend's child on her career, choose a newspaper, decide whether to fight an undemocratic, harsh, but fair administrative decision, trouble-shoot a malfunctioning vacuum cleaner, and turn down a thoughtful and appreciated invitation to spend the weekend at Mendocino. The Typical Educated Person argued politics, music, psychology, sports, and religion. Academic fields cover only a fraction of such stuff. And no student could cover but a tiny fraction of the needed fields.

The important point is that not all subjects are disciplines, especially disciplines that a given student could study. Even if it is agreed in the broad sense of "subject" that critical thinking is subject-specific, it does not follow that it is discipline-specific in a way that requires that critical thinking instruction be lodged in instruction in the disciplines.

So one common argument to support the lodging of critical thinking instruction within the disciplines does not work. Condensed, the argument goes as follows: "Thinking is always thinking about something. Thus, critical thinking is subject-specific. So critical thinking instruction must take place only within subject matter areas, the disciplines." This argument fails because it exploits the ambiguity of the word "subject" (the first occurrence of the word "subject" is broad in meaning; the third occurrence of the word has a narrow meaning, referring to the particular subjects—i.e., psychology, sociology, history, etc.—taken by a student). The argument contains the fallacy of equivocation.

Viewed in stark form like this, the argument looks too implausible for anyone to offer. Yet I often find embellished and extended forms of it in discussions of the topic.

I am not here saying that critical thinking instruction should not be part of the subject matter instruction that a student receives. I am only challenging one of the arguments alleged to show that such instruction should take place *only* as part of instruction in other subject areas. That conclusion does not follow from the fact that when we think, we must think about something.

A caveat: If we look far enough, then we might well find some course in some school, college, or university for each area of background knowledge in each act of critical thinking. That is, we might, for example, find somewhere a course in airport management, the subject matter of which includes the facts and principles that enable the traveler to understand the delay. And we might find a course in a law school or in a philosophy department that teaches the principles for a juror to use in figuring out whether a defendant lied about being threatened (though I do not know of any such course). But I am confident that cognitive psychologists like Robert Glaser would not advocate a course in airport management in order that the traveler understand the situation (one merely needs to read the newspapers), and juror Ennis never took a course teaching the principles for a juror to use in figuring out whether a defendant lied about being threatened. Furthermore, it would be absurd to advocate that we all take a course in everything about which we want or need to think critically.

GENERAL PRINCIPLES OF CRITICAL THINKING

Although I am firmly convinced that a thorough knowledge of the subject about which one is thinking is essential for critical thinking, *I also am convinced that there are general principles that bridge subjects, that have application to many subjects*. Here are several examples of such principles drawn from a large number embodied in the conception of critical thinking I have refined over the years:

1. A person's having a *conflict of interest* is a ground for regarding that person's claim with greater suspicion than would otherwise be appropriate.
2. It is a mistake to misdescribe a person's position, and then attack the position as if it actually were the person's position (the *"straw-person" fallacy*).
3. Given an "if-then" statement, *denial of the consequent* implies the denial of the antecedent.
4. The ability of a hypothesis to *explain or help explain the facts* lends support to the hypothesis, if the hypothesis is not otherwise disqualified.

The conflict-of-interest principle, though vague and requiring judgment in application, applies in all areas of activity with which I am familiar, including, for example, jury trials, certification of airplanes, appraisals of the state of the economy, recommendations of graduate students, interpretations of IQ studies, and, yes, even the hawking of materials for the teaching and testing of critical thinking.

Likewise, and obviously, the straw-person principle applies everywhere. It applies to politics, to medical research, and to appraisals of conceptions of critical thinking. You name the topic: the principle applies. But, of course, knowledge of the subject (including what the original person said) is needed to apply it.

Here are three examples of the application of the third principle, the one about denial of the consequent:

> If John is in school, then Mary is in school. But since Mary is not in school, we can conclude that John is not in school.

> If Shakespeare intended Iago to be a melodramatic villain, then Emilia, Iago's wife, would have at least suspected him to be a villain. But she did not suspect him to be a villain. So Shakespeare did not intend Iago to be a melodramatic villain.

> If a body in motion needs a continual impetus to keep it going, then this ball when thrown straight up in an automobile moving at constant velocity will move to the back of the automobile. I did throw it up that way, but the ball did not move to the back of the automobile. It came right back down in my lap. So it is false that a body in motion needs a continual impetus to keep it going.

Although it takes background knowledge to understand the significance of these arguments, the denial-of-the-consequent principle has wide application. It appears to be less subject-dependent than the fourth principle, the support-by-explanatory-power principle.

The fourth principle's wide application is evident from the following three examples: first, from a standard discipline, history. The hypothesis that Napoleon died of arsenic poisoning rather than cancer gets support from its ability to explain his nausea, chills, weakness, and increasing corpulence during his last few months. It also explains the traces of arsenic found in his hair—more support.

Second, from another standard discipline, English literature: the hypothesis that Emilia in Shakespeare's *Othello* did not suspect Iago to be a villain explains why she expressed surprise when Othello told her, "Thy husband knew it all."

Third, from my jury experience but no discipline that I have studied: the hypothesis that she loved him and was very jealous explains why the defendant stabbed the victim.

These four principles show that there are elements of critical thinking that are general and that bridge subjects. The conditions under which transfer, or subject bridging, occurs are my next topic. But it is important to remember that there are important features of critical thinking that are subject general, so to speak, just as their application is, I believe, at least in part subject specific.

44

My examples could be used to argue for the subject-specificity point that background knowledge of the subject is necessary for the reasonable application of a principle. For example, if you do not know about love and jealousy and how they move people, and if you do not know the particulars of that situation, then you are not in a good position to judge whether the hypothesis about the defendant's love and jealousy explains why she stabbed the victim. But I shall not argue here the need for background knowledge of this sort. It is not a controversial point among people who work in the area of critical thinking, although it is sometimes neglected.

TRANSFER

One matter that *is* controversial is the extent to which students transfer their knowledge of a general principle from one subject area to another. A vague general dictum of educational psychology is that transfer does not occur unless you teach for it. This time-honored principle is similar to the vague modern dictum that thinking is domain specific.

Vagueness arises in part from unclarity about whether two applications of a principle are actually in the same domain or whether a new application would actually be a case of transfer. The problem lies in the lack of criteria for deciding whether any two given topics are in the same domain. For example, are the hypotheses about Napoleon and the defendant in the same domain? One might think not, yet they are both about someone's doing something that could be illegal. By what criteria do we judge them to be in different domains?

Vagueness also arises from lack of criteria for deciding whether we have actually taught for transfer or not. In domain-specificity language, we might also ask, How many applications of a general principle in how many domains are required before we can be reasonably well assured of transfer? There are no clear criteria for deciding either of these questions.

Another uncertainty arises from the fact that some of the principles of critical thinking are more easily generalized (less domain specific) than others. From my teaching experience, I find much less domain specificity for the first three principles I mentioned than for the fourth. That is, I find students applying the conflict-of-interest, straw-person, and denial-of-the-consequent principles to new subjects more readily than the support-by-explanatory-power principle. In short, I have found that the first three principles seem to transfer more readily than the fourth.

These three kinds of vagueness (absence of a way of telling whether two topics are in the same or different domains, lack of a clear criterion for telling whether we have taught for transfer or domain bridging, and the variability among critical thinking principles in their transferability)

45

make research about the domain specificity and transferability of critical thinking instruction difficult indeed. They tempt me to retreat to the insights garnered from years of teaching critical thinking. Vague though it may be, here is one compilation of these insights: use many examples of many different sorts; go slowly; be receptive to questions and to students' original thoughts; press for clarity; arrange for students to engage each other in discussion and challenge; arrange for them to assume progressively greater control over and responsibility for their learning; encourage students to be aware of what they are doing and review what they have done; ask for a focus (often a thesis) and for reasons in any discussion, and encourage students to do likewise. I trust that if these principles are followed in a number of areas, transfer to new areas will occur.

But it is clear that transfer can occur and that we can go beyond domain specificity. Although I had never been on a jury before, I found myself exercising a wide variety of critical thinking skills in that courtroom situation.

Another way to look at the learning-transfer question is to think about the transferability and domain specificity of arithmetic and writing. Somehow it happens that we apply the principles of percentages, for example, to a wide variety of subjects: inflation, population increase, automobile finance contracts, aircraft fuel consumption, and income tax, for example. I did not study the application of the principles of computing percentages to these areas; yet I have transferred my grasp of these principles to them. Similarly, I did not write about critical thinking in my English classes; yet I am now managing to write complete sentences and to organize my thoughts in paragraphs in this essay. The principles of writing sentences and paragraphs and computing and comparing percentages are clearly not limited to the domains in which they were taught to me. Is there reason to think that it is different for critical thinking?

INCLUDING CRITICAL THINKING IN A CURRICULUM

It is relatively easy to add a critical thinking course to the curriculum in a college or university. It is very difficult to do so at the senior high school level. Middle schools and junior high schools tend to be more flexible, but there is not much flexibility where requirements are concerned. By and large there are no separate courses in critical thinking at the elementary level, though there are programs.

These are four practical facts that are important in making decisions about the inclusion of critical thinking in the curriculum at the four levels mentioned. Another fact is that students are understandably intolerant of being exposed to the same thing over and over again, and doing

46

so is a waste of resources. Furthermore, it is difficult for teachers to reach an adhered-to agreement among themselves about the total content of an area like critical thinking. It is also difficult to reach an agreement on the question of which subject matter areas should be counted on to have taught something which can be considered as a prerequisite in other subject matter areas, if the division of responsibility is not simple.

If it were not for the lower reading level, the relative immaturity, and the shorter attention span of elementary students, the elementary schools would be the best place to teach critical thinking, because one teacher generally has control over most of the subject matter and other experiences of the students for a whole year. A principle that is introduced in one subject or activity could then be applied in others under the guidance of the same person. Repeated application in a variety of situations would provide the ability and disposition to extend the learning to new situations. Furthermore, barring problems resulting from students transferring from one school to another—mobility among schools is admittedly a problem—coordination from one grade to the next could be easier because of possible interaction among elementary teachers.

It would not be politically feasible to introduce an extra course in "critical thinking" at the secondary level unless it were adopted by one department as part of its course requirements. Perhaps the English or the social studies department could offer instruction in "critical thinking" in required courses. A half-year course in "critical thinking" in one of these two departments (in the sixth or seventh grade and also in the ninth or tenth grade) could well provide summary and reinforcement of preceding work and a satisfactory introduction to further basic principles. Alternatively the same thing could be accomplished with two or three units at each grade level in the English or social studies sequence. Teachers of other courses in the secondary school could then depend on students' having developed these skills (just as physics and chemistry teachers now depend on an elementary algebra course to have conveyed some of the basic principles of algebra).

It would be inefficient to leave it up to each teacher in every course to *introduce* some principles of critical thinking: for example, that denial of the consequent in an argument is a valid form of reasoning. Teachers would find that some of their students know it well (though perhaps by a variety of names) and that others do not know it at all. So it would be good to have one central place where basic, generalizable ideas are reviewed and introduced. Of course, we cannot expect complete transferable learning (i.e., the ability to apply principles learned in one subject area to an entirely different subject matter) to occur from this one central course.

If and when critical thinking instruction becomes prevalent and successful in the elementary and secondary schools, then the need (for the sake of efficiency) for a separate course at the college level to introduce the principles of critical thinking will diminish; but the need for the practice of critical thinking within the other courses will not diminish, since critical thinking about the subject is an integral part of the proper study of most subjects.

In sum, showing that critical thinking requires some subject (or domain) does not make it necessary that it be taught only within one of the standard subject matter areas. However, the current practical situation in secondary schools (especially senior high schools) seems to call for the lodging of basic critical thinking instruction within the existing subject matter areas. (English or social studies departments could take on the responsibility for the review and introduction of the basic ideas of critical thinking.)

But the same practical considerations do not hold at the college level. At that level—at least until the secondary schools take care of it—a separate critical thinking course in some department (often the philosophy department) is practically feasible (but articulation with other courses in the university is often lacking and requires attention). This all assumes that subject-matter-specific, critical thinking instruction should take place in all elementary, secondary, and college subject matter areas.

The question of whether critical thinking skills transfer from one domain to another is vague enough to make useful research on the topic quite difficult. How do we tell whether two topics are in the same domain or subject? How many instances of teaching a principle in different domains are needed for learning transfer to occur, and how do we count them? And which critical thinking principles are we talking about? They seem to differ in their ease of transferability. Yet it seems that critical-thinking instruction does transfer to new situations—like serving on a jury—and it seems that similar principles from English and mathematics also transfer to new situations.

We do not have sample curricula in action in existing schools to test these suggestions about subject specificity and curriculum. Nor do we have trained teachers and quality teaching materials for implementing the sample curricula. These are jobs that need to be done soon. I hope that the current tidal wave of interest in critical thinking lasts long enough for the necessary research and development to take place.

The current emphasis in critical thinking is one educational trend that we need to preserve. Let us hope that fickle public interest provoked by the early errors of enthusiastic people and by the ignorance of instant experts and charlatans does not destroy this trend.

CONVERSATION WITH
DAVID N. PERKINS

David N. Perkins talks about the nature of creative thinking—what it is and is not, and how best to develop it. He begins by suggesting key errors about the nature of thinking. First, he suggests that solutions to problems do not come by waiting for inspiration—thinking is an active process, and successful problem solving requires actively working on a problem. Second, he feels that perhaps too much emphasis has been placed on problem solving; time must first be invested in problem finding: searching for problems of interest, rather than automatically working toward the technical solution of a problem posed. Perkins suggests a variety of activities that he sees as integral to active problem solving. He critiques creative thinking courses that emphasize fluency—making lists of new ideas without subjecting the ideas to a sense of standards. He maintains that "there's no such thing as creating in general," and feels that courses that attempt to teach general skills of creativity may not be useful.

In this chapter the initials JLS identify the name of the publication where it appeared originally: The Journal of Learning Skills, *Fall 1983. Reprinted with permission.*

David N. Perkins is Co-Director of Project Zero at Harvard University, Cambridge, Massachusetts.

JLS: Throughout your book *The Mind's Best Work*, you challenge some common assumptions about thinking. Could you give us an example or two which you think are critically important—key errors people make about the nature of thinking?

PERKINS: Well, I think one of the most important errors is the notion that you fill your mind with relevant information and then wait, and eventually the solution to a problem presents itself. Certainly my own view is that thinking is an active process: You make the most progress when you spend the most amount of time pushing around pieces of the problem in different ways and striving to resolve the problem. This is not to say that it's never a good idea to set a problem aside. It may very well be a good idea at certain junctures. But basically you make progress by working on a problem, not by sitting back and waiting.

Another common error is this: In popular parlance, and I think in the field of psychology also, there's a great stress on problem solving. Well, indeed problem solving is a very useful skill. But it can be argued that just as useful a skill is problem finding. One of the most notable characteristics of a skilled and creative scientist, for example, is that he or she selects very good problems to work on. The problems are meaty, important, they lead to further developments. In general it seems to be the case that people in their thinking do not invest enough time in problem finding—that is to say, exploring the possible problems they might ad-

49

dress, and choosing, with some care and thought, a problem to address. There's even some empirical evidence from the visual arts that the artists who produce the most creative products are those who spend the most time on problem-finding kinds of activities—that is, on searching for the sort of work they want to do at the moment, rather than quickly jumping into a particular kind of work and investing their efforts in its technical execution. So another important thing to keep in mind: reallocate some time to problem finding.

JLS: You've said that it's important to work actively at a problem, not simply sit and wait for its solution. What kind of activities does one engage in when working actively at solving a problem?

PERKINS: My list of activities is not unique. I take it that the following kinds of activities are routine and relevant: You try to remember related problems, problems that you've addressed before that may bear on the problem at hand. You perhaps try to put your information in different combinations, different arrangements—perhaps you make lists or diagrams. You may try alternative modes of representation—verbal versus visual, let's say, pictorial, three-dimensional even. You may make analogies: connect the subject at hand to something similar to it or sometimes to something quite remote from it. You may try to project yourself into the situation—in a physics problem, for example, imagining that you're the proton moving through the cyclotron. You may try to list lots of ideas; you may go through cycles of idea-generating and criticism, so that you produce and then sift. All of these kinds of processes, and no doubt a dozen others, are very common in any kind of generative thinking.

JLS: In your book you said that there are perhaps some problems with creative thinking courses. That students may be "trapped by their hypotheses" or these courses may promote long searches which, if they're not guided by standards and clear objectives, keep a problem open without reaching critical solutions. Would you comment on that and what you think about creative thinking courses in general?

PERKINS: One thing has to be said at the outset about creative thinking courses: they come in many kinds, and it's hard to generalize. Now there was a period—roughly speaking, the '60s—where there was a leitmotif that was common to most of the instruction in creative thinking. That leitmotif was that creative thinking was a matter of ideational fluency—cranking out lots and lots of ideas, and then of course being in a position to pick the best one, and solving the problem. Now my impression is that the stock in trade of instruction in creative thinking has broadened somewhat since then. On the question of ideational fluency, in particular, there are at least two problems with it. One is the following: Research shows that those who make long lists of ideas are not necessarily very good at picking out the best ones, and in fact may end up with no better a selection than the person who has tried from the outset just to list the three or four ideas that feel strongest. So one may simply be investing time to no purpose in making a very long list.

I'd like to qualify that, though. I'd like to point out that it depends on one's standards in what one is seeking. It really makes sense to make quite a long list, idea after idea, if it's quite clear in your mind that you haven't yet achieved something of the potential that you want. In other words, many times the process of invention is driven by a sharp sense of the standards one is trying to meet, and searches get long because the process is so driven.

JLS: Like a composer revising what he's written because he has an idea in mind and he's not quite gotten it yet.

PERKINS: That's a good analogy.

The second reason for caution in evaluating earlier creative thinking courses is that measures of ideational fluency originally were thought to reflect real-world creativity. If you scored high on an ideational fluency test, presumably you were creative in your writing, or your mathematics, or whatever your discipline was. And therefore, the logic went, perhaps if we can improve people's ideational fluency, we can improve their performance in real-world creative situations. Since then some more research has been done, and it turns out in fact that performance on ideational fluency tests does not correlate well with ratings of real-world creativity based on things like assessments by peers on one's contribution to a field, or listings of important publications—most any sort of measures you might want. This question has been looked at from various perspectives by various researchers, and by and large the consistent finding is that measures of ideational fluency do not reflect real-world creativity well. Consequently, the whole conceptual underpinning of instruction designed to improve ideational fluency comes under challenge.

JLS: Do you feel that there's a tendency to teach creativity out of context? Can you teach creativity in the abstract, or do you need a discipline, a concrete field in which to practice this behavior?

PERKINS: Let me give you some ideas of that based on knowledge and some based on conjecture. First, as a philosophical point, you have to be being creative about something. There's no such thing as creating in general. Okay. Different kinds of instruction highlight one or another discipline in which one is doing the creating. Some instruction highlights everyday problems—how to get along with your brother-in-law. Some instruction highlights business problems—how to resolve a labor dispute. Some highlight artistic pursuits—how to produce a provocative, inventive poem. In fact, if you look at the range of programs designed to do this sort of thing, you will find they all have favorite domains of creativity. Those programs that pretend to teach general skills of creativity almost always give problems from a limited domain. It is simply not the case that the problems they give range widely over the universe of creative problems. For example, it's often the case that a book designed to provoke creative activity might use puzzle problems of various sorts— where you have to fit a diagram together to achieve a certain constraint. Now there's no particular reason to believe that this sample of the range of all possible creative problems is particularly representative. Granted, then, any program has made a selection, often a rather narrow selection, of the kinds of problems it will deal with. A question arises: If you get good at being inventive in this context, will your inventiveness be improved in other contexts? In general, the lesson of a number of studies in contemporary cognitive psychology is that transfer is hard to come by— harder than you would think. Quite commonly, if you train a person and get them performing pretty well in one domain, they don't carry across these skills to another domain. That's one caution. My own feeling, therefore, is if you're interested in performance in a particular domain, teach in that domain. Don't teach something else and hope it will transfer. Teach directly to the task.

Nonetheless, it's possible that there may be transfer from one of these problem domains to others. Furthermore, transfer is a sticky thing. It seems that you have much better luck getting transfer if you deliberately provoke it—if you teach the person to transfer—show people how to apply things like new methods for solving puzzle problems to solving a set of real-world tasks. By and large, there have not been very many studies where teaching to transfer has been an explicit part of it. It's not clear how much transfer one might get if one taught for it explicitly. So my position at the moment is: One, teach to the task you're interested in, since we can't count on transfer. Two, let's experiment with teaching explicitly to transfer to see how much we can get.

JLS: Would you comment on the notion that concrete application is more likely to result in creative thought than practice in abstract concept making?

PERKINS: Contemporary psychology shows clearly that skill in any domain is highly dependent on a vast reservoir of experience. Take for example chess. Studies of master-level chess have demonstrated that the chess master relies on a kind of vocabulary of configurations of the order of 50,000. Using this vocabulary quite automatically and spontaneously, the chess master encodes the layout of the board. This is the mechanism by which he can memorize a board at a glance. Presumably this is also the mechanism by which he can search out various possible lines of attack and defense more efficiently than can the novice. He has these "chunks" to think with, whereas the novice can only think on a piece-by-piece level.

There is evidence that similar kinds of chunking occurs in almost any domain of skilled performance. Solving problems in physics or in mathematics, one develops a repertoire of paradigms and patterns of thinking and organizes one's problem solving in terms of those paradigms and patterns.

Now it's quite likely that there's no substitute for lots of experience in accumulating this repertoire which enables highly skilled performance. But there is another side to the story. That's the side of being generally organized and systematic about what one is doing. The novice not only does not have a very large repertoire, but many novices are also very disorganized in the way they go about trying to tackle a problem. A good example of this kind of perspective is that of Alan Schoenfeld, who's done work on mathematical problem solving. Schoenfeld distinguishes on the one hand managerial strategies for keeping track of what one is doing, and on the other hand a particular heuristic, like mathematical induction. Roughly speaking, one might call the heuristics he's referring to the repertoire of chunks, but there is this other thing, this managerial strategy. Even when the student is a novice, and has not accumulated a very large repertoire, it seems reasonable to encourage the student to be systematic, organized. In much more specific terms, it's reasonable to ask him to do things like the following: One, ask himself, "Am I making progress on the problem?" or "Can I think of another approach?" "Do I have a plan that I'm in the process of executing? If not, can I make my behavior planful?"

In conclusion, I'd say that there's no substitute for experience in the domain, but neither is it true that students right from the first have the kind of good management that also promotes effective problem solving.

JLS: You talk about thinking aloud experiments in terms of research throughout the book. You speak primarily of research done with experts—people who are successful in their disciplines. Could you tell us something about thinking aloud not as an experiment, but as an instructional technique, as Art Whimbey and Jack Lochhead are doing*, to

---

*Arthur Whimbey and Jack Lochhead are members of the Editorial Advisory Board of the Journal of Learning Skills. We have published articles on their work, Cognitive Process Instruction using pair problem solving, in two issues of JLS: Winter, 1982 and Summer, 1983.

53

help students become better and more systematic problem solvers by thinking aloud, externalizing their thoughts. People doing this kind of work feel that to externalize thought is to improve its functioning. What do you think about that?

PERKINS: On the whole, I view this kind of work very favorably, and take a somewhat Vygotskian view of it. That is, private thinking is in significant part an internalization of more public verbal and other interactions. By making important patterns of thinking public, by forcing them to occur in public—dialogue between two pair problem solvers, for example—or simply by having a person verbalize his thoughts—that begins to teach the person something about possible patterns of thinking. This kind of practice encourages the person to view patterns of thinking so made explicit as objects that he can adopt or not adopt, choose among, revise, and so on.

JLS: Along these same lines, Jack Lochhead has said, "Novice students, particularly poor ones, do not need to be taught methods which they can only follow in a mindless fashion. Rather they need to be taught to think about whatever problem solving method they happen to choose" (*JLS* Vol. 1 (2), 5). Would you comment on this?

PERKINS: Well, Jack is encouraging a kind of critical awareness of what one is about that I can't help but applaud.

JLS: How does this work relate to your own in this area?

PERKINS: I would say that my approach is very much in line with Jack's approach, and, in fact, with similar approaches which are widespread in the field. The idea of making explicit the thinking process at work is almost universal in this kind of instruction. As to just what you do exactly and what kinds of problems you pose, that varies from person to person and from population to population. One of the characteristics of Jack's work, for instance, is that he's working with remedial math instruction. He's working with people who are demonstrably below par in their mathematical competence. That means that you have to strike a slow pace, do things in an orderly, step-by-step, and not very brisk way to make progress. If you're dealing with a group of gifted students, or even a group of ordinary students, you may be able to pose problems of a scope and subtlety that would be entirely unreasonable for the students Jack is dealing with.

JLS: In *The Mind's Best Work,* you talk about a number of heuristics, for example, SQ3R. Would you tell us your central criticism of heuristics as they've been used so far, and how you think they might be best adopted by students?

PERKINS: There are a number of difficulties that get in the way of the effective use of heuristics. Perhaps one of the most important is the quality of the heuristics themselves. The fact of the matter is that very few of the heuristics that are commonly taught have been subject to rigorous testing. Furthermore, there is a problem with the track record of those that have been tested. It turns out that some that seem very plausible when tested turn out not to be very helpful. For example, as I mentioned earlier, it turns out that it isn't necessarily a good idea to generate as long a list of alternatives as you can when trying to solve a simple sort of problem, such as coming up with a title for a story. Likewise there's an extensive body of research on brainstorming—itself a particular approach to generating many ideas—and the research is quite equivocal as to whether or not brainstorming yields a better product. As a generalization, we simply have to be cautious about our intuitions as to the helpfulness of a heuristic. Heuristics that plausibly might help do not necessarily help. Eventually we can hope that psychologists will get around to doing the necessary research on which heuristics are the most powerful.

It also should be said that some heuristics seem so blatantly helpful that there's no great need to do heuristics on them. For example, the heuristic advice, "Understand the problem before you try to do it," is virtually unquestionable, and certainly many students do not take the trouble to determine whether they understand the problem before tackling it.

Another problem with heuristics is that they overshoot. Often they specify so full and detailed an approach to the problem that it seems not worth the effort. Like SQ3R. Now this depends also on one's context. If one is preparing for an exam in the forces behind the American Revolution and the events leading up to it, one might be well advised to use SQ3R to the letter. On the other hand, if one is trying to take in the gist of what happened, SQ3R seems to be too meticulous to bother with. Usually these kinds of hedges do not come with the presentation of a heuristic. Rather the student is told to "Do this." Fortunately, most people are sensible about heuristics. They hear them, try them a bit, and quickly start to revise and revamp them to each individual's personal needs. However, the problem is that the student doesn't always have the sense of which the most important parts of the heuristic are, and may not do such a hot job at editing it.

By far the larger problem with heuristics, however, is that students forget them. After a few exercises in class and some adaptation, out of the instructional context the student simply does not turn his mind in that direction again.

JLS: Like outlining.

PERKINS: Perhaps like outlining. Although that is probably a good case of a bad heuristic. The contemporary view of psychologists of writing seems to be that outlining is not very helpful, at least outlining as conventionally taught. So that particular heuristic may be well forgotten.

JLS: Well, the problem with many heuristics is that they are similar to outlining in the sense that they are not integral to people's thinking. Once the student stops doing the trick, he stops doing it totally—unlike learning to generate questions, for example, most heuristics do not become part of the student's thinking.

PERKINS: That makes sense to me.

JLS: A major problem with the educational system is that students are taught facts; they are not taught how to go about finding solutions to problems, generating problems, finding out what questions the field asks. On the other hand the business of discovery and invention is very different from this. The scientist explores, raises, and tests hypotheses, rejects them, generates new hypotheses. In schools, we don't teach this process, so we don't teach much about any given field. Rather, we teach the summary that a scientist has come up with—10 neat steps. Since we don't teach disciplines, it's hard for students to conceive of questions which are relevant to the disciplines they are studying. In fact, the way material is presented, it's very difficult for students to do anything other than memorize things. In light of this problem, do you think there are ways we ought to revise education—not only what is presented, but how it is presented?

PERKINS: I'm enthusiastic about that position. Furthermore, I claim that it's not even that difficult to engage students in much more meaningful inquiry than is ordinarily the case. Let me give you some examples. Take history, for example. Typically, instruction in history, as you put it, is a delivery of the facts. It's a "here's what happened" approach. There's very little attention to how we know what happened, what the process of historical inquiry is like. Now it might be said that history is relatively inaccessible; it all happened back there before 1900; what can the students reasonably do to pursue historical inquiry and get a feel for it? But why limit history to what happened before 1900? Or even before 1980? Suppose the task is to construct a history of the town meeting that happened three weeks ago. There are witnesses that can be interviewed; there are newspaper accounts, radio accounts, perhaps, minutes, possibly videotapes, audio tapes that can be looked at. That is, there's raw data. From the standpoint of learning the inquiry process of history, it's quite irrelevant that this particular town meeting was a very minor event, in a very minor place, important to hardly anybody else in the world. This context of the town meeting three weeks ago captures nearly all the dilemmas that the historian must face in trying to figure out when analyzing events that took place forty years ago—or even four hundred years ago.

Another example: It's thought that something like hypothetical deductive reasoning is completely outside the ken of a seven-year-old. Let me give you a problem that's entirely within the ken of a seven-year-old, that asks the child to generate an explanation for something. Here it is: I stand there and tell myself, "Lift one leg without moving any other part of my body." If I do that, I tip over. But here's a paradox: when people walk, they're standing on one leg at a time. Problem: Explain how it is that people can walk without falling over, even though they walk with just one foot at a time.

Well, the explanation of course is that you shift your balance as you walk from one side to the other. This is not inaccessible; it's easily demonstrated. For example, if you watch someone moving towards you, as he walks you can see the weight shift. Now there's no reason that the explanation for this phenomenon has to be in complex terms, citing Newton's laws. The child, observing the weight shift, can talk about it in his own terms. There are dozens of other very accessible phenomena that can be the occasions for explanation.

One would also like the student to be able to draw inferences from the explanation and check them to see if they occurred. Here's a problem from biology which calls for deductive reasoning. A sessile animal is an animal in the sea that is attached, anchored to something. For example, a coral is a sessile animal. Question: Why are sessile animals in the sea, but never on the land? This is a question you can answer not by looking in a textbook, but by reasoning about it—by thinking what the sea is like and what the land is like, and what makes a sessile lifestyle adaptive in the sea and not adaptive on the land. A reasonably alert high school student can come up with this explanation: In the sea, food is borne by the current. It's a reasonable design to sit there anchored to a spot and snap up food as it goes by. Air is a much less buoyant medium, and there are far fewer living things in it. Consequently, it's not feasible to sit in one place for the duration of a lifetime without moving at all and let your food be brought to you.

These examples can be taken as support for the notion that it's just not that hard to pose substantive problems, and even substantive occasions of problem finding, to youngsters, even to relatively young children. There is no real excuse for education to proceed along its fact-based path. It seems to me that education is in the business of "truth-mongering," and would do far better to go into the business of building minds.

CRITICAL THINKING ATTITUDES AND THE TRANSFER QUESTION

by Alma M. Swartz

As Alma M. Swartz suggests, the transfer of thinking skills across the curriculum and to everyday decision making is an important concern in the field of thinking skills improvement. Summarizing the views of a number of theorists on the question of thinking skills transfer, Swartz maintains that the emphasis on techniques to facilitate transfer is misplaced. Further, Swartz notes the importance of evaluating the presence of critical thinking attitudes in students. She offers an interview technique and an attitude inventory as instruments for this kind of evaluation, and suggests ways for teachers to interpret the instruments' findings.

The author is school psychologist for the Westford, Massachusetts, school system.

We have a good deal of evidence to support the concern that what children learn in school does not carry over into their everyday decision making. Some of the questions that have arisen out of this concern are as follows: Have critical thinking skills been taught in our schools? How do we know this? If they have been taught, why do they not seem to transfer to everyday reasoning? If we teach critical thinking in science, are these skills the same as or different from critical thinking in other areas? How can we ensure the generalization of critical thinking taught, for example, in history to other areas and to everyday decision making? Must we teach for transfer? If so, how?

Researchers investigating critical and creative thinking processes have different opinions about questions of transfer. McPeck (5) argues that we think *about* something when we think critically. He feels that different skills are used, depending on the focus of thought. For example, McPeck suggests that there is no reason to believe that the thinking skills used in mathematics will transfer to other fields or to daily activities. Beyer (1) also doubts that thinking skills transfer across disciplines or tasks. Perkins (6), while agreeing that thinking skills do not transfer easily, proposes a model for resolving the problem of transfer. He postulates two kinds of transfer which he calls "high road" and "low road," and suggests that high road transfer requires a more conscious effort, while low road occurs more automatically. Low road transfer, however, cannot be counted on to transfer skills to any great degree, because these skills are not used in a variety of areas. Perkins suggests that students practice in many areas to expand the possibilities for the application of thinking skills (low road transfer); further, he advises instructing students in the more deliberate acquisition of the general principles which underlie the critical thinking skills (high road transfer). In a similar vein, Swartz (7) suggests the need for integrating thinking skill instruction into the mainstream curriculum. He stresses the need to apply this instruction across the curriculum, so that students have a wide repertoire of thinking skills when they encounter an everyday problem or a problem in another area of study. Swartz maintains that thinking skills should be modelled by teachers in the classroom through practice, and that students should be asked to abstract thinking principles from real life situations. In contrast to many other theorists, Ennis (4) feels that critical thinking skills do transfer to other areas of learning. He is "convinced that there are general principles that bridge subjects," and suggests that teachers can provide numerous opportunities for students to develop and use critical thinking skills in the classroom.

The models and advice for teachers suggested by these theorists undoubtedly do advance the acquisition of thinking skills. Nevertheless, successful transfer demands more than exercising thinking skills in different settings: A precondition to the successful transfer of critical and creative thinking skills may be the development of critical thinking attitudes: for example, the tendency to be open-minded, to build on the ideas of others, etc. That is, if these critical thinking attitudes are not intact, instruction in thinking skills may not lead to the transfer of thinking skills to other life situations. When these attitudes (or dispositions) are present, transfer of specific skills may be facilitated; when absent, transfer is likely to be frustrated.

TRANSFER AND CRITICAL ATTITUDES

Searching our experiences with and understanding of children based on available research about their growth and development, we discover that children do think critically, if not in the classroom, then in the backyard while discovering how to build a fort (unencumbered by the need to prove to the teacher that they already know how to build a fort). If critical thinking is, as defined by Ennis, "reasonable, reflective thinking that is focused on deciding what to believe or do" (3), then children do it, and it is as absurd to say that we must teach it as it is to say that we must teach children to talk. Given emotional stability, adequate parenting, adequate cognitive capacity, and interactive experiences, the child will tend toward the acquisition of critical thinking skills. Critical thinking is an innate, species-specific trait which is generative in much the same way that language is generative; although we cannot specifically teach either, we can help foster their development.

The human tendency to critically assess the world and one's interactions with the environment, being innate, proceeds from a biological imperative. Evidence for this biological aspect of critical thinking may be seen in the attitudes and dispositions which underlie and impel critical and creative thinking, and in the generative capacity of critical thinking. The creative, spontaneous selection and combination of ideas with experience serves the development of the individual and ultimately the development of the species. As educators, we must keep in mind the natural human inclination to discover the environment and ourselves in it as well as our tendency to invent new ideas. Only when something interferes with cognition (neurological, emotional, societal, etc.) does the natural inclination to critically assess the world fail to develop to capacity.

If we continue to decide what problems the child should work on in any given moment, then we continue to decide out of our own experience, rather than the child's. This means that, as educators, we should stop thinking of critical thinking as something that must be taught, and begin thinking of it as something that must be facilitated. In order to facilitate such thinking, teachers should take care to ensure that good critical thinking attitudes are developed, for here is the means whereby the critical thinking skills, once internalized, will transfer.

Consider two four-year-old children negotiating a game of playing house. The girl suggests, "You be the daddy 'cuz you're a boy." The boy says, "And I'll drive this car to go to work." She says, "But I need the car seat to take the baby for shots—this doll's the baby. You need to get the car seat. Where's the yellow car?" We may recall from our own experiences with children how often this kind of problem solving takes place, and how frequently the game itself never gets played; the best part appears to be the planning—the problem solving itself being the motivation, especially at this developmental age. In the above example, we see two children engaged in reasonable, reflective thinking in order to decide what to believe or do. They don't say, "You be the mommy and I'll be the daddy," but give good reasons for their decisions, so that play will go smoothly.

We should also bear in mind the creative aspects of critical thought: that is, the child's ability to intuitively combine disparate ideas in a spontaneous way to solve a problem or critically assess a novel situation. These solutions may not always be novel to adults, or even to other children. However, the fact that this particular child has invented for him/ herself a new way of looking at the world is, in and of itself, a creative act. The first time a child successfully negotiates a flight of stairs, no one has taught him or her the law of physics, nor has anyone when he or she builds a tower of blocks. The child encounters, evaluates, and effectively judges.

Probably all of the experts in the field of critical thinking believe that attitudes or dispositions are important in teaching critical thinking skills. However, the focus has primarily been on the acquisition of discrete skills. When attitudes or dispositions are mentioned, modelling by the teacher is suggested as a way to help children acquire these by assimilation. Encouraging the dispositions as they arise is also a frequent suggestion. While this is good advice, it is not enough. Teachers need to be well versed in the critical thinking attitudes and dispositions, and need to know how to encourage children to develop these before they can begin to integrate critical thinking skills into the curriculum and hope for successful transfer.

Costa points out that children often do not use metacognition. "They seldom question themselves about their own learning strategies or evaluate the efficiency of their own performance. Some children have virtually no idea of what they are doing when they perform a task, and are often unable to explain their strategies for solving problems" (2). These children are apparently not using well-developed critical thinking dispositions, probably because teaching methodology has focused on content rather than thinking. Costa feels that children's use of metacognition is most likely to increase when "strategies of problem solving are . . . generated by the students" (2). He maintains that "when students experience the need for problem-solving strategies, induce their own, discuss them, and practice them to the degree that they become spontaneous and unconscious, their metacognition seems to improve" (2). I would suggest that Costa is describing the actualization of critical thinking dispositions here.

Responding to the neglect of critical thinking attitudes in the field of critical thinking, Ennis (4) has added a list of dispositions to his taxonomy of critical thinking skills. These are as follows:

1. Seek a clear statement of the thesis or question.

2. Seek reasons.

3. Try to be well informed.

4. Use credible sources and mention them.

5. Take into account the total situation.

6. Try to remain relevant to the main point.

7. Keep in mind the original and/or basic concern.

8. Look for alternatives.

9. Be open-minded.

   a. Consider seriously points of view other than one's own ("dia-logical thinking").

   b. Reason from premises with which one disagrees—without letting the disagreement interfere with one's reasoning ("suppositional thinking").

   c. Withhold judgment when the evidence and reasons are insufficient.

10. Take a position (and change a position) when the evidence and reasons are sufficient to do so.

11. Seek as much precision as the subject permits.

12. Deal in an orderly manner with the parts of a complex whole.

13. Be sensitive to the feelings, level of knowledge, and degree of sophistication of others.

It is certainly reasonable to suggest that certain critical thinking abilities will not, in and of themselves, transfer to other domains—for example, the skills involved in understanding and utilizing tables and graphs, designing experiments, or classifying specific data. However, a necessary condition for the transfer of these abilities may be the student's predisposition to their use as the need arises. We can open up the possibility of the transfer of even specific skills (such as understanding tables and graphs) if the student has developed the tendency to be open to adapting ideas to novel situations. The problem in asking teachers to work toward transfer by enrichment, modelling, and bridging alone is that it takes the responsibility away from the student. As Costa points out, children learn best when they take responsibility.

EVALUATING CRITICAL ATTITUDES

Not only do we need to focus more on the importance of the attitudes and dispositions which foster critical thought; we also need to develop methods for evaluating their presence in students. School districts will not want to incorporate the teaching of critical thinking attitudes without some means whereby the acquisition of these may be measured. Those of us who have been concerned about evaluation methods have come to understand the limitations of pencil and paper tests as a means of evaluating students. Multiple choice tests, we know, are not completely accurate, even when carefully designed.

The use of the interview technique for gathering data may be useful in uncovering critical thinking dispositions. In a recent twenty-minute interview with an adult, all of the dispositions emerged (although as interviewer I was not intentionally looking for these, but was attempting to discover something about his thinking in general).

The specific directions in this interview were to read a typical letter to the editor and report any thoughts which came to mind. Inquiring into someone's thinking places the person in a threatening situation, since the interviewer is in a position of control and authority. Therefore, the interview was deliberately open-ended; no leading questions were asked; further discussion was encouraged with smiles, nods, and other nonverbal expressions of interest whenever possible. (Allowing the subject to choose what he wishes to convey gives him a feeling of control, and he is able to take more responsibility for giving a good account of his thoughts.) Analysis of the protocol provided for the existence of the critical thinking dispositions:

- *Disposition #1.* (clear statement) "I had a whole bunch of questions but I didn't conclude anything .... it's not that I don't agree with that; I don't quite understand what she's saying there .... by the end of the letter I was mystified because some things I couldn't quite .... that was part of the whole process, trying to understand what she was saying ...."

- *Disposition #2.* (seek reasons) "I think there are legitimate reasons for rejecting it, as I said .... If those laws have beneficial consequences .... it depends on what the law is .... she may well be right, maybe there is something wrong with the restraint, but I'm not even sure that the reasons she gives, even if correct, support her conclusion, because it may well be that carnage due to lack of seatbelts is such a severe problem ...."

- *Disposition #3.* (well-informed) "I never knew that. I don't know whether she's right, but it made me wonder whether she's right and want to find out .... She'd have to give me some facts about the risks ...."

- *Disposition #4.* (credible sources) "The fact that it was a letter to the editor, okay, in and of itself, makes me read it with caution .... I've found very few letters to the editor that I've found convincing ...."

- *Disposition #5.* (total situation) "Well, she says, 'My car ...' .... I had a whole bunch of questions .... she makes a comment at the end that .... Let's see she says .... I also wondered what was behind the letter—whether she was affronted by the government putting restraints on her or whether she was genuinely worried about her safety in wearing seatbelts ...."

- *Disposition #6.* (relevant to point) The examples above support this.

- *Disposition #7.* (keep original concern in mind) The examples above support this.

- *Disposition #8.* (seek alternatives) "I suppose some people would break those laws, but if those laws have beneficial .... seems to me that, even if there's a chance of shorter .... she may well be right .... it may well be that, on the other hand...."

- *Disposition #9.* (open-minded) "... you know, my feeling was that I ought to hear the rest of what she has to say before I make a judgment .... until I fully understood what she was saying and I guess I feel it's not a good argument ...."

- *Disposition #10.* (take, change a position) "That represents a certain point of view that I don't share .... she'd have to give me some facts about the risks of injury .... I think there are legitimate reasons ...."

- *Disposition #11.* (seek precision) "I think it is justified for the government to do things that will force people, even in a free society .... present a danger to themselves .... for example, warning labels on bottles ...." (Examples above also support this.)

- *Disposition #12.* (order parts to whole) A general tendency, throughout the interview, to refer back to the letter, rereading and focusing on a given paragraph, relating this to the general topic.

- *Disposition #13.* (sensitive to knowledge, etc., of others) "I concluded that she had a concern which was similar to a concern my doctor had .... It's not that I don't agree, I don't quite understand what she's saying .... I never knew that .... made me wonder (see Disposition #8).

Most of the dispositions surfaced during the first half of the interview. With better planning for this specific purpose, an interview could be conducted which is shorter and more precise in its goals. One would not necessarily need to interview all school-aged children to discover if they have developed any of these dispositions. The interview could be used for those children who might not communicate these as openly as do other children.

Those who find the interview method time-consuming, or who do not feel qualified to judge the data gleaned from an interview, will seek other evaluation tools. One such tool might be an inventory of critical and creative thinking dispositions or attitudes which could be filled out by teachers and parents as a general guideline to be used in addition to interviews. The inventory in Figure 1, based on Ennis's list of dispositions in conjunction with some creative thinking dispositions, may serve this purpose.

This inventory may be adapted in a variety of ways by the creative teacher. It can be scored, then scrutinized for the kinds of patterns which emerge. For example, does the child who receives a lower score jump to conclusions? If so, can this be related to a general impulsivity, or is it a need to compete—to be the first to have a good answer? Teachers may want to discover how serious is their concern about a particular child. If this child's inventory shows very few "Never" responses, the concern is not as great as for the child whose protocol is filled with these. Teachers may also wish to use the inventory to assess how well their teaching strategies are affecting the children. The inventory may be given to children to evaluate themselves or each other. Some teachers may find it useful as a general teaching tool, or as a reminder for the students.

A general word of caution for persons wishing to use this inventory should be added here. First, anyone using an instrument to inquire into a student's thinking habits must be trained both in interview technique and critical thinking. Second, every precaution must be taken to ensure that the data is not misused or misinterpreted. It should be made clear to those seeking to evaluate children that these devices are best suited for the affirmation of certain critical thinking attitudes. One cannot assume that these are not present simply because they do not emerge in a particular interview—all kinds of intrusions can and do interfere which would render the results invalid or questionable. These concerns aside, a short interview with children who, for example, do not participate in group discussions may reveal that they have nevertheless developed good critical and creative thinking attitudes.

CONCLUSION

It is disturbing to think that the way we have organized our schools and trained our school teachers has often had the effect of stifling children's natural inclination to inquire. However, it is heartening to know that in the true spirit of critical thinking we acknowledge this inconsistency and want to remedy it; at the present time those in positions of power and educational leadership consider the situation in dire need of remediation. Those of us who work closely with children, teachers and researchers in the critical thinking field, know that an enormous effort must be undertaken. Broad changes will have to be made—ultimately by the teacher.

It is clear that authoritarian methods of teaching run counter to instill-

INVENTORY OF CRITICAL AND CREATIVE THINKING
DISPOSITIONS AND ATTITUDES

This inventory is intended for use as a general guide in discovering which critical and creative thinking attitudes may be present in middle and high school students. It will not identify definitely whether skills are *not* present: the absence of evidence for an attitude or disposition may simply mean that it is not manifest at this time.

Please respond to all items. In those instances where you are not certain, circle the number that most often applies, or the number that best describes the student.

SCALE: 1. Never   2. Sometimes   3. Frequently   4. Always

HOW OFTEN DOES THE STUDENT:

1. Listen to another person's point of view or ideas	1	2	3	4
2. Suspend judgment or resist jumping to a conclusion	1	2	3	4
3. Reason from a perspective other than his/her own	1	2	3	4
4. Remain generally objective/open-minded	1	2	3	4
5. Take a position, given sufficient evidence/reasons	1	2	3	4
6. Look for alternatives	1	2	3	4
7. Seek a clear understanding of the question/problem	1	2	3	4
8. Ask clarifying questions	1	2	3	4
9. Look for reasons/information	1	2	3	4
10. Make good use of resources	1	2	3	4
11. Make use of credible sources	1	2	3	4
12. Remain relevant to the point/topic	1	2	3	4
13. Take into account the total situation	1	2	3	4
14. Change his/her position, given evidence/reasons	1	2	3	4
15. Persist, seek precision	1	2	3	4
16. Accept criticism, incorporate ideas of others	1	2	3	4
17. Self-evaluate his/her own ideas	1	2	3	4
18. Fit parts of a problem together in an orderly way	1	2	3	4
19. Resist closure ("play" with ideas)	1	2	3	4
20. Take risks (even if his/her idea may be "silly")	1	2	3	4
21. Put together disparate ideas	1	2	3	4
22. Discover relationships, patterns	1	2	3	4
23. Build on someone else's ideas	1	2	3	4
24. Give good feedback to others	1	2	3	4
25. Remain sensitive to the feelings, knowledge, expertise of others	1	2	3	4

© 1985 Alma M. Swartz

Figure 1

ing critical thinking skills and attitudes in children. We must, however, make a distinction between authoritarian teaching and the teacher as authority, not only over the subject area, but also in the classroom. In this regard, it must be acknowledged that children need the guidance of these professionals in correcting misapplications of the rules of thinking (errors in transfer, perhaps), just as parents guide the child's language acquisitions, correcting the misapplication of rules which the child has internalized and automatically generalized. Of course, merely making corrections is not enough. Nor does teaching for critical thinking simply entail adding on another list of skills to the basic curriculum. If children are to become responsible, reflective adults in an increasingly complex world, teachers must understand the nature and importance of critical and creative thinking. Further, they must be willing to integrate this understanding into all aspects of teaching. Finally, administrators must strongly support teachers' understanding and promotion of critical thinking skills and attitudes.

In this overly compartmentalized world, it is not useful to separate the child's cognition from his/her affect, or creativity. The child is both a thinking and feeling person who brings to the classroom partially developed dispositions (attitudes, traits), partially developed habits of thought, and a backlog of experiences. In paying more attention to the role of critical thinking attitudes, we will create a more integrated, more natural, and more reasonable approach to facilitating critical thinking in children. Through the development of critical thinking attitudes, we may hope for the successful transfer of thinking skills, not only to problems in subjects other than the ones in which they were taught, but also to the more complex problems of the world in which these children will need to solve problems as adults.

REFERENCES

1. Beyer, Barry K. "Improving Thinking Skills—Defining the Problem." *Phi Delta Kappan* (March 1984).
2. Costa, Arthur L. "Mediating the Metacognitive." *Educational Leadership* (November 1984).
3. Ennis, Robert H. "Critical Thinking and the Curriculum." *National Forum: The Phi Kappa Phi Journal* (Winter 1985): 28–31.
4. Ennis, Robert H. "Goals for a Critical-Thinking/Reasoning Curriculum." *Illinois Critical Thinking Project*. Urbana, Ill.: University of Illinois, June 21, 1985.
5. McPeck, John E. *Critical Thinking and Education*. New York: St. Martin's Press, 1981.
6. Perkins, David N. "Thinking Frames: An Integrative Perspective on Teach-

ing Cognitive Skills." Paper presented at the Practitioner's Conference on Teaching for Critical and Creative Thinking, University of Massachusetts, Boston, July 1985. (Forthcoming in *Teaching Thinking Skills: Theory and Practice*, edited by J. Baron and R. Sternberg. New York: W. H. Freeman.

7. Swartz, Robert J. "Critical Thinking Programs and the Problem of Transfer." Paper presented at the Harvard Thinking Skills Conference, 1984. In press.

THINKING ACROSS THE DISCIPLINES: METHODS AND STRATEGIES TO PROMOTE HIGHER-ORDER THINKING IN EVERY CLASSROOM

By Diane F. Halpern

Diane F. Halpern's chapter discusses three important aspects of integrating thinking skills instruction into content classrooms: developing higher-order thinking attitudes in students, implementing activities designed to encourage higher-order thought, and using exams and homework assignments that require and test for thinking. Halpern suggests that students live up to our expectations—if we encourage memorization, they will stay at that level; conversely, students can learn how to use facts, to discriminate between relevant and irrelevant information, and to make informed value judgments. To foster improved attitudes about higher-order thinking, Halpern suggests teaching students to question facts; learn from errors; monitor their own thinking processes; and teach each other.

The author is Associate Professor of Psychology and Associate Dean of Undergraduate Programs, California State University, San Bernardino.

> Most people would sooner die than think.
> In fact, they do.
> —Bertrand Russell

Traditionally, instruction in how to think has been a neglected component in American education. Students were more often taught what to think than how to think. Education within most academic disciplines has primarily been concerned with presenting students with the "facts" on a variety of topics—the "knowing that"—while offering little on how to utilize this information or how to discover facts on their own—the "knowing how." Domerique (cited in Parnes, Noller, and Biondini [6, p. 52]) summarized this situation well when he said, "Some people study all their life, and at their death they have learned everything except to think."

Students are expected to learn, remember, make decisions, analyze arguments, and solve problems without ever being taught how. There has been a tacit assumption that students already know how to think. Yet, as most teachers know, this assumption is not warranted. In recent years there has been increased concern with enhancing the critical thinking abilities of students in all areas of the curriculum. Although most people agree on the need for higher-order thinking instruction, few educators have been trained in the instructional methods and strategies needed to attain this goal. The focus of this chapter is to provide some practical suggestions and ideas that can be used in almost any classroom to enhance thinking. Three basic topics, each concerned with a different aspect of thinking will be addressed: (1) how to develop a thinking attitude in students, (2) classroom activities designed to encourage higher-order thought, and (3) examinations and homework assignments that require and test the thinking skills we want students to acquire.

HOW TO DEVELOP A THINKING ATTITUDE IN STUDENTS

One of the main indicators of a higher-order thinking attitude is the desire and motivation to expand the effort needed to learn complex material. Thinking well is hard work, and students find that they can often rationalize sloppy thinking habits. Some students are not convinced that higher-order thinking is worth the effort; others simply are not aware of the fact that they will have to work hard at thinking. They do not understand the relevance of much of their course work and cannot understand why they should exert the effort to think critically about the material that is being presented. In order to counteract these attitudes, begin each class period with interesting relevant examples to motivate students to consider the material being presented. Encourage students to ask questions and to anticipate outcomes. Asking good questions is an important thinking skill in any academic context, and one that should be fostered every day.

Too often, students learn with catechistical techniques. Most report that they learned their foreign language vocabulary words through rote memorization. Unfortunately, they probably also learned their history facts, geometry proofs, and chemistry the same way. If you doubt the accuracy of this statement, present a group of students with some information to be learned and watch how they go about learning it. You will find that many students will begin by listing the facts and then proceed to repeat them over and over in the hope that somehow they will "stick." This sort of learning is not conducive to the deeper level thinking we hope to promote because it does not create connected knowledge structures or complex representations in memory.

Students need to know that there are better ways to learn and to engage spontaneously in learning activities that will lead to more meaningful storage and recall. All teachers can encourage a positive deeper-level

70

thinking attitude by sending a clear message to students that knowing the facts in a subject area is only the first step. They also need to know how to apply them, when to question them, and how to relate them to other topics. It is these subsequent steps, utilizing and synthesizing the facts, that are the hallmark of critical thought. It is considerably more difficult, for example, to explain the mutual effects that certain historical events had on each other than it is to list the events in chronological order, and because it is more difficult, students will make more mistakes on this sort of task. You can teach them that these mistakes are opportunities to learn and not failures. Encourage students to view difficult material as a challenge and not a frustration. Help them develop the attitude of a deeper-level thinker.

Teach students to monitor their own thinking processes. In cognitive psychology, we call this "metacognition," or knowledge about what you know. Knowing what you know, and more importantly, knowing what you do not know is the most critical of the thinking skills. In order to develop basic thinking skills, it is necessary for students to direct their attention to the processes and products of their own thought. They need to become consciously aware of the way they think and to develop the habit of assessing the end products of their thought processes—the solution they have arrived at, the decision they have made, the inference they believe to be true, or the judgment they have formulated. In short, they need to be mindful of how and what they think.

Allow students the opportunity to teach each other. The effort involved in teaching is similar to the effort required in learning. No matter what subject matter you teach, there is no reason why you should be the only teacher in the room. Leave class time before each exam to form mixed-ability study groups (based on your own assessment of ability level) in which students review specific material. All teachers have probably had the experience of never really understanding a topic until they have taught it. The same is true for students.

CLASSROOM STRATEGIES AND ACTIVITIES DESIGNED TO ENHANCE HIGHER-ORDER THOUGHT

Thinking instruction is predicated on two assumptions: (1) that there are clearly identifiable and definable thinking skills that students can be taught to recognize and apply appropriately, and (2) that if these skills are recognized and applied, students will be more effective thinkers. Be clear about which thinking skills you want to emphasize in your classes. A general list of skills that would be applicable in almost any class would include understanding how cause is determined, recognizing and criticizing assumptions, analyzing means-goals relationships, assessing degrees of likelihood and uncertainty, incorporating isolated data into a wider framework, and using analogies to solve problems. The following short list is a suggested guide to accomplishing these objectives:

1. *Decide which thinking skills you want to emphasize in class.*

One of the first things to do if you want to encourage critical thinking in your classroom is to decide which skills are important in your subject area domain. For example, in history these would be some important thinking skills: understanding cause-and-effect relationships among events, the importance of time as an underlying dimension in everything that happens in history, questioning the sources of information that could also include propaganda and other attempts to persuade. Whatever your field, pay attention to the controversies. Too often, in many classes, students are given simple answers to complex questions. There can be no simple explanation to a question about the rise of the Nazi party or the causes of mental illness or the efficacy of Reaganomics. Encourage students to ask the important questions in your field and to think beyond the information presented. Have them relate what they have learned in your class to something else they have learned previously.

2. *Identify comprehension pitfalls in your subject matter domain.*

Once you have listed some goals or objectives, think about common pitfalls, the kinds of problems that commonly occur in understanding concepts in your academic discipline. The pitfalls vary with the nature of the subject matter. A common problem in mathematics and the sciences occurs when students rely on formulas they do not understand. A student may be able to substitute numbers for the algebraic symbols, then work through the appropriate arithmetic and arrive at the correct answer without ever understanding the principles involved or the meaning or importance of the answer.

One comprehension pitfall for students in the sciences and in mathematics is reliance on a technical jargon. Too often, they believe that scattering these terms in a discussion is evidence that they understand the concepts, when in fact their understanding of the phenomena involved is shallow and consists mainly of the ability to label events. Too often, students are taught to memorize formulas with little understanding of when and how to apply them.

Here is another example of a discipline-specific thinking problem. One course that is required of many college students is statistics. Most students have little trouble doing problems that are all the same type. All texts put t-test problems in one chapter, chi-square in another, and so on. The difficulty arises when students have to decide for themselves what type of analysis to use since problems in real life do not come neatly labeled with chapter references. Whatever academic area you teach, be aware of the "comprehension glitches" within your discipline and find ways to guide students around these pitfalls.

3. *Require students to be active participants in the learning process.*

Thinking is not a spectator sport. Very little, if any, learning ever occurs in a passive manner. There are several ways you can keep students actively involved in the learning process: pause frequently in your lecture to ask probing questions, require them to consider the pros and cons of each side of an issue, or demonstrate the phenomena you are describing.

There are numerous possible class activities that will help bring home the point that you want students to remember and use. In a psychology class, you could have Freud debate Maslow, in physical education your students could measure the effects of different types and levels of exercise on heart rate and blood pressure, in education they could compare recall rates when they are allowed to take notes during a lecture and when they are not. These sorts of exercises also make classes more enjoyable for both the students and the instructor. Remember that certain demonstrations are possible on the computer that never were possible before. You can show students certain wave forms in physics that students could only imagine before the computer age. Students can "see" how binomial distributions approximate normal ones in less than a minute with a suitable computer program. Take advantage of all of the new technology available.

4. *Make abstract concepts concrete and relevant.*

Much of the material we find ourselves teaching is theoretical and, admittedly, somewhat dry. This is a fact of life and we should not make high school and college classrooms look like *Sesame Street*. However, even the most theoretical and basic research issues can be related to something more concrete (and thus easier to understand and remember). Whenever possible, ask students to apply an issue to a relevant everyday occurrence and/or generate examples to show where it can be applied.

Another way of accomplishing the same result is to use an analogy— taking a totally new and unfamiliar concept and relating it to something known and familiar. For example, if I tell you that the atom is like a miniature solar system, and if you know a great deal about the solar system, this analogy can help you integrate information about the atom. Research in this area has shown positive comprehension effects with other simple analogies such as "The lymph system is like a sponge in the way it stores and moves liquids" or "The heart is like the filter system in a swimming pool." Also encourage students to generate their own analogies to understand difficult material. This general thinking skill is particularly useful when the material is abstract and difficult.

5. *Use think-aloud protocols to model your own thought processes.*

Whenever you are working a problem on the board or just thinking in class, try to think out loud. Verbalize the information you are considering and the steps you are mentally going through in solving a problem. Students can learn the thinking process by observing how you, as an expert thinker, go about solving problems. Say out loud statements like, "I need to decide which formula is appropriate when we have three groups of subjects and interval level measurement," or, "I need to think about the unknown in this equation," or, "I need to decide which sources of information are most convincing or reliable." Thomas Good, an authority on math education, has found that mathematics students learn best when the teachers actively work with them and model out loud the problem-solving process. It seems that when teachers think out loud, they provide "a structure and a way of thinking about the material . . . so [students] can better understand the relationships" (2, p. 7).

Be sure to use a simple, straightforward style to communicate difficult ideas. Mark Twain said this best when he said, "Eschew surplusage." Avoid technical terms and jargon when introducing new topics. Add new terms slowly with special care to provide good definitions. Be sure to use the chalkboard. It will help slow you down and will provide visual support to your presentation.

EXAMINATIONS AND HOMEWORK ASSIGNMENTS THAT REQUIRE AND TEST HIGHER-ORDER THINKING SKILLS

Now that we have considered encouraging a higher-order thinking attitude in our students and strategies for incorporating deeper-level thinking activities into the classroom, how do we know if we have been successful? If you began with an explicit list of thinking skills that are important in your discipline, then designing test items that tap these skills should follow naturally. Let's consider the specifics of designing measures of higher-order thinking ability within specific disciplines.

Multiple-choice and fill-in-the-blank tests do have valid and appropriate uses. While it may be possible to recognize or even recite a correct answer without understanding very much about the concepts being tested, multiple-choice and fill-in-the-blank test items allow us to test for detail and close reading in ways that essay questions do not. Even if this were not true, they would still be a necessary evil whenever teachers find themselves confronted with fifty students in a class, professional articles half-written, a two-hour curriculum committee meeting, and a soccer game to coach at four o'clock. They obviously meet some of our own needs by reducing grading time considerably.

Essay questions, even of the short-answer variety, should also be included as part of every assessment package. This is true in just about every class including mathematics classes. An excellent technique is to require students to write about the rationale and procedures in math courses. I firmly believe that unless a student can explain in words when, why, and how to perform a math procedure, then he or she does not understand it. It is a simple matter to solve an equation and a much more difficult one to make sense out of what one has done. Conversely, teachers can require some diagramming or other abstract representation in courses that are primarily language-based. An example in the health sciences would be a schematic model of the multiple influences that contribute to or protect against heart disease. An education example would be an abstract representation of the way stereotypes influence teacher expectancies. Verbal and schematic descriptions can be used to supplement each other in almost any course.

Do not accept superficial or skimpy answers. Be sure that students know from the first day of class that you expect high-quality work and that you will not be satisfied with less. Students live up to or down to teachers' expectations of them. Ask complex questions that will require thought. Of course they need to know the facts, but they also need to know how to use the facts and when facts are irrelevant or not even facts. Be sure that you give students opportunities to demonstrate these skills. Describe a novel situation and ask them to apply something they have learned in your class or ask them to generate novel situations in which certain principles apply.

When assigning homework, include reading or study guides to help students focus on the issues you believe are the most important. The kinds of instruction that you include in your study guides will determine what students do with the assigned readings. Be sure that you are providing them with ample opportunities to practice their thinking skills. The guides should tell them to generalize certain principles, compare two or more theories, synthesize several empirical findings, and define key concepts. In short, they should serve as guides for students to think critically about their homework assignments.

Add some humor to everything. In statistics, a generally grim course, have a "joke du jour." Start every hour of class with a joke. Assign students to bring in jokes on specified dates. Take the jokes seriously because they are an important part of the learning process. They need not be wonderful jokes. Moaning about a bad joke can be as useful as laughing at a good one.

Encouraging students to think is the most important task we will ever attempt as teachers. It is time to show the skeptics that they are wrong and that improvement in the ability to think critically can be an outcome of education.

REFERENCES

1. Berger, Dale; Pezdek, Kathy; and Banks, William. *Applications of Cognitive Psychology: Computing and Education*. Hillsdale, N.J.: Lawrence Erlbaum Associates. In press.
2. Cordes, C. "Search Goes on for 'Best' Ways to Learn Science." *American Psychological Association Monitor* (April 1983): 7–8.
3. Halpern, Diane F. *Thought and Knowledge: An Introduction to Critical Thinking*. Hillsdale, N.J.: Lawrence Erlbaum Associates, 1984.
4. _____. *Sex Differences in Cognitive Abilities*. Hillsdale, N.J.: Lawrence Erlbaum Associates, 1986.
5. Kahane, H. *Logic and Contemporary Rhetoric: The Use of Reason in Everyday Life*. Belmont, N.J.: Wadsworth Publishing Co., 1980.
6. Parnes, S. J.; Noller, R. B.; and Biondini, A. M. *Guide to Creative Action: Revised Edition of Creative Behavior Guidebook*. New York: Charles Scribner's Sons, 1977.

PRACTICE IS NOT ENOUGH*

by Barry K. Beyer

Barry K. Beyer maintains that the kind of thinking instruction that occurs in most classrooms will not effectively develop students' thinking skills. Beyer notes that in most classrooms, thinking instruction is a matter of teachers' instructing students to "think"; giving students practice exercises from worksheets or textbooks that require them to think; journal writing; debate; and providing thought-provoking assignments. While these activities are useful in helping students use their reasoning skills, Beyer feels that "practice is not enough": students need to learn how to think. Beyer suggests that thinking skills be explicitly introduced by classroom teachers. He provides two models for introducing thinking skills into the classroom, both of which provide for modeling of the skill (either by the teacher or by other students) and explaining the steps in using the skill.

The author is Professor of Education and American Studies, George Mason University, Fairfax, Virginia.

Most classroom teachers teach thinking. At least they believe they do. Teachers almost daily do many different things to foster thinking in students. Which of the following techniques are most used in your school to teach thinking?

1. Asking questions, sometimes questions structured in a sequence that seeks to move students from fact-giving to information-processing to applications.

2. Having students fill out ditto worksheets of multiple-choice questions that require them to think.

3. Encouraging students to "Think!" when a question is asked, to "Think again!" if the answer is slow in coming, and even to "Think harder!"

4. Having students write out answers to the "Questions for Further Thinking" that appear at the end of textbook chapters.

5. Engaging students in inquiry or problem-solving processes of hypothesizing in response to assigned problems and then checking out the validity of their hypotheses through discussion, further reading, and perhaps library research.

---

6. Having students write frequently, either journals or other types of writing.
7. Organizing debates in which students argue the pros and cons of subject-related problems or issues.
8. Giving students useful rules to follow, such as "Work as quickly as you can!" or "Use all the information given!"
9. Providing challenging assignments and questions.
10. Engaging students in continued student-to-student discussion, questioning, and interaction.

These techniques seem to be the most commonly used methods for teaching thinking in our classrooms today, as they have been in the past. Yet in spite of our continued use of such techniques, the National Assessment of Educational Progress, not to mention business and governmental commissions, reports that graduates of our schools seem less capable of engaging in skillful thinking than is desirable. Why? The major reason is our reliance on these very methods. We have long assumed that these methods teach thinking. They do not.

What these methods, singly or in any combination, do and often do well is encourage, stimulate, and provide opportunities for students to think. Indeed, most to them actually put students into situations where they have to exercise or practice their thinking as best they can. Unfortunately, if the goal is to improve student thinking, practice is *not* enough.

It takes more than practice to develop proficiency in thinking (1). This is not to say that practice is not important in achieving this goal. It obviously is important. But other things are equally or more important. To develop fully student proficiencies in thinking, classroom and school climates must support student and teacher thinking. Attitudes and dispositions that support and drive skillful thinking must de developed and reinforced. There must be deliberate and thoughtful study of the subject matter and knowledge bases that inform thinking. Finally, and perhaps most importantly, helping students improve their thinking requires the actual *teaching* of thinking.

Practice does not constitute the whole of teaching. In fact, practice alone is but a fraction of the instruction needed to develop proficiency in thinking. Research suggests that practice becomes most useful in improving thinking only when it is combined with at least three other methods (2). These include explicit introductions to the specific skills that constitute thinking, instructive guidance as students practice executing these skills, and teaching these skills to transfer. By incorporating these three techniques into what is conventionally presented to enable students to practice thinking, teachers can sharply enhance student proficiencies in thinking. This chapter suggests some practical ways to accomplish this task.

EXPLICIT INTRODUCTION OF THINKING SKILLS

Whenever students are expected to learn a new thinking skill, the skill should be introduced as explicitly as possible. This means that a teacher should provide instruction in how to execute the skill, with a minimum of interference from subject matter. Too often teachers assume students can engage effectively in the skills they need to think. Just as often, teachers assume that simply by executing a skill to learn more about a subject, students automatically learn the skill. However, neither of these assumptions is supported by most teachers' experiences or by research (3).

Research on skill learning and teaching suggests that in the initial stage of thinking-skill learning, students need to overlearn the skill. This requires, first, a direct focus on what psychologist R. E. Snow describes as the "component processes and skills" involved in the thinking tasks to be undertaken or learned, on the specific operations and rules that constitute the overall task (4). When "how to do it" is embedded in content, students naturally attend to the content and simply are not aware of the skill they may be employing. Explicit focus on the components of a skill in its introductory stage is essential to help students develop the conscious awareness of how the skill works that is preliminary to becoming proficient in its application (5).

Research also suggests three additional techniques useful in introducing any thinking skill (6). Modeling demonstrates the procedures and principles involved in executing the skill and provides students with cues that highlight these components as they are demonstrated (7). Student articulation and discussion of these components are also helpful at this point, especially in helping students to think through what constitutes a skilled operation (8). Finally, student discussion of what they do in their heads as they execute the thinking skill (metacognition) raises to a level of consciousness how their thinking occurs; this is important in helping students take informed control of their own thinking (9). These three techniques characterize what reading researcher Ann Brown calls "informed training" and "self-control training"—as opposed to the "blind training" typified by the techniques listed at the beginning of this chapter (10). Researchers Walter Doyle and Barak Rosenshine refer to teaching that includes these techniques as "direct instruction" (11).

Teachers can implement these techniques in several different ways to introduce any thinking skill. For example, they can use the principles of Piagetian-based developmental learning advocated by researchers such as

79

Irving Sigel (12) and Robbie Case (13). Or they can use more didactic, directive teaching as described by Doyle and Rosenshine (14). These two approaches are best conceived of as prototype strategies on either end of a range of strategies useful in introducing thinking skills. Many variants of these approaches may be found within this range.

A developmental strategy introducing a new thinking skill might proceed through six steps:

1. The teacher introduces the skill by writing its label on the board, having students name the skill aloud, getting synonyms from the class or providing them him/herself, and seeking examples of where students may have engaged in this operation before, in classwork or outside school.

2. Students are then asked to engage in the skill without any further instructions. If, for example, the skill is to make an analogy, the teacher and students find or devise a working definition of analogy, identify appropriate synonyms, and give examples of analogies encountered earlier in the course or in daily life. Then they make some analogies of their own or on assigned topics.

3. Students next discuss the analogies they made or attempted to make and reflect on and discuss these. In the course of the discussion, difficulties may become evident: they may have skipped steps in the procedure, or selected items that were too similar, or had difficulties in mapping the inferred relationships.

4. The teacher clarifies and models those parts of the procedure that students could not execute well, explaining the principles behind the steps being demonstrated.

5. Students then return to the original task. They may repeat it by incorporating the teacher's explanation, or they may produce new analogies following the original procedure with the teacher's modifications.

6. Students conclude the lesson by reflecting again on how they engaged in analogizing, to articulate the basic steps in the procedure and important rules or principles to follow in employing this thinking skill.

When a skill is judged too difficult for students and when the teacher understands exactly how to execute it, a quite different strategy can be used to introduce it. In launching this five-step directive strategy:

1. The teacher introduces the skill in the same manner used in the previously described strategy—writing the label on the board, developing synonyms and a definition for the skill, and helping stu-

dents recall similar examples of where they may have performed the skill or seen someone do it earlier.

2. The teacher then describes how an expert executes the skill, instead of asking students to practice it. A teacher who chooses this strategy to introduce making an analogy would at this point explain step-by-step how the skill is executed, perhaps as outlined by researchers Patricia Alexander or Robert Sternberg (15).

3. The teacher next demonstrates the skill with whatever contributions students care to volunteer, highlighting important operational cues as the demonstration proceeds.

4. After discussing reasons for executing the skill procedures and any relevant knowledge, the teacher then has students apply what they have seen, heard, and discussed to executing the skill themselves.

5. To conclude this introductory lesson the teacher guides students in reflecting on and discussing the extent to which they followed the steps modeled for them, what they did mentally to execute the skill, any modifications they thought they were making in the modeled procedure, and what they learned about the skill.

These two introductory strategies share a number of common features. Both require approximately a class period, anywhere from 30 to 45 minutes depending on the complexity of the skill, the abilities of the students and their previous experience with the skill, and the type of subject matter serving as the vehicle for applying the skill. Both strategies provide for modeling the skill: the developmental strategy by students who do it reasonably well in the two applications of the skill, and the more expository strategy by the teacher. Both strategies explicate the steps in the procedure by which the skill is executed by both students and teacher. Both strategies involve students in thinking about and discussing what they do in their heads as they execute the skill.

Most importantly, the focus throughout each strategy is on the skill. The introduction to each lesson clearly establishes learning the skill as the lesson objective. It also helps students develop the mental set needed to call up previous experience related to the new skill. Thereafter, each strategy focuses exclusively on the components of the skill. In spite of temptations to engage in discussion of subject matter, especially where students offer inferences of questionable validity, the teacher must, in such an introductory lesson, put discussion of subject matter aside until the next lesson and keep student attention on the attributes of the skill. Concluding the lesson by reflecting on or reviewing how the skill works and the rules that guide its explanation completes both strategies. This ensures continuing, explicit attention to the skill throughout its introduction.

One of these strategies or a variant can be used to introduce a thinking skill whenever a teacher senses that students cannot execute well a thinking skill they need to complete a subject matter task or whenever the teacher wants to introduce a skill new to the students (16). A teacher who has command of these strategies can use them on the spot, switching to them whenever appropriate. Regardless of which particular strategy is used, for best results it should include the features of a skill introduction described here. Use of such a lesson contributes immeasurably to student understanding of and increased proficiency in any thinking skill.

GUIDED PRACTICE

Of course no student should be expected to demonstrate proficiency in a particular thinking skill simply on the basis of one introductory lesson on it. Unlike the teaching of information, which can usually be presented in a single lesson, teaching a skill requires continued attention to the skill over an extended period of time. Research suggests these followup skill lessons should be frequent, require relatively small amounts of time—usually interpreted to be approximately 20 minutes—and be spaced out intermittently over a period of time. Moreover, as Benjamin Bloom and other experts have noted, these lessons should provide immediate instructive feedback and correction for the students (17).

To promote proficiency in a skill, lessons that follow an introduction to a skill ought to offer not only practice in executing the skill but continued teacher and peer feedback and instruction in how to execute it. Such instructive feedback can precede, follow, or be simultaneous with application of the skill. Here is one strategy useful in providing such guided practice:

1. The teacher **reintroduces** the skill to be used, exactly as in the introductory lesson strategies—with its name, some synonyms, a definition, and examples of its use.

2. The teacher, with student help, **previews** how to execute the skill by reviewing what students already know about the steps to go through and what rules or principles need to be followed.

3. The students **apply** the skill to the same type of data as used in the introductory lesson, periodically checking what they are doing against what they articulated earlier as they previewed the skill, taking corrective steps as needed.

4. The students **reflect** on how they executed the skill, especially on any obstacles they encountered and how they dealt with them, and on any modifications they made in the skill.

These activities customarily take 20 minutes. Once the activities have been completed, students can move to a discussion of the subject matter products generated by their application of the skill.

A number of guided practice lessons using strategies like those outlined here should follow any lesson introducing a thinking skill. Although there are no specific guidelines presented in the research as to how many, a teacher will know when to move into conventional student self-directed practice or use of the skill by observing when the students reach a level of proficiency where a detailed introduction of the skill and previewing and reviewing skill attributes are no longer necessary (18).

SELF-DIRECTED PRACTICE

Once a thinking skill has been explicitly introduced and students have had sufficient guided practice to attain self-directed autonomy in applying the skill, self-directed practice in or exercise of the skill becomes appropriate. It is at this point that the techniques listed at the beginning of this chapter prove most useful. By engaging in activities initiated by or built around these techniques, students have an opportunity to exercise on their own the thinking skills they are learning. But without prior explicit introduction and guided practice as described here, such techniques will be more like testing than teaching.

TEACHING TO TRANSFER

Contrary to common assumptions, thinking skills do not transfer automatically to contexts or settings that differ from the context in which they are initially developed. Thinking skills are very much tied to the contexts in which they are initially experienced. Thus, in order to help students generalize a thinking skill—to be able to apply it or transfer it to a variety of subjects, settings, or contexts—teachers must explicitly show them how. Teachers must provide instruction in a thinking skill in a variety of contexts after it has been mastered in the initial context. Too often the teaching of thinking ignores this important step (19).

Teachers can do several things to help students learn how to transfer a newly learned thinking skill. First, teachers who initiate instruction in a new skill, after providing guided practice to the point where students can apply the skill effectively on their own, can show them how to apply the skill in different contexts. Teachers who wish students to apply a skill in their subject area that was introduced in another subject can do the same thing. This requires use of almost the same kinds of strategies used to conduct an introductory lesson in a skill. Indeed, using a previously learned skill in a new context usually appears to students as if they are learning a new skill. To do this effectively, a teacher can do the following:

1. Introduce the skill, as in the preceding strategies.
2. Review what students know about the skill.
3. Explain and demonstrate how the skill is executed in the context to which it is to be transferred.
4. Have the students apply the skill in this new context, providing corrective feedback as needed.
5. Have the students reflect on what they did in their heads as they executed the skill.

This strategy differs from the directive introductory strategy only in its second step. Here students review what they already know about executing the skill before they try to apply it in the new context. Thus they have to concentrate on only one new thing—the context—when they apply the skill.

Once a previously learned skill has been reintroduced in a new context or setting, students must receive guided practice in applying the skill in this context until they achieve the appropriate level of proficiency. As they demonstrate this level of proficiency, guided practice must be mixed between applications of the skill in the original context and in the newer context to which it is being transferred. As students apply the skill, with appropriate corrective feedback, to a variety of contexts, they move toward generalizing the skill. Once this has been accomplished, students can engage in self-directed application of the skill, initiated by teacher questions, writing assignments, or other techniques commonly used to foster practice in thinking. Teaching a thinking skill to transfer actually duplicates the process of introducing a new skill from scratch to initial mastery, as it moves from introducing it, through guided practice, to autonomous application or self-directed practice.

MAKING PRACTICE PAY OFF

Developing student proficiencies in thinking requires considerably more than simply making students think. It requires more than encouraging or exhorting, more than questioning and discussing, more than stimulating and challenging. All of these techniques are useful in engaging students in thinking, but they fail to show them how to think more skillfully than they otherwise do.

For practice to pay off in improved student thinking, it should be combined with explicit introductions to the major skills that constitute thinking, repeated guided practice in executing these skills, and the teaching of these skills to transfer. By incorporating these three techniques into teaching strategies that include practice and applying them to the teaching of thinking, teachers can accomplish what they have long sought to accomplish, the fullest possible development of our students' abilities to think skillfully on their own.

REFERENCES

1. John McPeck, *Critical Thinking and Education* (New York: St. Martin's Press, 1981), 78; Sydelle D. Seiger, "Reaching Beyond Thinking Skills to Thinking Strategies for the Academically Gifted," *Roeper Review* 6, no. 4 (April 1984): 185–88.
2. Michael I. Posner and Steven W. Keele, "Skill Learning," in *Second Handbook of Research on Teaching*, ed. Robert M. W. Travers (Chicago: Rand McNally, 1973), 805–31; Barak V. Rosenshine, "Teaching Functions in Instructional Programs," *Elementary School Journal* (March 1983): 335–53; Jack Lochhead and John Clement, eds., *Cognitive Process Instuction: Research on Teaching Thinking Skills* (Philadelphia: Franklin Institute Press, 1979).
3. Hilda Taba, "Teaching of Thinking," *Elementary English* 42, no. 5 (May 1965): 534; Edward M. Glaser, *An Experiment in the Development of Critical Thinking* (New York: Bureau of Publications, Teachers College, Columbia University, 1941), 69; James P. Shaver, "Educational Research and Instruction for Critical Thinking," *Social Education* 26, no. 1 (January 1962): 14, 16.
4. Quoted in Norman Frederiksen, "Implications of Cognitive Theory for Instruction in Problem Solving," *Review of Educational Research* 54, no. 3 (Fall 1984): 382; see also McPeck, *Critical Thinking*, 18, and Robert J. Sternberg, "How Can We Teach Intelligence?" *Educational Leadership* 42, no.1 (September 1984): 47.
5. Catherine Cornbleth and Willard Korth, "If Remembering, Understanding, and Reasoning Are Important . . .," *Social Education* 45, no. 3 (April 1981): 278; McPeck, *Critical Thinking*, 18; Rosenshine, "Teaching Functions."
6. Jane Stallings, "Effective Strategies for Teaching Basic Skills," in *Developing Basic Skills Programs in Secondary Schools*, ed. Daisy G. Wallace (Alexandria, Va.: Association for Supervision and Curriculum Development, 1983), 1–9; Ann Brown, Joseph C. Campione, and Jeanne D. Day, "Learning to Learn: On Training Students to Learn from Texts," *Educational Researcher* 10 (February 1981): 14–21; Sternberg, "How Can We Teach Intelligence?" 38–50; Benjamin Bloom, *Human Characteristics and School Learning* (New York: McGraw-Hill, 1976).
7. David W. Pratt, *Curriculum Design and Development* (New York: Harcourt Brace Jovanovich, 1980), 313; Posner and Keele, "Skill Learning"; Rosenshine, "Teaching Functions."
8. Rosenshine, "Teaching Functions."

9. Brown and others, "Learning to Learn"; Sternberg, "How Can We Teach Intelligence?"; Elizabeth Bondy, "Thinking About Thinking," *Childhood Education* (March/April 1984): 234–38; Arthur L. Costa, "Mediating the Metacognitive," *Educational Leadership* 42, no. 3 (November 1984): 57–62.

10. Brown and others, "Learning to Learn," 15.

11. Walter Doyle, "Academic Work," *Review of Educational Research* 53, no. 2 (Summer 1983): 159–99; Barak V. Rosenshine, "Content, Time and Direct Instruction," in *Research on Teaching*, ed. Penelope L. Peterson and Herbert J. Walberg (Berkeley, Calif.: McCutchan, 1979), 28–56.

12. Irving Sigel, "A Constructivist Perspective for Teaching Thinking," *Educational Leadership* 42, no. 3 (November 1984): 18–22.

13. Robbie Case, "A Developmentally Based Theory and Technology of Instruction," *Review of Educational Research* 48, no. 3 (Summer 1978): 439–63.

14. Doyle, "Academic Work"; Rosenshine, "Content, Time and Direct Instruction."

15. For a description of the analogy-making process, see Patricia A. Alexander, "Training Analogical Reasoning Skills in the Gifted," *Roeper Review* 6, no. 4 (April 1984): 191–93; Sternberg, "How Can We Teach Intelligence?"

16. For additional similar strategies, see Barry K. Beyer, "Teaching Critical Thinking: A Direct Approach," *Social Education* 49, no. 4 (April 1985): 297–303; Reuven Feuerstein, *Instrumental Enrichment* (Baltimore: University Park Press, 1980); Superintendent of Public Instruction, *Development of Problem-Solving Skills for Vocational and Educational Achievement: Student Workbook* (Olympia: Washington State Department of Public Instruction, 1976).

17. Bloom, *Human Characteristics*; Rosenshine, "Teaching Functions," 340–41; Posner and Keele, "Skill Learning," 807, 813–14.

18. Posner and Keele, "Skill Learning."

19. Brown and others, "Learning to Learn," 15; Bryce B. Hudgins, *Learning and Thinking* (Itasca, Ill.: F. E. Peacock Publishers, 1977), 142–72; Herbert J. Klausmeier and J. Kent Davis, "Transfer of Learning," *Encyclopedia of Educational Research* (New York: Macmillan, 1969), 1483–93: Herbert Simon, "Evidence on Transfer," in *Problem Solving and Education: Issues in Teaching and Research,* ed. D. T. Tuma and F. Reif (Hillsdale, N.J.: Erlbaum Associates, Publishers, 1980), 882–84; David N. Perkins, "Thinking Frames," paper presented at ASCD Conference on Approaches to Thinking, Alexandria, Virginia, August 6, 1985.

LEARNING TO LEARN: IMPROVING THINKING SKILLS ACROSS THE CURRICULUM

by Marcia Heiman

> Marcia Heiman discusses the development, structure, and effects of the Learn-
> ing to Learn Thinking Improvement Program. The program began nearly 20 years
> ago with research at the University of Michigan. Successful learners were asked to
> talk aloud their thinking while engaged in a wide variety of academic tasks. It was
> discovered that the following thinking skills are common to good learners: they ask
> questions of materials they read and hear, continually raising and testing hypothe-
> ses; they devise informal feedback methods to assess their learning progress; they
> break down complex ideas and tasks into manageable components; and they are
> goal-directed in their approach to learning. Over several years' time, these skills
> were translated into practices that proved to be highly effective for unsuccessful
> students.
>
> This chapter is reprinted with permission of the Association for Supervision and
> Curriculum Development from Educational Leadership, September 1985.
>
> The author directs the Learning to Learn Program, Boston College, Chestnut
> Hill, Massachusetts, and is coeditor of this book.

When I was in high school I hated school. I never read nothing, never
did no school work. I dropped out of school as soon as they let me.

I couldn't get no job, so I decided to see if college was better. I went
for my GED, and came to Roxbury Community College. I didn't do
good my first semester here—I failed two courses. Then I took Learning
to Learn, and things really changed. I had to think about my school
work. Reading was like playing some game—looking for the answers to
my questions. I'm a business major, and now I can do even hard subjects
like economics and accounting. It's like I think better. Math was a jum-
ble for me. Now I see how to do the parts and how they fit together.

Used to be I couldn't see no future for me. Now I can see my way to a
four-year college education. I just wished I took Learning to Learn in
high school, so I didn't need to waste no time like that.

—student at Roxbury Community College

During the 1960s, a group of researcher-clinicians at the University of
Michigan took a nontraditional approach to improving students' learning
strategies. Rather than using a diagnosis-and-remediation model, which

at best results in only a year's gain in a year's time, the Michigan group sought to discover skills that are critical to successful learning. If skills of successful learners could be identified and translated for use with less successful students, the group felt that learning gains might be more rapid.

Over a period of several years, these researchers observed the learning behaviors of successful students as they verbalized their thinking while solving a variety of complex academic tasks. They found that good learners:

1. "Program" their learning for content courses—identifying the component parts of complex principles/ideas and breaking down major tasks into smaller units.
2. Ask questions about new materials, engaging in a covert dialogue with author or lecturer, forming hypotheses, and reading or listening for confirmation.
3. Devise informal feedback mechanisms to assess their own progress.
4. Focus on instructional objectives, identifying and directing their study behaviors to meet course objectives.

The Michigan group translated these skills into a series of exercises that students could apply directly to their academic work. I joined the group in 1967. Since then, as director of a number of college learning centers, I have sought ways to apply the four general skills to a wide range of academic areas and to adapt the techniques to students of varying entry skill levels. In 1979, I was joined in this work by Joshua Slomianko, who has helped put the skills into the framework of a cohesive system and found applications to new contexts. The resulting combination of skills and instructional materials constitutes Learning to Learn (LTL).

Learning to Learn has three stages: *input* (gathering information), *organization* (arranging information for further analysis), and *output* (student demonstration of mastery of the material). Students learn to build general learning skills and subject-specific skills into their daily school work. After a few months of adapting these skills to their coursework, most students report that they become involved with school work and that they begin using the skills automatically. For example, one student said, "I used to fall asleep in class and over my books. Now I want to know what's going on. I ask myself, 'What's the teacher after now? Is he answering my questions, or is this something new?'" As students begin to "play" with the material in their courses and discover their own variations of the skills, they increasingly view the skills as aspects of two central learning tools: generating questions and breaking down complex ideas and tasks into simpler, more comprehensible parts.

As a result of work done with educationally disadvantaged college students reading as low as the 5th grade level, the U.S. Department of Education's Joint Dissemination Review Board approved Learning to Learn for national dissemination. Data from controlled studies show that the program has significant, long-term effects on students' grade point averages, the number of academic credits they complete per semester, and their retention in school. For example, a study conducted with students reading at the 6th grade level at Roxbury Community College showed that LTL students earned a 2.9 grade point average; comparable students who received traditional remediation (for example, content-course tutoring or basic skills support) earned a 2.2 grade point average (Heiman, 1983). LTL students also completed significantly more academic credits per semester. Three semesters after treatment was completed, 70 percent of the LTL students were still in college or had graduated, as compared with 40 percent of non-LTL students.

LEARNING TO LEARN IN SECONDARY SCHOOLS

Learning to Learn has now been piloted by teachers in several Boston-area high schools. In 1985-86, the program is being fully implemented in a number of schools, including Winchester High School, West Roxbury High School, and the Massachusetts Pre-Engineering Program at Boston Latin High School in Massachusetts; Kings Park Junior and Senior High Schools on Long Island; and Taft High School in Cincinnati.

Learning to Learn is most effectively built into students' academic work in two ways:

1. *In the content classroom.* In both junior and senior high schools, teachers incorporate LTL skills directly into their classroom teaching. The following vignettes illustrate this process:

- Robert Stone's 10th grade chemistry class has been assigned Chapter 7, which discusses the relationship among temperature, pressure, and volume of gases. Students work in pairs, generating questions from the text and using an active method of reading to solve problems. In this way, their chemistry texts become "dictionaries" that help them solve the sample problems in the text.
- Amy Anderson's 6th graders will be studying a unit on Africa. Working in small groups, they have identified questions to which they would like to find answers. Their questions will be the basis of small-group "research" projects, in which they will find answers to their questions in an encyclopedia. Each group has at least two "resource" persons who read at the 4th grade level or higher.
- Albert Hart has just given a brief lecture on Greek city-states to his 9th grade social studies class. Students took notes on his lecture.

Later, working in pairs, students will help each other fill in missing notes and generate questions from those notes. They will then use their questions to read-to-find-answers in the textbook chapter on Greek city-states.

As these illustrations suggest, Learning to Learn has a wide range of applications for content classrooms. Classroom management problems are minimal because student motivation is high. By looking for answers to their own questions and breaking down complex ideas into manageable units, students gain a sense of mastery over their academic work. Their information search becomes personal, as they are working to achieve goals they have set for themselves.

2. *As a credit course.* In the senior high school, Learning to Learn is also offered as a year-long credit course. Students are required to adapt the appropriate LTL skills to content-area courses taken concurrently with LTL. Students learn how the skills relate to each other by learning principles on which they are based and how to vary the skills for a wide range of academic tasks. The course is designed to make students independent learners in any academic course, whatever its structure.

Learning to Learn is available to schools through a combination of training workshops and instructional materials. Content-area teachers receive field-relevant instructor manuals, which review those skills most suited to a particular discipline, suggest ways of using the skills as classroom activities or homework assignments, and provide sample lesson plans. Manuals are available for teachers of social studies, English, mathematics, physical science, and biology/earth science. In addition, student workbooks are available in these areas (such as *Learning to Learn Social Studies*).

A detailed manual provides teachers of the LTL credit course with step-by-step instruction in the content and structure of the course. In addition, a student workbook gives students practice in using LTL skills and suggests ways to adapt them for use with content classwork.

POSITIVE OUTCOMES

Learning to Learn has positive outcomes for students, teachers, and school administrators. Students become more actively engaged in their work and can improve their basic skills (primarily in reading, writing, and listening), content-course grades, and reasoning skills. Improved student motivation and a higher level of student classroom participation, in turn, have a positive effect on teacher morale. Schools that fully use the system can expect to realize some of the following results: improved student scores on competency exams, improved student retention through graduation, and more students going on to post-secondary schools.

One reason for the system's effectiveness is that it provides students with an environment conducive to active learning. Students are not simply advised to improve their organization, motivation, and interest in school. Rather, as the student quoted in the beginning of this article suggested, students develop tools for turning academic work into a kind of "game" in which they predict questions and answers. The dichotomy between "real world learning" and "book learning" begins to diminish for many students as they see the relationship between the kinds of learning they do in daily life and academic settings.

The useful effects of Learning to Learn appear to be a product of its basic approach to higher-level learning: the skills that are central to the system (generating questions, identifying essential parts of complex situations, looking for feedback on progress, directing behavior toward clear goals) are part of *all* learning. Learning to Learn works because we are teaching children to bring their own highly developed intellectual strategies into a setting—formal education—that has often seemed alien ground.

REFERENCE

Heiman, M. "Learning to Learn," Joint Dissemination Review Panel Submission. Washington, D.C.: National Diffusion Network, 1983.

A STRATEGY FOR DEVELOPING DIALECTICAL THINKING SKILLS

by Joel Rudinow and Richard Paul

Joel Rudinow and Richard Paul discuss the importance of reflective self-criticism and the ability to reason sympathetically within alternative frames of reference. In a series of exercises students learn to argue in and be sympathetic to positions—frames of reference—different from their own. The class is divided into groups according to students' initial positions. The instructor functions as moderator, creating an atmosphere that encourages mutual awareness and responsiveness. After experimenting with the alternative positions, students can defend both their own views and those of others. The ability to sympathetically articulate an opinion other than one's own, and perhaps to consequently alter one's own opinion, is seen as essential to the critical thinking process.

The authors are with the Center for Critical Thinking and Moral Critique, Sonoma State University, Rohnert Park, California.

Among the most difficult yet important intellectual skills currently taught in Critical Thinking courses are those we would call dialectical. These include the ability to reflect critically on one's own thinking and the closely related ability to reason sympathetically within frames of reference distinct from, and even opposed to, one's own. The instructional strategy we will present here is appropriate for students at grades 9 through 16 studying in a variety of disciplines. We wish to stress, however, that the abilities our strategy is intended to cultivate are latent and important to cultivate at the earliest stages of formal education. Accordingly, we encourage instructors in the elementary grades to consider adapting our recommendations to the needs and maturity levels of their students. Before we turn to the details of our strategy, let us briefly discuss the nature and importance of these abilities.

Reflective Self-Criticism: To think about one's own thinking, to make one's own thinking the object of one's thinking, particularly with a view to discovering its limitations and weaknesses—this is what we mean by "reflecting critically on one's own thinking" or "reflective self-criticism." The difficulty inherent in reflective self-criticism is both deep and obvious: reflective self-criticism requires a level of provisional or hypothetical detachment from one's own views, but since the critic and

92

the thinker are identical, this detachment frequently seems psychologically or even conceptually impossible. And yet not only is detachment from one's own views a possibility, but also it and the reflective self-criticism it makes possible are essential to intellectual self-guidance and to autonomous intellectual growth. In other words, the abilities to detach oneself from one's own views and to reflect critically on one's own thinking are fundamental to learning to think for oneself. Indeed, one's awareness and grasp of one's own views are based in large part on one's understanding of the ways one's views relate to and diverge from the views of others.

Reasoning Sympathetically Within Alternative Frames of Reference: There is no better way to demonstrate to students that detachment from one's views and reflective self-criticism are possible and beneficial than to have them *do* these things. And a good way to get students to do these things is to have them engage in a process of sympathetic reasoning within frames of reference that differ from their own.

Again we stress that this can be done in modest ways with simple and elementary examples, or it can be done at advanced levels with highly complicated examples. The level of difficulty can be adjusted by the instructor to the special needs and capacities of the students, and the details of what follows adjusted accordingly.

To reason sympathetically within a frame of reference different from one's own requires that one engage in hypothetical reasoning, that one be willing to entertain, as true, hypotheses that one is not already convinced are true. And this is good exercise for the mind, indeed! One needs to be able to entertain and to rationally evaluate hypotheses of which one is not already convinced in order to learn anything at all. Fortunately the capacity to think hypothetically is as genuine as the drive (to which it is dialectically opposed, but which typically overrides it) to remain confined egocentrically or ethnocentrically within one's own frame of reference.

Let us now present our instructional strategy for exercising and encouraging these abilities. We recommend that wherever possible instructors work with issues that touch the students' own interests and concerns, for the reason that students are more readily, and deeply, and genuinely motivated to apply themselves to tasks whose relevance to their interests and concerns they can see and understand. Of course, an instructor may wish to work to interest a class in those particular issues the *instructor* may feel are of paramount importance. Indeed, there are many moral and social issues that arguably all students need to develop an interest in. This interest can be developed by leading students to see the connections between their interests and desires and these larger questions. Fortunately, however, there is generally no need to inhibit student input on this account. An instructor with a wide range of current interests can usually find a lot to encourage in the interests and concepts of the average group of students. And the flexibility of mind of the instructor who is willing to allow a community of interest to evolve in response to student initiative is a useful model to exhibit early in the game. We recommend that students be invited to suggest issues they would like to see discussed, and that they participate in the selection of issues for class exercises from the list of such suggestions. At early primary grades, and also with particularly shy groups of students, there may have to be extensive priming of the pump. Materials may have to be brought in by the instructor to generate student awareness of issues which they come to see as related to their experience. We recommend that the instructor guide the selection process toward issues about which the class exhibits considerable diversity of opinion, rather than toward issues about which there is general agreement. Ultimately, students need to deal with their shared ethnocentricities by discovering and reasoning within divergent points of view and value systems.

Once an issue has been selected, there are a number of ways, depending on the size and setting of the class, instructor's preferences, and so on, to structure class discussion so as to encourage and develop dialectical thinking skills. An example will illustrate some general guidelines which will help students—and therefore their instructors—succeed.

Suppose the class is initially divided into groups corresponding to the initial position each student takes on the issue. There may, of course, be as few as two such groups or as many as there are students in the class (though this latter possibility is even less likely than it is manageable, due to the psychological safety that comes with being a member of a group). We recommend, as an instructive subsidiary exercise, that the instructor take as much time as needed to assist students in articulating as many distinct positions on the issue as necessary, so that every student feels comfortable identifying with one or another position.

In a recent case involving a class which included students from a variety of Latin American and Pacific Rim origins, a small contingent of Palestinian Arab students, and a group of American students, the students elected to discuss the issue of terrorism. It is worth remarking how the class framed the issue for discussion. It quickly became apparent that there were competing understandings of terrorism underlying the students' interest in the issue, and this posed an initial obstacle to discussion: how to formulate a question that we could all discuss without initially prejudicing the discussion against one or another of these competing understandings. An early formulation—"What should the

United States government do to put a stop to terrorism?''—failed to win a consensus because it would have prejudiced the discussion against those students who thought that terrorism might be a justifiable last resort for occupied or exiled peoples. The class formulated and considered several options before shortly arriving at a formulation which it found reasonable by consensus: "How should the phenomena of terrorism be understood and responded to?"

At this point two positions emerged: first, that terrorism is the use of violence against innocent civilian noncombatants and as such is morally unjustifiable, and warrants strong preventive and retaliatory measures; and second, that what is called "terrorism" is in reality the understandable and justifiable response of occupied and exiled peoples to unprovoked military aggression. It is hard to imagine two positions more at odds. It is interesting, therefore, that before proceeding to generate and examine the arguments, the class also produced an intermediary position: that armed resistance to military aggression within one's homeland must be distinguished from the indiscriminate use of violence against civilian noncombatants outside one's homeland, and that in any case the response to either sort of violence ought to stress diplomatic negotiation.

Our experience indicates that students are likely at first to avoid isolation and exposure and rather to gravitate toward each other in large numbers. Let us suppose, therefore, that the class is polarized into two groups corresponding to antithetical positions on the issue.

Each of the resulting discussion groups is now assigned the task of preparing a defense of its position, to be presented before the assembly of the class as a whole by representatives of each group. The goals of the task include (1) that each group be prepared to deliver as clear, concise, and compelling a rationale for its position as it can devise; (2) that each group be prepared to interrogate the other position(s) as deeply and incisively as possible; and (3) that each group be as fully prepared to answer questions and respond to criticisms of its own position. The instructor should be aware (and in due course make the students aware) that the second and third of these goals involve reasoning—though not yet (necessarily) sympathetically—within the frame of reference of the opposition, and further that the mature critical thinker incorporates the second and third goals into the first. In addition to preparing the case in favor of its position, each group is to select its team of three representatives and assign them distinct roles, corresponding to the three goals above.

Once the discussion groups have made their preparations, the class is reassembled for a discussion among the representatives of the positions. As moderator, the instructor is in a position to guide the discussion in the direction of mutual awareness and respect by facilitating and stressing reciprocity (or mutual responsiveness) between the teams of representatives, by pointing out such problems as straw-man interpretations of opposing points, and so on. It is well worth reviewing the discussion together as a group before proceeding to the next step.

Each of the discussion groups is now assigned the task of preparing a defense of the (or a) position to which it was initially opposed, the rest of the exercise to be carried through as before. This step is crucial. Its importance lies in the fact that it makes it extremely difficult to avoid considering an alternative frame of reference *sympathetically*. Whereas it may, up until now, have been tempting and adequate to examine the opposed position simply with a view to discovering its limitations and weaknesses, it now becomes necessary to attend to its strengths. More important still, it now becomes necessary to probe and challenge the position one initially identified with, to engage in reflective self-criticism.

In our experience, students frequently find this crucial step quite difficult, especially in connection with emotionally charged topics such as terrorism. The results of the exercise, though, have been very encouraging. In reflecting on their experience, our students—regardless of their initial positions on terrorism—reported a wide range of beneficial effects of the experience on their thinking and their approach to issues generally.

We have found it useful to reinforce the exercise through the use of audio and video recording technology.* First of all, a retrievable and verifiable record of the discussions is a great help in analyzing the arguments with students after the fact. And such records also contribute directly to reflective self-criticism by allowing the participants to review and critique their own performances.

We have also found it useful to vary this strategy in several ways; for instance, have students discuss the issue in pairs, making sure that each student has an opportunity to practice each of the three activities mentioned above from two antithetical positions; then have students each compose essays in dialogue form, first defending one or another position on an issue, then critically examining the initial thesis and its defense, and finally responding to these criticisms and objections either by meeting them or by adjusting the original position.

The strategy outlined here is not without risk. Since a great deal of the content of discussion is left up to the students and the instructor's role is in large measure responsive, the instructor must be prepared to deal with a wide variety of situations which may arise. At the same time, however, the instructor may look forward to the opportunity to recognize

---

*For information concerning the Center's Critical Thinking Video Library, contact: Center for Critical Thinking & Moral Critique (Attention: Joel Rudinow or Richard Paul), Sonoma State University, Rohnert Park, California 94928.

and reward deep and authentic insights arrived at by students. Recently, in a dialectical essay responding to the question "Should all college students be required to take a basic course in Critical Thinking?" a student majoring in Communications wrote:

> Is a required course in Critical Thinking at the college level the most effective means of teaching individuals how to defend themselves against "intellectual trickery and self-delusion"? (Critical Thinking course description, Sonoma State University Catalog, 1982–83). Prior to taking this course, I would not have questioned the validity of such a requirement. In fact, I had only a faint idea about what the course entailed, and I signed up for it simply because it *was* required. Since taking Critical Thinking, I have begun to analyze, criticize and more carefully evaluate the ideas presented in all my courses, including this one, and including the idea that this course is worthwhile. Critical Thinking has taken me beyond learned belief systems into the area of developing my own. . . .

Here the student has recognized and appreciated the value inherent in a discipline which questions itself as well as everything else. The student demonstrates that she understands the connections between such a discipline and freedom of thought and between freedom of thought and responsibility for one's own thinking.

It is worth dwelling on these connections briefly to dispell a common worry among teachers: that an atmosphere that encourages questioning may actually undermine discipline and contribute to the deterioration of classroom morale. The instructor should bear in mind that Critical Thinking *is* a discipline, and it is, therefore, not to be confused with unruly contempt for authority. To encourage the one does not necessitate tolerating the other.

Finally, the abilities to engage in reflective self-criticism and to reason sympathetically within alternative frames of reference are essential to the discipline of critical thinking and, therefore, also to the goals of the Critical Thinking course. Unless these abilities and the commitment to exercise them are established in the student, any systematic analytical or argumentative skills the student may acquire in the course are prone to degenerate into sophistry.

REFERENCES

Benderson, Albert. "Critical Thinking." *Focus* 15 (1984).

Easley, J. "A Japanese Approach to Arithmetic." *For the Learning of Mathematics* 3, no. 3 (1983).

Easley, J. "What's There to Talk About in Arithmetic?" *Problem Solving* 5 (1983).

Easley, J. "Is There Educative Power in Students' Alternative Frameworks?" *Problem Solving* 6 (1984): 1–4.

Easley, J. "A Teacher Educator's Perspective on Students' and Teachers'

Schemes: Or Teaching by Listening." Paper presented at the Conference on Thinking, Harvard University Graduate School of Education, 1984.

Passmore, John. "On Teaching to Be Critical." In *The Concept of Education*, edited by R. S. Peters, pp. 192–211. London: Routledge and Kegan Paul, 1967.

Paul, Richard W. "Human Factors in Learning." In *Proceedings of Sixth Annual Rupert N. Evans Symposium, April 25-26, 1985*, edited by Hazel Taylor Spitze. Urbana–Champaign, Ill.: Office of Vocational Education Research, University of Illinois, 1985.

Paul, Richard W. "Bloom's Taxonomy and Critical Thinking Instruction." *Educational Leadership* (May 1985).

Paul, Richard W. "Critical Thinking and the Critical Person." In *Proceedings of the Harvard University Conference on Thinking*. Hillsdale, N.J.: Lawrence Erlbaum Associates, 1984.

Paul, Richard W. "The Critical Thinking Movement in Historical Perspective." *National Forum* (Winter 1985).

Paul, Richard W. "Teaching Critical Thinking in the 'Strong' Sense: A Focus on Self-Deception, World Views, and a Dialectical Mode of Analysis." *Informal Logic* (May 1982).

Paul, Richard W. "Dialogical Thinking: Critical Thought Essential to the Acquisition of Rational Knowledge and Passion." In *Teaching Thinking Skills: Theory and Practice*, edited by Joan Baron and Robert Sternberg. New York: W. H. Freeman, 1986.

Paul, Richard W. "Critical Thinking Research: A Response to Stephen Norris." *Educational Leadership* (May 1985).

Paul, Richard W. "Critical Thinking: Fundamental to Education for a Free Society." *Educational Leadership* (September 1984).

Paul, Richard W. "The Socratic Spirit: An Answer to Louis Goldman." *Educational Leadership* (September 1984).

Paul, Richard W. "A Review of Critical Thinking and Education by John E. McPeck." *Informal Logic* (Spring 1986).

Peters, R. S. *Reason and Compassion*. London: Routledge and Kegan Paul, 1973.

Scriven, Michael. *Reasoning*. New York: McGraw-Hill, 1976.

Scriven, Michael. "Critical for Survival." *National Forum* (Special Issue on Critical Thinking) (Winter 1985).

Siegel, Harvey. "Critical Thinking as Educational Ideal." *Educational Forum* (November 1980): 7–23.

STRATEGIES FOR ACTIVE INVOLVEMENT IN PROBLEM SOLVING

by Joseph S. Karmos and Ann H. Karmos

Joseph S. Karmos and Ann H. Karmos argue that "good problem solvers tend to be more active than poor problem solvers." In an effort to create more active learning habits in students, the authors use a set of procedures that involve student participation in problem solving. For example, students are asked to draw pictures or diagrams of the problem under discussion, or they are asked to write simulations. In addition, a set of specific problem-solving strategies is employed: thinking aloud, using trial and error, working backwards from the end of a problem, and systematically listing all possible outcomes of an event. Karmos and Karmos find that time management can influence problem solving—helping students persevere is often a matter of scheduling and listing priorities. They note that many of the problem-solving strategies help the teacher become a better resource for students. For example, when students talk aloud their problem solving, the teacher can identify deficiencies in their reasoning.

The authors are with Southern Illinois University, Carbondale, in the Department of Educational Psychology and the Department of Curriculum and Instruction, respectively.

The importance of problem solving is receiving more attention than ever before. Business and industry list it as an essential skill for dealing with the future (1). Educators are looking for ways to effectively teach it in classrooms.

One thing we know is that good problem solvers tend to be more active than poor problem solvers (5). They create mental pictures, relate problems to familiar or concrete experiences, ask themselves questions, think aloud, brainstorm, make diagrams or flowcharts, and use physical aids to thinking. But not enough active problem solving is occurring in classrooms. In the April 1983 *Kappan*, John Goodlad remarked that teacher talk was by far the dominant classroom activity. "Teachers rarely encouraged student-to-student dialogue or provided opportunities for students to work collaboratively in small groups or to plan, set goals, determine alternative ways of achieving these goals, and the like. The emphasis was on recall, not on problem solving or inquiry" (3, p. 552).

This chapter describes several classroom procedures and specific problem-solving strategies that encourage students to be·active problem solvers. Students learn to be active by participating in problem solving. They

99

learn to use their personal resources by working on lots of problems and being exposed to a wide variety of different strategies.

SOME PROCEDURES FOR ENCOURAGING ACTIVE PROBLEM SOLVING

For many instructional purposes it is appropriate for a teacher to demonstrate a specific method for solving a class of similar problems. For example, finding the area of a circle given the diameter of the circle is a routine kind of problem which is efficiently solved by using a formula. The ability to solve such routine problems is important because it arms the student with skills for solving more complex problems. But if students are to be prepared to solve non-routine problems, different instructional procedures are needed.

One procedure is to present a problem and ask each student to draw a picture or some representation of the problem. The teacher asks a number of students to copy their representations on the chalkboard. The class examines each one and asks for clarification of the picture if necessary. From viewing each other's thinking, students learn different ways to organize information. They also gain confidence in their own problem-solving abilities when the teacher is accepting of several different approaches to the same solution. We have used the following nonroutine problem for this process in grade four through college level:

> A mother St. Bernard had two pups. She ate ten pounds of dog food per day, and each pup ate two pounds per day. The dogs' owner bought a one-hundred-pound bag of dog food. One pup was sold after the third day. The other pup was sold after the seventh day. For how many days did the one hundred pounds of dog food last?

On page 101 is a fourth grader's St. Bernard drawing, which is typical of what many fourth graders have produced. Note that the student did not solve the problem, but her drawing brought her so close that the teacher was able to reinforce her thinking skills and ask good questions that led the class to the correct solution.

Simulation is another excellent procedure for active problem solving, and it is applicable at any grade level and for any subject area. Simulations are particularly useful for experiences with decision-making and interpersonal skills. The following example is from business education:

> You are a member of an office staff for a company whose president made a decision to trade in all the existing office equipment and replace it with a system of equipment from one company. The office staff had been asked for input on such matters as new procedures, workflow, job responsibility, training for use of new equipment, and guidelines for implementing the new procedures. Nevertheless, after the new setting has been used for six weeks, some prob-

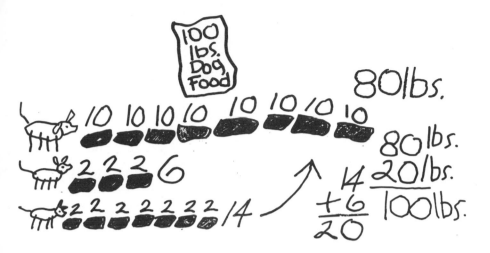

lems have arisen with job satisfaction and the staff is meeting to search for solutions. You are one of the following staff members. *Sandra Miles* was Mr. Hamblin's secretary. Her duties were to keep his calendar, take his calls and serve as receptionist for his callers, process all his paperwork, and retrieve information from his files. Her new title is *office manager*. She is now responsible for directing the workflow from all the executives. Since there was no cross training, she is unable to retrieve information when Don, the information processor, is gone. Sandra also supervises all the work of the office staff. She is beginning to feel that she lacks supervisory skills. She is also frustrated with the pressure to resolve problems which have arisen with the rest of the staff, and that is the reason she has called this meeting. *Don Feldman* was Mrs. Longan's secretary. His duties were similar to Sandra's. Don's new title is *information processor*. He was eager to be trained on the new equipment and is enjoying the challenge of problem solving for what the new equipment could do for his work load. But Don is having problems with his back and his eyes. He complains of the glare on the screen. In addition, his equipment was placed in a small room adjacent to the main office and he misses the contact with the rest of the staff. *Charlene Henry* was moved from her job as clerk/typist to that of *receptionist*. She takes all incoming calls on the switchboard and receives clients. She is having difficulty with retrieving information for customers and dealing with their irritation when they feel that they are being slighted. *Mason Tyler* was the clerk/typist who was primarily responsible for the filing system. His new position is *records clerk* and he has full responsibility for storage and retrieval of records. Like Don, he misses contact with the rest of the staff, but also is running into problems with the increased flow of paper resulting from the new system. Another problem is that no system has been identified for filing information stored on disks. Mason feels pressured to respond efficiently to requests for information. Your staff meeting has begun, and the entire staff has agreed that the office environment is depressing and that these unresolved problems are beginning to cause friction. Your group has agreed to use a five-step model for problem solving: (1) identify, understand, and prioritize the problems; (2) brainstorm for solutions; (3) select tentative solutions; (4) determine how to implement the solutions (who does what, when); and (5) discuss what people have learned about themselves individually and as a group. The staff has also agreed to set a date for reevaluation of the solution. You are a member of the office staff—proceed with the problem solving.

A second example is a simulation written by an elementary school teacher for her social studies class.

Destitute on the Desert. You are with a group of scientists who are doing scientific research in the desert. When you are 200 miles from your headquarters, the engine in your vehicle blows up. Since survival depends on reaching your headquarters, the most critical items available must be chosen for the 200-mile trip. Below are listed fifteen items. Your task is to rank them in terms of their importance to your group in its attempt to reach your headquarters. Write a "1" by the most important item, a "2" by the second, and so on. The items are these: tent, map of the desert, sun glasses, flashlight, blankets, sharp knife, extra shoes, first aid kit, signal flares, five gallons of water, magnetic compass, one can dehydrated milk, two 45-calibre pistols, food concentrate, box of matches.

For these open-ended procedures, an extensive collection of nonroutine problems is an essential resource for teachers. More and more substantive problems are becoming available commercially and in professional journals. As teachers provide opportunities for students to work in groups, in pairs, or individually, problems can be selected that are appropriate for emphasizing and illustrating specific problem-solving strategies.

SOME SPECIFIC PROBLEM-SOLVING STRATEGIES

Thinking Aloud

When using this strategy, people say aloud their thoughts while attempting to solve a problem. Expressing thoughts, especially at sections of a problem where difficulties or hesitancy arises, is a good way to avoid skipping steps in reasoning, jumping over important information, or being unaware of the point at which being bogged down occurred.

Thinking aloud while solving problems requires practice. At first, many students find it difficult to vocalize their thoughts as they work problems. However, students do get used to expressing in words the steps they take, and then gain confidence in talking out the problem in front of the teacher and other students. This technique is used in full class settings, in small groups, and in one-to-one discussions between student and teacher. The choice of setting depends on the nature of the problem, the students, and the teacher.

From thinking aloud, students learn to listen to each other, to locate breakdowns in reasoning, to learn where the stumbling point is, to realize how different people approach the same problem at the same time.

Students and teachers are often amazed at how much they can learn from each other by thinking aloud.

Using Trial and Error

Trial and error is often underestimated as a problem-solving strategy, but it can be a key strategy in the solution of some problems. Trial and error can be applied systematically by simply trying different solutions to see if they work. More often than not, however, the search can be narrowed by taking into account relevant knowledge and, by inference, reducing the number of solutions to be tried.

Trial and error can also be advantageous in getting a feel for a problem. Trying out a reasonable guess, even if it does not work, can give valuable information. For example, if trying to find a decimal approximation for the square root of 2, one might try 1.5 (1 is too small because 1 x 1 = 1, and 2 is too big because 2 x 2 = 4). Since 1.5 x 1.5 = 2.25, 1.5 is too big, but that is valuable information because it directs the next attempt to a number between 1 and 1.5. Teachers should encourage students to make reasonable guesses at times and should specify for them the value of what was learned from trial and error and how an error can narrow the search for a solution.

This same way of thinking about the information gained from an imperfect attempt can be applied to solutions of interpersonal problems. Suppose a father and his daughter are applying the problem-solving process to the condition of her room, particularly in regard to the dirty clothes on the floor and on the furniture. An idea to try might be to put a clothes hamper in her room. Both would agree that this is a trial solution to be evaluated, say in three weeks. If the solution is not the right one, the attempt still will help to clarify the problem and will lead to a better solution.

One roadblock to becoming a good problem solver is reluctance to take a risk. Many adults have been conditioned over the years to believe that there is some strategy or way to proceed in solving a problem that they think they should have learned, and if they can't remember how to solve this kind of problem, they simply give up. Teachers are confronted with this attitude frequently when their students complain that they haven't had this yet. Indeed, there are many specific approaches to problems that can be learned. But good problem solvers are not hampered by the conviction that there is only one way to solve a problem. They do not rely on some outside authority but have confidence in their own ability to generate ideas. Teachers can encourage students to become self-reliant by freeing them to make reasonable guesses and to use trial and error to gain insight into a problem.

Working Backwards

Sometimes it is easier to solve a problem by working backwards rather than attacking the problem head on. As an example, consider the following problem from Moshe Rubenstein's *Patterns of Problem Solving* (4, p. 19):

Problem—How many tennis matches of single elimination must be played by 1025 players before a winner is declared?

Most of our students start at the beginning by figuring there would be initially 512 games with one player getting a bye. Next there would be 256 matches with 1 bye, then 128 (1 bye), 64 (l bye), 32 (1 bye), 16 (1 bye), 8 (1 bye), 4 (1 bye), 2 (1 bye), 1 (bye), finals. The sum of 512, 256, 128 . . . 4, 2, 1, 1 is 1024.

It is much more direct and general to start from the end and view one winner and 1024 losers, and note that each loser would play one losing game in a single elimination tournament. So there would be 1024 matches.

This working-backwards technique not only yields a solution; it also displays a unique strategy that can be used for many problems. The solution path for the tennis match problem is more important than the answer since the path yields a general method for solving such problems—work backwards. The solution is known for any number of N players; that is, N – 1.

Working backwards has many useful applications. Suppose you are writing a position paper to convince your boss to accept a particularly crucial idea. In thinking about how to draft the paper, you might begin by working backwards and ask yourself, "What kinds of questions would the boss ask me? What would be the boss's major objections? How do I keep from offending the boss?" By working backwards, by starting with the goal, you can write a more convincing paper.

Finding All the Possibilities

Another important strategy for problem solving is to have a systematic way of listing all possible outcomes of some occurrence. The system must ensure that all possibilities are listed and also that only those possibilities that make sense from the structure of the problem are listed.

Thinking exercises about drawing marbles from bags are useful for developing orderly ways to exhaust all possibilities, and they can be generalized to fit a large number of actual situations. An example: Suppose there are four marbles in a bag, numbered 1, 2, 3, and 4. What are all the ways to draw out the marbles one at a time if, once a marble is drawn, it is not returned to the bag? One could actually make a list of the ways with the help of a running conversation with oneself.

"O.K. Suppose I take out the 1 first. I'll list the ways if 1 is drawn first and 2 is drawn second." (1234, 1243) "Now what are the ways for 1 first and 3 second?" (1324, 1342) "Now, 1 first and 4 second." (1423, 1432) A similar conversation goes on with oneself to list the ways if 2 is drawn first (6 ways), if 3 is drawn first (6 ways), and if 4 is drawn first (6 ways). So there are 24 ways in all.

Another skill for finding these 24 possible ways is to draw a tree.

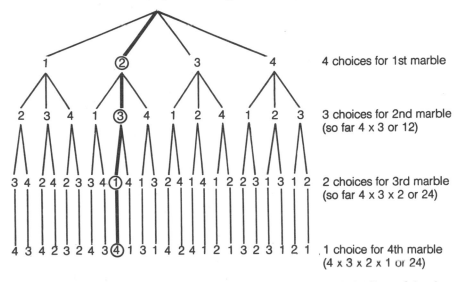

There are 24 paths down this tree and the one that is indicated in the drawing represents the combination 2314.

The skill of drawing a tree to determine all possibilities is an important one. Suppose all the possible ways to arrange ten digits (without replacement, as in the example above) were critical information for the solution to a problem. Listing all the possibilities would be formidable and the tree would be impractical to draw. But by *reducing the problem to a simpler problem* (another problem-solving strategy), one could realize that there is a pattern for finding the number of combinations. The tree for the four-digit problem makes it clear that there are 4 x 3 x 2 x 1 or 24 ways to arrange four digits. So it is logically sound to compute 10 x 9 x 8 x 7 x 6 x 5 x 4 x 3 x 2 x 1 to find the number of ways to arrange ten digits (without replacement).

This kind of thinking is a useful problem-solving skill. The four-digit problem has the same structure as figuring out, for example, these problems:

- How many different ways can 4 colors be used to paint a car if the colors for the body, the top, and two parts of the trim are arranged differently? (24 ways)
- What is the probability of drawing a "winning number" 2 1 4 3 from a box containing four chips labelled "1," "2," "3," "4"? (1/24 or 1 of the 24 possibilities)
- How many different routes are there that reach all of 4 cities only once and that could originate in any of the four cities? (24) One such route, (1) Cleveland to (3) St. Louis to (2) Kansas City to (4) Chicago, is shown below. The illustration shows that regardless of the city of origin, any other city can be reached next, making this situation analogous to the 4-digit problem.

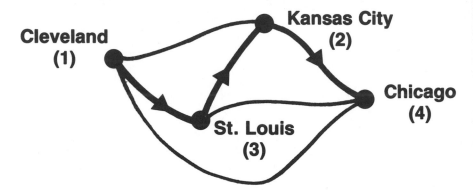

Often the number of ways to do something or the likelihood of an event occurring is important information for solving a problem, not only in mathematics, but also in other subject matter areas. It is a skill that can and should be taught as one of many problem-solving strategies.

Time Management

Time management can influence problem solving. Poor scheduling can result in insufficient time for thinking through a problem, or perhaps never even getting to the problem. An appropriate amount of time must be allocated for reflecting on the problem, for considering different ways to approach a solution, and for reviewing and critiquing the steps used. The pressure that can result from poor scheduling can cause subpar problem solving by limiting the amount of planning time and the time available for patient deliberation. A student's patience and perseverance are often keys to good problem solving. Good time management skills are a necessary condition.

One might recommend to students that they keep a chart of their activities to use as a basis for managing their time better. Time priorities often have to be set each day and a chart or list can help. Some students do not manage their own time well enough to acquire an essential piece of knowledge, get to the library, or talk to someone who can help them. Allocating specific blocks of time to specific tasks according to their importance and the time they require is a useful skill. Systematic reflection on one's use of time and on how much is lost if time is used inefficiently can lead students to modify their own behavior.

Time management requires scheduling, but flexibility in following a schedule is also important. For example, there is a problem-solving strategy that is useful when one has come to a dead end or exhausted all ideas for approaching a problem. Wickelgren calls the strategy *incubation* and it means simply to get away from the problem for a while (6). It is a common experience to sleep on a problem and to solve it with a new insight the next day. Even when time is limited, as in taking an exam, going on to other problems and then coming back can be useful. Teachers can model this strategy from time to time by leaving problems with students instead of rushing to solve them before the bell rings.

The key to time management, then, is to recognize the need for time to gather information, to try different ideas, to critique solutions, and also to have the flexibility in one's schedule for some incubation time.

Reasoning Critically and Logically

By observing students when they talk aloud about their problem solving, checking their papers, and observing their activities, the teacher can discern the extent of their deficiencies in logical and critical reasoning.

One of the major problems students have is dealing with ambiguities in the English language. For example, consider the real-life story of a famous mathematician who had to take a driving examination. He had memorized many statements from a booklet, including "It is illegal to park within fifteen feet of a fire hydrant." As part of the test, he was given some true-false statements, one of which was "It is illegal to park within nine feet of a fire hydrant." The mathematician checked "true" on the grounds that if the statement he had memorized was true, then the statement on the test was true. The examiner, however, claimed that the correct response was "false," since the statement in the booklet explicitly mentioned fifteen feet and not nine feet, even though the mathematician was correct, according to the rules of logic.

Students need to be given more practice and guidance in dealing with the logic of problem solving. A particular emphasis should be placed on teachers' giving them many sound, appropriate problems to work and listening to them reason aloud. As a resource for this activity, the authors strongly recommend *An Introduction to Logic* by Exner and Kaufman (2).

Critical reasoning is another area of student deficiency. Students often lack skills to assess expressed ideas, beliefs, and statements that one encounters daily through the media and through remarks made by people in such forms as opinions, reports, and rumors.

The process of critical inquiry must be an impartial one. Judgments and evaluations are delayed until the data have been collected. Observations, people's opinions, and collected information should all be assessed before decisions are made. The aim is to be objective, avoiding preconceived versions of the results. The process should be open enough to invite further inquiry if people are not satisfied and problems are not solved. Also, in critical inquiry, people's feelings are often involved. Respect for people's personal dignity must be remembered when people are the objects of the inquiry.

Another important part of the critical inquiry is evaluating the assumptions being made during the inquiry. If assumptions are not clearly in mind, then invalid conclusions can be drawn, inappropriate decisions made, or people's feelings hurt.

People can improve their critical reasoning skills. It is evident from the authors' experience that there is no substitute for practice. Students must be given good situations, problems, and simulations from which to develop and sharpen their skills.

Gathering, Recording, and Analyzing Data

The first step in problem solving is to understand the problem. When full information is presented to a student, understanding the problem involves reading carefully, eliminating extraneous information, and, for some problems, drawing a sketch or a diagram or organizing given data in a table. These steps are obvious in solving the usual kinds of problems students are given in school. Unfortunately, most problems encountered in one's life at work, at home, or socially are not so neat. Crucial or helpful information is often missing and the problem solver must have skills not only for obtaining necessary information, but also for recognizing what information is needed. Later in life, students may need this skill for problems like "What steps can I take to effect a behavior change in person Y?"; "To cut costs and maintain sales volume, where can money best be saved in the production of product X, packaging or advertising?"; "What is the best solution for a problem involving a disagreement between labor and management?"

Data gathering can occur on many levels. In some cases, *unstructured observation* is useful. For example, simply watching a production line for an hour could help a person generate ideas for a more structured efficiency study; or a task-oriented group could be observed for clues about group discord. More analytical data gathering involves the use of *checklists* or *coding* of events or behaviors. Once data are collected, a second skill is to *summarize* the information in meaningful form. If the information is quantitative, data from a checklist can be recorded in a variety of graphs, tables, or figures. Nonquantitative observations can be categorized or written up as a case study. The skill of selecting a way to represent data interacts with a third skill, *analyzing observational results*.

Social and interpersonal problem solving can also require data gathering. Much of this must be done via observation of people and their interactions. For resolving conflicts between two people, the needs of both persons must be known, and good listening skills can provide much of the necessary data. Many interpersonal problems involve needs, preferences, or values of groups of people. Useful information can be collected via interest surveys, evaluation forms, or other questionnaires.

If instruction in problem solving is to be transferable to real-life problems, students must learn to gather relevant information, and they must be armed with the tools they need for recording and analyzing their observations.

SOLVING REAL PROBLEMS

Problem-solving skills should be an integral part of the curriculum in all subject matter areas. Teachers can emphasize the importance of problem-solving skills by looking for opportunities for students to solve problems that occur in their everyday lives. Active involvement in meaningful problem solving is invaluable and should occur at all grade levels. Following are some examples from our own observations:

- a high school biology class in which the problem of too much noise during lab periods was solved by the students in such a way that they monitored themselves and increased their productivity;
- a fourth grade teacher facilitating a rule-setting session during the first week of school; class rules were determined to satisfy students and the teacher, and consequences were agreed upon;
- a first grade teacher dealing with two students who were disputing the ownership of a red felt pen; she directed the students to go out in the hall, settle the matter, and report their solution to her; they did.

Valuable lessons are learned when teachers facilitate problem solving when natural opportunities arise. Such learning experiences with real problem solving are often remembered above all others.

REFERENCES

1. Daniels, H., and Karmos, J. *Skills for Adapting to Change*. Carbondale: Southern Illinois University, 1983. ED 237 687.
2. Exner, R., and Kaufman, B. *An Introduction to Logic*. St. Louis: CEMREL, 1978.
3. Goodlad, J. I. "The Study of Schooling: Some Implications for School Improvement." *Phi Delta Kappan* 13, no. 6 (April 1983): 552–58.
4. Rubenstein, M. *Patterns of Problem Solving*. Englewood Cliffs, N.J.: Prentice-Hall, 1975.
5. Whimbey, A., and Lochhead, J. *Problem Solving and Comprehension*. Philadelphia: Franklin Institute Press, 1979.
6. Wickelgren, W. A. *How to Solve Problems*. San Francisco: W. H. Freeman, 1974.

RESTRUCTURING WHAT WE TEACH
TO TEACH FOR CRITICAL THINKING*

by Robert J. Swartz

Robert J. Swartz argues that critical thinking can only be taught successfully if it is fully integrated into content-area teaching: add-on approaches will not be effective. He provides several examples of how the curriculum in content-area instruction can be restructured to allow for the infusion of critical thinking skills into classroom work. Swartz suggests that, through analogy and guided practice, students at all grade levels can learn essential critical thinking skills; further he maintains that these skills can be applied to all academic areas, as well as to real-life situations. In addition, he sees critical thinking skills working in combination with creative thinking skills.

The author is Co-Director of the Critical and Creative Thinking Program, and Professor of Philosophy at the University of Massachusetts, Boston. (A shorter version of this chapter appeared in Educational Leadership *(May 1986) and is forthcoming in* Thinking Across the Curriculum, *the 1986 Yearbook of the Massachusetts Association of Supervisors and Curriculum Developers.)*

AN APPROACH TO BRINGING CRITICAL THINKING INTO THE CLASSROOM

The phrase "critical thinking" is used in educational circles today almost as often as "computers" was three years ago. However, bringing critical thinking into classrooms that are steeped in efforts to help children learn all the facts they can is not at all like bringing in a new piece of equipment that we can learn to use in an hour. Add-on approaches to critical thinking in the curriculum—even if based on the introduction of one of the many new curriculum packages available today—will be a frustrating experience if they are surrounded in other parts of the curriculum by much the same teaching we see every day. Further, given the variety of different things that are now called "critical thinking," it is hard to know whether even these add-on curricula will really help students to develop the critical thinking we hope for.

In contrast, teachers who have taken the time to think through what critical thinking means, based on their own experience and their study of others' attempts to make this notion clear, have turned away from relying on prepackaged curricula and have risen to the challenge to infuse critical thinking into their teaching by restructuring the same content that they have been teaching. The results are often exciting, always enervating, and constantly being refined in ways as numerous as individual teaching styles. Once teachers embark on this road, there is no retreating, and teaching for critical thinking eventually permeates their teaching as naturally as reading and writing do, and in ways that no prepackaged curriculum can duplicate.

In this paper I will illustrate this process by first starting with some of its products, the classroom work of a number of teachers who have infused critical thinking into their teaching. What critical thinking actually involves will emerge from this look at what teaching for critical thinking has become for these teachers. We will see that it is more than many well-meaning educators who use this term take it to be. We will also see that it is nothing esoteric that we need a massive amount of technical expertise to master. We do it often, as do our students, but we can all do it better, and we can certainly teach our students to do it more systematically and pervasively than they normally do. Teaching for critical thinking in this way brings out the best in teachers and ultimately in their students.

TEACHERS TEACHING FOR CRITICAL THINKING

The following examples, drawn from a number of Massachusetts teachers who use this approach to bring critical thinking into their classrooms, will illustrate its potential. These examples are typical of what other teachers in other cities as far apart as Baltimore, Maryland, and Irvine, California, are doing.

Kevin O'Reilly, a high school American history teacher from the Hamilton-Wenham school system, starts his lessons about the reliability of sources of information in history by staging a scuffle in the corridors outside his classroom and then trying to ascertain what happened by asking students who were in the vicinity. The differences in the accounts his students give are like the variety of accounts that were given about who started the firing in the Revolutionary War at the Battle of Lexington in 1775. The attempts by these students to determine which of the eyewitnesses gave the most accurate account of the scuffle, and their reflections on why one account is better or worse than another, arm them with certain critical skills they draw on again and again in Kevin's classroom. These skills relate to the reliability and accuracy of eyewitnesses, of observation, and of sources of information in general. In the immediate context of their study of the Revolutionary War, these skills put Kevin's students in an excellent position to make informed critical judgments about the accuracy of various textbook accounts of this incident which other students in other classrooms are directed to read simply to get the facts.

These skills are, of course, important not only in the study of history. They are important in ascertaining the credibility of a vast amount of information passed to us through a variety of sources in everyday situations, usually through the media. Kevin tries to teach so that these skills will not only be helpful in reading history, but in this broader arena of the everyday lives of his students; he tries to help them *transfer* these skills out of his immediate classroom setting into their everyday thinking by the use of analogy and guided practice on different examples (1).

Kevin's overall approach—that of restructuring traditional content to teach for thinking—is an approach that is not restricted to American history or to high school. Cathy Skowron, a first grade teacher in the Provincetown Elementary School, uses the same technique when she follows up a reading of the tale of Chicken Little with a discussion, prompted by her questioning, of whether the other animals should have trusted Chicken Little, and how they could have determined her reliability. Here Cathy bases her lesson on the same critical thinking concept, that of the reliability of sources of information, but structures her lesson in a grade-appropriate way. Many teachers just use the Chicken Little story and others like it to read from in order to help students build their listening skills and perhaps their vocabulary. Cathy restructures the way she uses the same material to teach for critical thinking by integrating questioning techniques keyed to her goal of helping her students think about the reliability of sources of information. There are a multitude of other contexts, in other subject areas, and at other grade levels, in which the same skill can be taught, reinforced, and elaborated.

Cathy Skowron also prompts her students' thinking about whether Chicken Little had good evidence that the sky was falling herself. Could there have been something else that made whatever hit her on the head do so other than the sky falling? What could it have been and how could we find out what actually caused this?

Causal explanation and causal inference involve a cluster of different critical thinking skills from those involved in thinking about the reliability of basic information we get from others or through observation—skills at the use of evidence in reasoning about cause and effect—that are also crucially important in our everday lives. Accurate judgments about what caused what are necessary in our attempts to control our environment, whether it be the immediate environment of our daily lives or the broad environment of the natural world in which we live. They are also crucially important in assessing the many claims people make directed at influencing our beliefs about the effects of certain courses of action—especially the purchase of various products through advertising.

Causal explanation also plays a role in determining responsibility. Whose fault something is depends in part on whether the person in question caused what we are concerned about. But it involves more than just determining what caused what, and there is no substitute for good, clear, critical thinking about such questions. Another teacher, this time a high school English teacher in the Groton school system, Cathy Peabody, asks these questions of her students in thinking about the play *Romeo and Juliet*. Usually in English classrooms this play is read for vocabulary building, plot analysis, and the study of character. Cathy, recognizing that it is a play in which chance, emotion, misunderstanding, and deliberate intent interweave in a causal web to bring about the tragedy, uses it to help her students develop critical thinking skills concerning causality and responsibility. What was the complex web of causes that led to the tragedy of the two lovers? Who, if anyone, was responsible? The depth of the activities that she prompts starting with questions like these brings her students to the depths of questions about causality and responsibility, building on the same core of inferential skills that Cathy Skowron introduced in her elementary school classroom. And she, too, helps them see analogies in their own experience as does Kevin O'Reilly, so that transfer of these skills will be facilitated.

There are a multitude of similar opportunities across the curriculum for restructuring what is taught to teach for the cluster of critical thinking skills related to the use of evidence and reasoning about cause and effect: well-founded explanation, prediction, and generalization. This is not such a difficult thing to do once we think about it a little. Teachers who take the time to think through what these skills involve usually find that many already existing curriculum books that claim to include activities on these skills have an inadequate conception of them.

Restructuring traditional content is, of course, not the only way that a teacher can bring critical thinking into the classroom. Being sensitive to real-life situations in which these skills are important can prompt teachers to structure entirely new activities into their teaching that involve the same critical thinking skills that Cathy Skowron and Cathy Peabody base their lessons on. The technique is the same: infusing teaching for critical thinking into content material based on an understanding of the requisite skills and utilizing special thinking-skill-oriented techniques. This way of bringing critical thinking into the classroom complements and can reinforce what teachers do in restructuring traditional content. They are especially important in teaching for the transfer of these skills.

In the fourth grade classroom of Phyllis Cooper in the Dennis-Yarmouth school system, for example, there is a similar concern about accurate appraisal of cause and effect. While Phyllis does restructure traditional material as Cathy Scowron does, on this occasion she focuses the attention of her students on a specific problem about the school lunchroom. What is causing the fact that students are more and more unable to finish their meals by the end of the period, and that there is a rise in anxiety and agitation in the lunchroom that everyone has noticed over the past two weeks? What can we do about this? This kind of research applies the same skills of casual inference to an actual situation. The concept of causal inference that Phyllis helps the students to use and the standards they develop of good causal judgment are the same as those employed by Cathy Peabody and Cathy Skowron, though again grade-appropriate.

There are, of course, a multitude of other real-life issues that teachers can bring into the classroom that are rich in opportunities to teach for critical thinking. These activities can go hand-in-hand with using the same techniques in restructuring traditional material to build in a focus on critical thinking. When this is done, the important thing is consistency in the use of the specific skill(s) involved, the use of the same terminology, and helping students see the analogies in the various examples that are used to teach for specific skills.

Such activities should not be a substitute for restructuring what we ordinarily teach, however. Without restructuring the content of our mainstream instruction, such activities tend to separate teaching for thinking from where we want students to exercise and develop good thinking most: through the teaching we do in the core of the curriculum. As exciting as they may be, their impact will be minimal. Juxtaposed against restructured teaching, however, they become powerful adjuncts. The real challenge for teachers in the thinking skills movement is such restructuring. The examples presented show how we can meet that challenge.

THE CONCEPT OF CRITICAL THINKING

The teachers mentioned, and the lessons they have developed, are only a small sample of a growing number who have produced critical-thinking-oriented lessons and units that are equally exciting. They all reveal a rich concept of critical thinking that many now feel is amenable to the skills approach these teachers have adopted. Thinking critically impacts on questions about what we should believe and do. Practicing it involves the use of certain skills, and understanding what these are and their appropriate application can lead to their being integrated into our daily teaching routines in ways that are bound to impact on the lives of our students outside school. Skills related to discriminating reliable and unreliable sources of information, accurate observation, good and bad

115

reasoning and inference (involving the use of both evidence and deduction), and the array of skills necessary to achieve the clarity we need to assess these processes effectively are now recognized to be part and parcel of critical thinking. The important thing about these skills, in contrast to other thinking skills, is that their effective use involves us in the development of viable standards which we can use to make these discriminations. These, too, should be the results of clear critical thought, and not be simply taught to students in traditional ways.

Critical thinking skills presuppose others involving perceptual and conceptual abilities, and such skills as the ability to categorize, classify, recognize patterns that can also be the subjects of thinking-oriented lessons. They also work hand-in-hand with other skills often called creative thinking skills. Besides lessons directed at specific critical thinking skills, students should be given opportunities to use whole clusters of different skills, including both critical and creative thinking skills, in thinking through complex issues. This will avoid the dangers of fragmentation to which skills approaches inevitably give rise. Contrary to what some have argued (2), combining a skills approach with such more holistic approaches is not only possible but practical; the combination yields an approach to teaching thinking that is more powerful than either.

But skills alone do not make a good critical thinker. Teachers must also recognize something that thinkers from Plato onwards have underscored in endorsing critical thinking as a way of life: that critical thinking must involve a whole cluster of thinking attitudes and dispositions: being open-minded, considering other points of view, looking for all available evidence, for example. Teaching for critical thinking, therefore, involves more than just routinely teaching students new skills. It must also involve helping them develop these key attitudes of thought (3). For this to happen effectively, students must be given opportunities to explore, investigate, make errors and correct them, and take risks. The changes necessary in classroom teaching to bring this about add a dimension to teaching for critical thinking that is of great importance to develop in systems firmly committed to critical thinking instruction as a goal.

It is clear that this conception of critical thinking is a richer conception than is usually captured by taxonomies that locate critical activities under one, or a small number of, heading(s) such as "evaluation." This conception is finely tuned to incorporate such skill areas as reliable/unreliable sources, observation, and causal reasoning. The most comprehensive taxonomy of critical thinking skills available today that includes this fine tuning is that developed by Robert Ennis (4). While many approaches to teaching for thinking which incorporate only broader categories such as "evaluation" sometimes promote interesting classroom approaches, there is often too little discrimination between the variety of skills that we call upon for different types of critical determinations in critical thinking (5). This results in little or no direct instruction about many of these important skills. In this we sell our students short. Breaking free of reliance on such broad categories and thinking through the different things we must do in the variety of circumstances calling for critical thinking provides a deeper appreciation of what is truly important, and exceptionally teachable, in teaching for critical thinking.

The richness of the application of this concept must strike us here as well. Some have argued that true critical thinking must be practiced only on a small set of special problems—for example, philosophical problems— and that to teach for critical thinking we must bring philosophy into the classroom (6). I feel that such problems as the free-will/determinism problem are wonderful and intriguing issues for students to grapple with, and excellent vehicles to stimulate good, clear, critical thinking. But to restrict critical thinking to just these issues robs us of a wealth of viable applications of critical thinking. Indeed, more than that, it makes it seem that critical thinking skills applied to issues about the accuracy of what we read in the morning newspaper are misapplied. The critical thinking concepts the teachers cited in this chapter use as a basis for their lessons show not only how familiar we all are with critical thinking, but also how various the applications of this concept are in our daily lives. Bringing this into the classroom is exactly what teaching for critical thinking should be.

BRINGING CRITICAL THINKING INTO THE CLASSROOM

How easy is it for teachers to do what is described in this chapter? It can't be done overnight, but it doesn't take years. We are all familiar with what it is to think critically, but this familiarity needs refinement, broadening, and must be constantly in our consciousness. Teachers exploring issues critically is an ideal way to provide raw material for the kind of look at this concept that can serve as the basis for the three lessons described above. But it does more: it models what the same teachers will want to help their students do. So here we have one important ingredient in adopting the approach this chapter focuses on. But this is not enough.

The lessons commented on were all developed with the conscious intention of translating the teacher's understanding of certain critical thinking concepts into classroom activities that would help students use and understand the critical thinking skills involved. Time is needed to refine this process. Essential to it is an exploration by teachers of key critical thinking skills such as distinguishing reliable from unreliable

117

sources, or the use of evidence in such activities as making well-supported predictions and generalizing, and a sensitivity to the scope and variety of their application in nonacademic and academic contexts. Ideally, this should happen in a setting in which groups of teachers work together to bounce their ideas off each other, perhaps supported by an ongoing relationship with a critical thinking specialist. Bringing the results of classroom applications back to this group is a further help in detecting things that can be improved.

This approach to bringing critical thinking into the classroom can be called the *conceptual-infusion approach* (7). It is the most powerful approach to bringing teaching for critical thinking into classroom activities. It requires more than individual teachers' wanting to bring critical thinking into their teaching. Any school system that sets the infusion of critical thinking into mainstream instruction as a goal must be willing to provide the time and support needed for this enterprise to succeed. Without this we will have only second-best. And why should we settle for that?

REFERENCES

1. Kevin O'Reilly, *Critical Thinking in American History* (Beverly, Mass.: Thinking Press, 1984). Mr. O'Reilly has published four volumes of lessons in American history.
2. William A. Sadler, Jr., and Arthur Whimbey, "A Holistic Approach to Improving Thinking Skills," *Phi Delta Kappan* (November 1985).
3. John Dewey, *How We Think* (Boston: Houghton Mifflin, 1933), 31–33.
4. Robert Ennis, "Goals for a Critical Thinking/Reasoning Curriculum," *Educational Leadership* (October 1985).
5. Such broad and unrefined categories appear in Bloom's Taxonomy, as well as in the work of many concerned with creative thinking; see, for example, Sidney Parnes and others, *Guide to Creative Action* (New York: Charles Scribners Sons, 1976).
6. Matthew Lippman, "Philosophy in the Classroom," *Educational Leadership* (September 1984).
7. Robert J. Swartz, "Teaching for Thinking: A Developmental Model for the Infusion of Thinking Skills into Mainstream Instruction," in *Teaching Thinking: Theory into Practice*, ed. J. Baron and R. Sternberg (New York: W. H. Freeman and Co., 1986).

DEVELOPING METACOGNITION IN COMPOSITION WITH PEER RESPONSE GROUPS

by Lynn Langer Meeks

Lynn Langer Meeks discusses using peer response groups to improve elementary school students' writing. The class is student-centered: students work with partners or in groups, reading, praising, offering suggestions and asking questions about each other's writing. Working together and externalizing their thinking helps students develop an internal control editor. Through talking aloud, students learn to listen to the internal voice that is the core of all writing. In a peer response group class, the teacher models the questioning and revising techniques that are central to this process. The teacher is a classroom resource, walking around the room, answering questions when asked, reinforcing appropriate behavior.

The author is Assistant Professor of English, Utah State University, Logan.

TIME: January

PLACE: Third grade classroom

SCENE: Students, gathered in small groups, are engaged in an intense discussion. They hardly notice their teacher who walks around the room listening and answering questions.

OVERHEARD:

Elizabeth: Why did you smell the floor?

Brent: I wanted to see what it was.

Elizabeth: You mean, you just bent down and thought, "Oh, it smells like chocolate?"

Brent: Yes.

Stacy: Well you should write *chocolate* in, because I don't think anybody's going to know what you're talking about. You know, you just smelled the floor? You just got down on your hands and knees and went [sniff]?

Fara:	[reading] "Daffy the dolphin swims all day." What else does he do? Does he eat all day?
Holly:	No.
Fara:	Does he like fish?
Sean:	So, should I put down, "Copy Cat plays with my dad's socks"?
Brent:	Why don't you put in that she didn't have any babies?
Sean:	No, she's only a kitten.
Brent:	Oh, you mean a little one? Or a big one?
Holly:	No, that doesn't sound good.
Fara:	Put "in the hot."
Holly:	Okay. [reads] "In the hot summer breeze because Daffy..."
Fara:	You could put "to cool down."
Holly:	Wait. I want to work on this last line. Wait.
Fara:	[suggesting] "In the hot summer breeze to cool down."
Holly:	No, 'cause water is cool. Plus there's a breeze.

The third graders are helping each other revise their compositions with a technique called peer response. Through instruction, the students have learned to think metacognitively about writing: they have conscious steps and strategies that they use when they write, and they have developed inner voices that help them to revise (25).

Students taught to collaborate during revision learn to function at what Piaget (29, 30) called the formal operational level (25). As a result of their interaction during revision, specifically during peer response groups in which students read each other's writing and make suggestions for improvement, students learn to manipulate ideas, to reason on the basis of verbal statements, to suggest alternatives for language, and to make recommendations for change (25).

WHAT ARE PEER RESPONSE GROUPS?

Even though peer response groups go by different names—peer revision groups, editing groups, peer tutoring, writing groups, or writing collaboratives—the peer response concept is the same: students meet with partners or in groups to help each other revise their writing (20, 23, 25). Regardless of the name, peer response groups have three things in common:

1. Students read each other's writing.
2. Students praise each other's writing.
3. Students offer suggestions and ask questions to help improve each other's writing.

WHAT IS THE PURPOSE OF PEER RESPONSE GROUPS?

A peer response group's major purpose is to teach students to write better compositions through teaching them to think metacognitively, and through encouraging them to have a positive attitude toward their writing.

HOW DO PEER RESPONSE GROUPS WORK?

Peer response groups allow students to take more responsibility for their writing. In addition, by helping each other revise, students learn to look at their own and others' writing from the reader's perspective. By receiving praise and suggestions for improvement, students become more confident in their ability to write. When students feel responsible for, have perspective on, and show confidence in their writing, they have a better attitude toward writing, and they produce better writing (15, 21, 25).

WHAT CLASSROOM ENVIRONMENT SUPPORTS PEER RESPONSE?

Peer revision groups function more successfully in a classroom where writing is important. The class should be student-centered, rather than teacher-centered, and have a workshop atmosphere in which the teacher and students see themselves as writers, and in which the teacher gives the students responsibility for writing rather than taking the role of the sole writing authority (17, 19).

WHAT IS THE TEACHER'S ROLE IN PEER RESPONSE?

The teacher organizes peer response groups and models the procedure, questioning techniques, and revising. During the peer revision sessions, the teacher walks around the room, keeping students on task, answering questions, and reinforcing appropriate behavior (25).

HOW DOES MODELING DEVELOP METACOGNITION?

Modeling revision is the concrete demonstration of an abstract concept. It is essential to their development of metacognition that students understand that writing is a recursive, messy process. Students need to be aware of the trial-and-error nature of composition—that most writing is the result of the continual struggle to make meaning where there was no meaning. In order to understand the recursive nature of writing, students need demonstrations. Both revision and questioning techniques should be modeled (25).

Revision Techniques: Teaching Students to Be Messy

Crossing out, underlining, drawing arrows, cutting and pasting—ways of changing text should be modeled. Students need to understand the impermanence of drafts, that anything can be changed, moved, left out and then later put back in. Students need to see how to be messy in order to be clearer (7).

Questioning Techniques: Revising from a Reader's Point of View

Another value to modeling is that it teaches the students to look at their writing from the perspective of a reader. Students need to be taught to ask the same questions about the content of their text that a reader might ask. Learning to ask questions—"Does this make sense?" "Have I used the best possible order to present my information?" "Do I need to include more details?" "Have I written too much or too little?"—is essential to developing metacognition (25, 34).

WHY IS IT IMPORTANT TO HAVE RULES FOR PEER RESPONSE?

Students are more successful and efficient at peer revision when they are guided by a set procedure (25). The rules serve two functions:

1. They reduce entropy by creating a format for the students to follow.
2. They focus students on relevant features of revision and give them a hierarchical order with which to approach revision (10, 22).

WHAT ARE THE PEER RESPONSE RULES FOR ELEMENTARY STUDENTS?

1. Read your paper to your partner. Read exactly what you've written.
2. Ask what words your partner likes: Listen and *underline* them.
3. Ask what ideas your partner likes: Listen and *underline* them.
4. *Read* your paper *again* to your partner.
5. Ask your partner for suggestions to make your paper easier to understand.

122

6. Write down on your paper the suggestions for improvement your partner gives you.
7. *Thank* your partner for the help.
8. *Be proud of your work.*

FINAL EDITING

Look for these:

CAPITALS	QUOTATION MARKS
SENTENCE ENDINGS	INDENTED PARAGRAPHS
"ANDS" THAT GET OUT OF HAND (25)	

WHY SHOULD STUDENTS HAVE COPIES OF EACH OTHER'S WRITING?

Peer revision groups are more successful when students have copies of each other's compositions and underline words and ideas they like as well as make revisions (25). When the editors revise their copies along with the author, the editors make more comments and more relevant comments. There is less repetition in the groups because each student has a record of what had been said before; therefore, groups that actively mark all copies stay on task more efficiently (25). Another positive effect of both editors and authors making revisions on their copies is that the idea of revision is reinforced and so is the student-student teaching.

WHY SHOULD STUDENTS READ THEIR COMPOSITIONS ALOUD?

When students read aloud, they can hear their mistakes. Most changes that students make in peer revision groups are based on whether the writing under discussion sounds all right. Initially students rely on their internalized rules rather than on specifically taught external rules to tell them if their writing is correct (28). Reading the compositions aloud several times during the peer response process gives students a chance to put their tacit knowledge about language to work. Students hear their words differently when they read them aloud.

WHAT TEACHING TECHNIQUES CAN SUPPLEMENT PEER RESPONSE?

As a complement to peer revision, individual conferences are an important way to model peer group behavior and to reinforce the students' sense of power and accomplishment. The conferences are student direct-ed, just as the peer revision groups are. Students follow the same proce-dure: they read their compositions aloud; the teacher responds first with positive comments. In order to give control of the conference to the stu-dents, the teacher asks the student what kind of response the student wants: ideas, mechanics, or content revision (19).

HOW CAN TAPE RECORDING AND VIDEO TAPING HELP STUDENTS LEARN PEER RESPONSE TECHNIQUES?

Audio and video are essential parts of the techniques for teaching peer response. The audio and video tapes of students interacting in their peer revision groups become the basis for refining teaching and modeling. The audio and video tapes of successful groups can be used as models for other groups and as reinforcement to the groups who have performed successfully.

HOW DO PEER RESPONSE GROUPS DEVELOP METACOGNITION ABOUT COMPOSITION?

Developing Internal Locus of Control: When Teachers Give Up Power Without Giving Up Authority

Central to the ability to revise and work in peer revision groups is the concept of internal locus of control. The power to create, revise, and evaluate text should reside with the student, not the teacher. This sense of control over writing comes from knowledge about composition process as well as self confidence in writing ability (25).

Metacognition: Thinking About Writing

Metacognition is essential to developing internal locus of control. Me-tacognition is self-awareness, the ability to consciously think about the act of writing: to plan, make word choices, and revise with a sense of purpose (11). This ability is the result of knowing how an individual's unique writing process fits into the larger writing process. Knowing how to plan writing, how to reflect upon it, and how to revise it from a read-er's point of view creates self-confidence.

The Internal Editor: The Audience Within

A result of modeling and working in peer revision groups is the development of the internal editor. The internal editor is another name for audience awareness. Helping students develop an internal voice with whom they converse during the revision process is essential to developing their internal locus of control (25). When students read their compositions to their peers and hear the questions that their peers ask, they internalize those questions and ask those same types of questions of themselves as they are writing and revising (34). The peer revision group becomes a demonstration of reading the text from a reader's point of view. The demands of the audience become internalized because students have had immediate audience response to their writing.

SUMMARY

Peer response is a method of teaching writing which ultimately develops students' metacognition and internal locus of control. When students develop metacognition about writing, their internal locus of control also develops because students understand that writing is a process that they can control; they become responsible for their own learning; they rely on their internal editor, and relying on the internal editor encourages continued dialogues with the inner self.

Peer revision groups are certainly not the only way to help students develop metacognition and internal locus of control, but peer revision groups create an atmosphere—and are created in an atmosphere—where talk is essential to writing. The peer revision rules are designed to reduce confusion and focus students on the important features of peer revision. The peer revision rules become the scaffolding (4) for the questioning strategy which begins the cycle of internal editor/metacognition/internal locus of control.

Ideally, the peer community is an integral part of the cycle. For Carl Bereiter

> the idea of a community of scholars holds promise. Translated into practical terms, this would mean turning the classroom into a social setting for mutual support of knowledge construction, a setting that could eventually be internalized by the individual student (4, p. 221).

Students best learn about writing in a classroom that is student-centered and writing-centered where rules exist to support a process rather than dictate behavior, and where students working together become what Bereiter called a "mutual support of knowledge construction" (4, p. 221). This implies, as Janet Emig (14) and A. N. Applebee (1) pointed out, that even though most classrooms are teacher-centered, peers are still the most important audience for students' writing. It also implies that the "teacher-centered presentation of composition...is pedagogically, developmentally, and politically an anachronism" (4, p. 100).

REFERENCES

1. Applebee, A. N. *Writing in the Secondary School: English and the Content Areas.* Urbana, Ill.: National Council of Teachers of English, 1981.

2. Barritt, L.S., and Kroll, B.M. "Some Implications of Cognitive-Developmental Psychology for Research in Composing." In *Research on Composing: Points of Departure,* edited by C.R. Cooper and L. Odell, 49–59. Urbana, Ill.: National Council of Teachers of English, 1978.

3. Beach, R. "The Pragmatics of Self-Assessing." In *Revising: New Essays for Teachers of Writing,* edited by R. A. Sudol, 71–83. Urbana, Ill.: National Council of Teachers of English, 1982.

4. Bereiter, C. "Toward a Solution of the Learning Paradox." *Review of Educational Research* 55, no. 2 (1985): No. 201–26.

5. Burtis, P. J., and others. "The Development of Planning in Writing." In *Explorations in the Development of Writing,* edited by B. M. Kroll and G. Wells, 120–53. New York: John Wiley and Sons, 1983.

6. Butturff, D. R., and Sommers, N. I. "Placing Revision in a Reinvented Rhetorical Tradition." In *Reinventing the Rhetorical Tradition,* edited by A. Freedman and I. Pringle, 99–104. Conway, Ark.: L and S Books, 1980.

7. Calkins, L. M. "Children Learn the Writer's Craft." *Language Arts* 57 (1980): 567–73.

8. Calkins, L. M. *Lessons from a Child: A Case Study of One Child's Growth in Writing.* Ann Arbor, Mich.: University Microfilms International, 1982. No. 8226743.

9. Calkins, L. M. "Learning to Think Through Writing." In *Observing the Language Learner,* edited by A. Jaggar and M. T. Smith-Burke, 190–99. Urbana, Ill.: National Council of Teachers of English, 1985.

10. Campbell, J. *Grammatical Man: Information, Entropy, Language and Life.* New York: Simon and Schuster, 1982.

11. Costa, A. L. "Mediating the Metacognitive." *Educational Leadership* 42, no. 3 (1984): No. 57–62.

12. Don Carlos, P. H. "Family Structure, Locus of Control, Reading Achievement, Manifest Anxiety, and Self-Esteem in Children." Ph.D. diss., Arizona State University, Tempe, 1981.

13. Donaldson, M., ed. *Children's Minds.* Glasgow: William Collins Sons, 1978.

14. Emig, J. *The Composing Process of Twelfth Graders.* Urbana, Ill.: National Council of Teachers of English, 1971.

15. Friss, D. "Writing Class: Teachers and Students Writing Together." In *Teaching Writing: Essays from the Bay Area Writing Project,* edited by G. Camp, 292–98. Montclair, N.J.: Boynton/Cook, 1982.

16. Gere, A. R., and Stevens, R. S. "The Language of Writing Groups: How Oral Response Shapes Revision." Paper presented at Conference on College Composition and Communication, New York, 1984.

17. Graves, D. "We Won't Let Them Write." *Language Arts* 5 (1978): 635–40.

18. Graves, D. *Writing: Teachers and Children at Work.* Exeter, N.H.: Heinemann Books, 1983.

19. Graves, D. "Patterns of Child Control of the Writing Process." In *The Development of Children's Imaginative Writing,* edited by H. Cowie, 219–32. London: Croom Helm, 1984.

20. Healy, M. K. "Using Student Writing Response Groups in the Classroom." In *Teaching Writing: Essays from the Bay Area Writing Project,* edited by G. Camp, 266–91. Upper Montclair, N.J.: Boynton/Cook 1982.

21. Johnson, D. W., and others. *Circles of Learning: Cooperation in the Classroom.* Alexandria, Va.: Association for Supervision and Curriculum Development, 1984.

22. Marder, D. "Revision as Discovery and the Reduction of Entropy." In *Revising: New Essays for Teachers of Writing,* edited by R. A. Sudol, 3–12. Urbana, Ill.: National Council of Teachers of English, 1982.

23. Mayher, J. S.; Lester, N. B.; and Pradl, G. M. *Learning to Write/Writing to Learn.* Upper Montclair, N.J.: Boynton/Cook, 1983.

24. Meeks, L. L. Cassette recordings. Unpublished raw data, 1983.

25. Meeks, L. L. "Developing the Internal Editor: Peer Revision in a Third Grade Class." Ph.D. diss., Arizona State University, 1985.

26. Moffett, J., and Wagner, B. J. *Student-Centered Language Arts and Reading, K–13.* 2d ed. Boston: Houghton Mifflin, 1976.

27. Mohr, M. M. *Revision: The Rhythm of Meaning.* Upper Montclair, N.J.: Boynton/Cook, 1984.

28. Murray, D. M., and Graves, D. H. "Revision in the Writer's Workshop and in the Classroom." In *The Development of Children's Imaginative Writing,* edited by H. Cowie, 139–53. Manuka, Aus.: Croom Helm, 1980.

29. Piaget, J. *The Language and Thought of the Child.* New York: Harcourt, Brace, 1926.

30. Piaget, J. "Appendix: Piaget's Theory of Intellectual Development." In *Children's Minds,* edited by M. Donaldson, 129–45. Glasgow: William Collins Sons, 1978.

31. Shafer, R. E. "Children's Interactions in Sustaining Writing: Studies in an English Primary School." Department of English, Arizona State University, Tempe, 1980. Typescript.

32. Smith, F. *Writing and the Writer.* New York: Holt, Rinehart and Winston, 1982.

33. Stanford, G. *Developing Effective Classroom Groups: A Practical Guide for Teachers.* New York: Hart Publishing Co., 1977.

34. Wong, B. Y. L. "Self-Questioning Instructional Research: A Review." *Review of Educational Research* 55 (1985): 227–51.

BASICS IN BLOOM

by Norma J. Hoelzel

Norma J. Hoelzel uses Bloom's taxonomy to develop students' question-generating skills. She illustrates how all levels of the taxonomy can be translated into student-generated questions by average students. In her system, the upper levels of Bloom's taxonomy are not limited to use with gifted students. She finds that students become more active learners as they improve their question-asking skills and become less dependent on the teacher for stimulation: "They use the taxonomy not only to reinforce basic areas of study, but also to expand and challenge themselves and their classmates in many other areas of study."

The author teaches fifth grade at the Vineland School, DeSoto, Missouri, school district.

Developing the ability to think, and thus to question, is the basis for all other learning. In the very early elementary grades mechanical rote and memory work commonly take precedence. However, we should consider the fact that in a high-tech world, it might be wise to begin the teaching of expanded thinking skills at an early age. Unfortunately, it is well known that elementary and secondary educators stress memorization. This is an important and necessary skill. However, analytical thinking should also be developed if students are to be adept at reading comprehension and problem solving, necessary in all academic studies, and if they are to participate fully in a technological society.

Finding the best way to help students think analytically should be of interest to teachers on all levels of learning. One effective way is to utilize the Benjamin Bloom Taxonomy of Thinking Skills. Unfortunately, all six levels of the taxonomy are not always used in the regular classroom. Normally, teachers use the first three levels: knowledge, comprehension, and application; however, use of the upper levels—analysis, synthesis, and evaluation—is often expected only in classes for the gifted. And when the taxonomy is used, we usually find it with teacher-directed activities, where the teacher asks the questions. Commonly, the assumption is that teachers ask questions and students answer them based on memory and rote learning.

Teachers ask a tremendous number of questions. One study reveals that primary school teachers ask 3½ to 6½ questions per minute! Elementary school teachers average 348 questions a day....yet...the typical student asks approximately one question per month. (Sadker, Myra, and Sadker, David. "Questioning Skills." In *Classroom Teaching Skills,* 2d ed. Lexington, Mass.: D.C. Heath & Co., 1982. Edited by James M. Cooper and others. p. 150.)

How well might students learn by developing their own skills of questioning, thus possibly exploring areas that might not be brought to light by the classroom teacher.

It is challenging to work with a process that encourages students to utilize Bloom's Taxonomy themselves. They use the taxonomy not only to reinforce basic areas of study, but also to expand and challenge themselves and their classmates in many other areas of study. The challenge and excitement of learning comes when they begin doing this themselves, and do not always have to depend upon the teacher for stimulation.

To understand this process, one must first understand the definition of the levels of Bloom's Taxonomy of thinking skills.

Bloom's Taxonomy is probably the best known system for classifying educational objectives as well as classroom questions. There are six levels of Bloom's Taxonomy and questions at each level require a person responding to use a different kind of thought process [taxonomy is another word for classification]. (Sadker and Sadker, "Questioning Skills," p. 151.)

These levels are as follows:

KNOWLEDGE: This is the learning and repeating of information from memory—unfortunately, this information is often quickly forgotten.

| label | repeat | list | recall | recognize |
| who | what | when | where | define |

COMPREHENSION: The student must have some knowledge and some understanding of subject and be able to restate information in her/his own way. The majority of classroom time is spent on this level.

| describe | explain | identify | report | compare |
| illustrate | review | contrast | compare | locate |

APPLICATION: The student must be able to explain and apply rules in answering questions or problems.

| solve | choose | use | select | schedule |
| employ | classify | operate | translate | demonstrate |

ANALYSIS: The student is required to think critically, to break information into parts and be able to offer evidence to support conclusions.

| detect | infer | determine | question | solve |
| analyze | test | conclude | criticize | diagram |

SYNTHESIS: Students produce an original product or idea of their own; they make predictions to solve problems.

propose	assemble	organize	develop	design
produce	plan	predict	arrange	collect

EVALUATION: The student now judges the value of the information collected and offers a solution for the problem.

decide	evaluate	judge	value
estimate	rate	measure	assess

Initiating the use of this taxonomy in developing these questioning skills was a comparatively simple exercise in a self-contained class made up of 25 fifth grade students ranging in abilities from learning disabled to gifted, with reading achievement scores ranging from 2.4 to post-high-school level. Our school district is mostly rural, centered in a small Missouri community with students transported to school from a 50 square-mile area. The district offers special classes for students needing remediation in reading, language, math; for the learning disabled; for students needing special education; and for gifted students. Pull-out classes for the gifted were started two years ago. This group was named the Discovery class, and of course, since it is new and it is well-known that the students going to this class are upper-level students, all students think they want to participate. In initiating the learning of these questioning skills, I capitalized on this fact.

To capture student interest, I first explained that some of the study skills I was about to introduce were skills commonly used only by the teacher in the Discovery classes. I further explained that this method was probably not utilized by the students themselves in any other classrooms in the way that they would be expected to use it. They were told that they were the first students with whom I had tried this method of teaching, and that they—not the teacher—would be asking most of the questions.

Once I had their interest, their attention was then focused on a set of wall charts which gave each level of Bloom, with verbs which a student might use on each of the six levels. Then we progressed through each level of the taxonomy, using very simple questions based on a subject we had been studying in social studies, cotton. For example:

KNOWLEDGE: Name states where cotton would most likely be grown in the United States.

COMPREHENSION: Explain why cotton grows best in these particular areas.

APPLICATION:	Illustrate five uses of cotton in today's society.
ANALYSIS:	Debate the advantages of cotton vs. wool.
SYNTHESIS:	Predict what the effect on our society would be if cotton had never become a product of our agriculture.
EVALUATION:	Assess the value to our society of the invention of the cotton gin.

As we worked our way through the charts and examples, student interest increased rapidly. It was especially exciting to see all students on every level participate enthusiastically in this exercise.

The next step was to turn the questioning over to the students, based on the same subject, beginning with the knowledge level again and progressing on to the evaluation level. Students were asked to choose another verb on each level, rather than using the one we had just used. I was surprised at the quality of questions these students immediately began to fire at each other, and the overall interest it created in the subject itself. All students were eager to take part, as they were thinking for themselves, with no threat of asking wrong questions.

Once all students had an opportunity to question, and I was reasonably sure that all had sufficient understanding of the method, an assignment was given relating to the study of weather, which we had just completed in science class. I was very pleased with the results. Some examples of student activities follow:

KNOWLEDGE:	Define barometer. Recall and name cloud types. How does air affect weather? How does an anemometer work? What is it called when it rains, sleets, or snows?
COMPREHENSION:	Illustrate a barometer and an anemometer and explain how they are used. Compare air moisture with air pressure. Explain the troposphere. Explain how an anemometer is useful.
APPLICATION:	Draw a scene of the three cloud types and name the kinds of weather associated with each one. Design a machine to predict rain. Write a play about what you would be doing outside today. Plan and write a weather report for today. Demonstrate how you might feel on a cumulus cloud day.

131

ANALYSIS:	Debate living in and out of the atmosphere.
	Discuss the advantages and disadvantages of being a weather reporter.
	Dissect the clouds.
SYNTHESIS:	Think of a way to walk in the clouds.
	Invent a new name for weather.
	Think of a way to make air pressure, and list the steps necessary.
	Decide whether you'd prefer the climate in Missouri or the climate in Florida and explain why.
	Predict what life would be like without thermometers.
	Predict what would happen if there were never any clouds.
EVALUATION:	Decide what happens to a weather vane when a storm blows in from the west.
	Assess what might happen to your home if the wind speed reached more than 117 km/hr.
	Compare the weather in our state with that of one of the southeastern states.

Students then presented their exercises to other students to complete. Exercises using the verb "debate" became a favorite choice. Students who feared giving oral presentations before the class could readily get up and debate without any fear at all. The student who had to think of a way to walk in the clouds chose to invent a magic cloud to float around and see the world, until he came to Africa where he planned to squeeze out the much needed rain for the starving people in that area. (The unusual idea often surfaces during this kind of activity.)

This exercise has been used in this class for the study of Halley's comet and the human body, and in reading comprehension exercises, language arts, and social studies. We also use it on holidays. We decided to do "Halloween in Bloom." The students had great fun with this, discovering information they would not have otherwise covered. Many students chose Dracula, witches, or goblins for their subject, but one student decided to produce her activities based on the bat. First of all, she found out just what a bat was, when it fed, and where it lived. Then she illustrated what a bat looked like and built a mobile of one flying in the air. Next she dramatized how a bat flies. To analyze the bat, she actually dissected one (on paper), showing all of its body parts. On the synthesis level, she created a new name for the bat, "Nightflyer"; discussed a way to talk with a bat; and decided to choose a new color for the bat. Last of all, she predicted what could happen if the world had no bats at all. When this student completed her exercise, she had a real understanding of the bat and had developed some new ideas relating to it. Sharing this knowledge with her classmates was great fun for her.

My students have found this to be a challenging and enjoyable way to learn. They especially like to share their activities with other classmates in both individual and group projects. The class is developing valuable comprehension and questioning skills, but most importantly, they are developing a healthy respect for each other as they solve and work through the activities presented to one another.

For the very young primary classes, color-coded charts for each level of Bloom could be used for easier identification of level, and simple verbs could replace the ones used for upper grade activities.

The results of using this method have been very gratifying. Students learn to ask questions and to answer them intelligently as they share with each other. Ideas and facts are revealed which are often new to the students, some of which probably would not have been covered using traditional methods. Minds are stretched in unforeseen ways, and results are often refreshingly surprising. The shy or timid student gathers confidence in the free and open atmosphere this method creates. In short, all students become more active learners, engaged and interested in what they are learning. Thus, the exercise and refinement of thinking skills can and does occur when students know, understand, and use this process.

TEACHING THINKING TO TEACH LITERATURE WHILE TEACHING LITERATURE TO TEACH THINKING

by Natalie C. Yeager

Using Bloom's taxonomy, Natalee C. Yeager shows how teaching thinking and the study of literature "can be combined to the enhancement of both." For example, discussing the interpretation stage of thinking, she suggests using Venn diagrams to help students learn to compare and contrast characters in a novel; or constructing charts to compare survival methods of central characters in adventure stories. Syllogisms can be used to help students identify and analyze the assumptions made by some of the characters in their reading. Students can engage in deductive reasoning by solving matrix puzzles based on episodes in a novel; or they can discover something new to them through a synthesis activity. Yeager shows how literature can be used to provide content for these thinking skills exercises. She feels that combining literature study with thinking skills practice helps students more deeply understand what they read, and impacts positively on their attitudes, sensitivity, and values.

The author is Gifted Coordinator, School District #17, Jacksonville, Illinois.

Productive learning, according to Hilda Taba, should contribute to more than one objective and thus provide for multiple learnings (25). The teaching of thinking and the study of literature can be combined to the enhancement of both. Examples from literature will motivate students in the development of critical thinking skills, and using those skills will lead to a deeper understanding of literature.

The definition of critical thinking used in this study is taken from *Classroom Questions: What Kinds?* by Norris Sanders:

> A precise and useful definition of the phrase is that it includes all thought processes beyond the memory category. A teacher who offers his students appropriate experiences in translation, interpretation, application, analysis, synthesis, and evaluation can be assured he is providing instruction in every intellectual aspect of critical thinking. (23, p. 6)

Sanders's categories are based on Bloom's *Taxonomy of Educational Objectives* (6). Sanders has changed Bloom's lowest level, "knowledge," to "memory" to make it a thinking skill as are the other levels. Sanders points out that the levels are both sequential and cumulative. Thus, each level, including memory, is important in its own right and also as a component of higher levels of thinking. He warns against getting bogged down on exact classification because many questions seem to fall between two categories.

Translation is the ability to change the form in which ideas are expressed. This includes summarizing, illustrating what has been read, mapping, graphing, and expressing ideas in a drama. Students who have completed the reading of an example of literature can benefit from performing these activities. For instance, students who have read about Taran and Eilonwy's escape from the Spiral Castle in Lloyd Alexander's *Book of Three* (1) will increase the clarity of their imagery if they diagram the structure of the castle. Or they might be asked to put these adventures into play form. A way of using an additional translation experience is to have the students illustrate the main events in the play. If the play is then recorded on a tape and the pictures are shown with an opaque projector, the audience will share a narrated filmstrip.

Interpretation is the ability to see relationships. This includes being able to compare, infer, generalize, and understand simple cause and effect. Interpretation includes on a common-sense level many of the same elements that are dealt with more formally in analysis.

Literature contains many possibilities for comparison. In discussion and in writing assignments students can list or describe the likenesses and differences of two or more characters or situations in a single book, in different books, or in a series of books.

A Venn diagram is an instructional technique that can be used to help students learn to compare and contrast. Two intersecting circles can be drawn on the chalkboard and the name of a book character placed in each circle. Students are then asked to list as many attributes as they can for each character. When it is found that both characters share a certain quality, that quality is written in the intersection of the two circles and eliminated from the separate sides. After this has been done as a large group so that they understand the method, students can work in small groups, again using a Venn diagram, to determine the likenesses and differences between two different characters, settings, or plots.

Retrieval charts (25) are another technique for comparing and contrasting. In this way, for instance, students can compare their lives with the life of Nomusa, the Zulu girl in *Thirty-One Brothers and Sisters* (18). (See page 136.)

Another retrieval chart might compare the survival methods of the Indian girl Karana in *Island of the Blue Dolphins* (20) with those of Timothy, the West Indian in *The Cay* (26). Venn diagrams and retrieval

	Nomusa	Students
Type of home		
Family structure		
Jobs for girls		
Jobs for boys		
Food		
Entertainment		
Love for family		

charts can be used as the first step in developing generalizations. Students look for similarities among the examples and for cause-and-effect relationships. Generalizations are usually qualified by a degree of probability (17).

Literature provides many examples of cause and effect. What caused a character to do what he or she did? What result did he or she hope to achieve by that act? The combination of a Venn diagram and mind mapping (29) can lead students to a better understanding of cause and effect as well as of the characters and events in a book. For instance, in *No Promises in the Wind* (11), what were the causes and effects of Josh Grondowski's decision to leave home?

Application is the ability to use skills and knowledge in a new situation. Students are applying their skills any time that, with a minimum of direction, they do something that they have previously learned. In a broader sense, every time students read a novel, they are using the many levels of reading skills they have previously acquired.

Application thinking also occurs when students get involved in projects and use skills they learned in an earlier situation. When students read *Key to the Treasure* by Peggy Parish (21), they learn several different codes. If they are asked to write a message using one of the codes and then exchange their messages with other students, their thinking is application.

136

In the future world described in *Konrad* (19), parents can order a child from a factory, specifying the characteristics they wish the child to have. Students can find out what qualities their parents, teachers, and friends would choose for an ordered child by conducting a survey. In doing this they would be learning and applying the skills needed to conduct a survey. By keeping the responses for the three groups separate, students would have the data needed to apply their graphing skills to construct graphs. They could also make Venn diagrams for the purpose of comparing and contrasting.

Sanders says that *analysis* is primarily logical reasoning, and students should be aware of the rules they are following. Students who have been taught to use syllogisms will find them helpful in discerning the assumptions made by some of the characters in literature. At the beginning of *The Cay* (26), Phillip's thinking could be analyzed thus:

> Major premise: All black men are inferior.
> Minor premise: Timothy is a black man.
> Conclusion: Timothy is inferior.

The conclusion is valid according to the rules of logic, but students who have read *The Cay* realize that it is false. They can then reason that if the conclusion is false and the minor premise is true, the major premise must be false. A similar example can be found in *Walk the World's Rim* (5). The Indian boy Chakoh has been taught that all slaves are cowards because they have allowed themselves to be captured in battle. He then learns that his best friend Esteban is a slave. Students can chart Chakoh's conclusion and then see what must be changed if he is to regain his friendship. The fallacy of his original premise is clearly established when he learns that Esteban was sold into slavery by his parents to get money so his brothers and sisters could eat. In this instance, the fact that Esteban was black was not a concern. This example can be diagrammed as shown:

> The largest circle, A, includes all cowards. Circle B—which includes all slaves—is placed inside A to show that all slaves are cowards. Circle C, designating Esteban, is inside Circle B—because he is a slave and, therefore, a coward.

The diagram would be changed to reflect Chakoh's discovery that Esteban was not a coward taken in battle.

> Circle A still includes all cowards, and Circle B all slaves. But since only some slaves are cowards, Circle B is only partially inside Circle A. Esteban fits into the part of Circle B that is not inside Circle A. Therefore, he is not a coward.

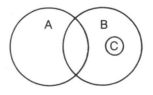

Whether the use of Venn diagrams is categorized as interpretive or analytic is partly a matter of complexity. A clearly analytic task would be to compare and contrast the philosophies of the two major groups in *Gammage Cup* by Carol Kendall (12). The members of the ruling class of a fictitious town are known as Periods. Their authority is challenged by several free-thinking individuals who have the good of the entire community as their goal. The philosophies of the two groups are not explicitly stated and must be inferred from an analysis of the behavior of the various characters.

Students engage in deductive reasoning when they solve matrix puzzles. These can be constructed with names and other information from a book. The solutions require both deductive reasoning and a knowledge of characters and events in the book. The following puzzle is based on *Escape from Warsaw* by Ian Serraillier (24). The book is about children who fled the Nazis, and describes their adventures in various countries. In one episode the children receive clothing, although the author does not specify what items each child received.

Deductive Reasoning Puzzle

Four children—Bronia, Edek, Jan, and Ruth—are left homeless by the Nazi invasion of Poland. Each is given an item of clothing by the Polish Relief Agency: boots, a hat, mittens, or a sweater. When they finally reach their parents, each tells of an adventure in a different country: Bavaria, Germany, Poland, and Switzerland. Use the clues below and the matrix on page 139 to find which item of clothing each received and which country that child tells about.

- No one's country, clothing, or name starts with the same letter.
- Jan tells about the farmer who found the children in his barn. (Bavaria)
- Bronia tells about Ivan, the Russian sentry. (Poland)
- Edek tells about his experiences in prison. (Germany)
- Edek's gift keeps only his hands warm.
- A girl receives the sweater.

Defining analysis more broadly than Sanders, Bloom (6) says that it is the breakdown of a communication into its parts so that one can see how it is organized. This definition provides a particularly rewarding approach to the study of literature, for example, when applied to books that have unique organizational plans.

In *Time Cat* (4) Lloyd Alexander gives the proverbial nine lives to the black cat Gareth, who is enabled to go back in history to nine different places and times. Simply by referring to the table of contents, students

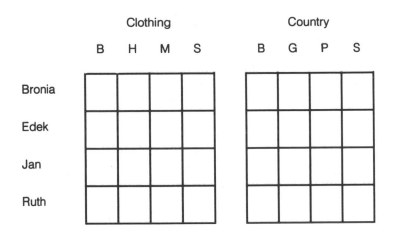

	Clothing					Country			
---	B	H	M	S		B	G	P	S
Bronia									
Edek									
Jan									
Ruth									

can see that there are two chapters for each visit. By analyzing the themes of each visit students discover how Gareth is able to help the people living at that time. For instance, Awin is a girl living on the Isle of Man in 1588. Her awareness that the Manx cat lacks a tail helps her to accept the fact that one of her eyes is blue and the other brown.

Madeleine L'Engle uses a delightfully intricate plan in *A Swiftly Tilting Planet* (15). This is a difficult book, and students understand it more clearly when they analyze the way it is organized. Meg's mother-in-law recites an ancient rune to protect them from danger. Each line of the rune calls upon a specific power for good, such as the sun, to stand between them and the powers of darkness. Each line provides the key for help in a different adventure as Charles Wallace goes back into history to help people struggling in various situations.

Lloyd Alexander forecasts events in *The High King* (3) when Hen Wen, the oracular pig, uses letter sticks to make a prophecy: stones will speak, night will turn to noon, and rivers will burn with frozen fire before the sword Dyrnwyn will be regained. Each of these seemingly impossible things then happens in the story and students, discovering the structure of the story, are excited each time they encounter another episode.

Synthesis activities stimulate students to engage in imaginative, original thinking, to discover something that is new to them. This category includes most of the elements usually encompassed by "creative thinking." Synthesis thinking often leads to a product of some sort—art, drama, writing, a plan for an invention, or a solution to a social problem.

Literature is itself a product of synthesis thinking, and immersing students in good literature gives them a foundation for their own creative expression. Good literature gives students models of good writing and demonstrates that characters can be brought to life. It introduces them to all kinds of people and their achievements and problems and to a variety of responses to diverse situations.

Teachers have a double responsibility in nurturing creative thinking. First, it is important that the classroom be a place where children know that diverse ideas will be accepted. Antoine De Saint-Exupery's little prince (8) experienced rejection when he drew an elephant that had been eaten by a boa constrictor. Adults called it a hat and advised him to give up drawing. Students also may find that their original ideas are not understood by classmates or teachers, and some, like the little prince, may learn to express only ordinary, unimaginative ideas.

Second, teachers must provide activities designed to help students grow in their creative abilities. E. Paul Torrance has identified four components of creativity: fluency, flexibility, elaboration, and originality (27). A student's abilities in each of these areas can be developed through instruction and practice. Brainstorming is a technique that can be used to develop all of these components. Students are asked to list as many ideas as possible (fluency). As soon as a student shifts to a new category of answer or a different point of view (flexibility), the teacher can point this out and encourage others to do the same. Elaboration takes place when students build on their own or others' ideas—making modifications of some kind. Originality is perhaps the most difficult to teach. Original ideas usually come near the end of a brainstorming session after most of the commonplace ideas have been expressed. A delightful book to share with students as an example of fluent, flexible, and original thinking is Mary Ann Hoberman's *A House Is a House for Me* (10). In fast-moving rhyme, the author tells of many different kinds of houses. Students who previously had brainstormed for all the kinds of houses are particularly impressed by the wealth of ideas in this book.

Literature presents many opportunities for involving students in synthesis thinking. In *Ben and Me* (13) by Robert Lawson, Amos, a mouse, claims that he was really responsible for many of the achievements credited to Ben Franklin. In a second book, *Mr. Revere and I* (14), Paul Revere's life is described by his horse. Students can analyze the structure of these books and consider what steps Lawson had to go through in order to write his books. They then can choose a different person and tell his or her story from the point of view of some other animal.

Students who have read *The First Two Lives of Lukas-Kasha* by Lloyd Alexander (2) can be assigned to list as many characteristics as they can of Lukas-Kasha in each of his first two lives; then they can look for causes for each of the changes that he undergoes. At the end of his second life, the boy is brought back to the scene of his first life, but he rejects this and sets out to begin a new one. Students will have an opportunity for synthesis thinking if they write about Lukas-Kasha's third life.

C. S. Lewis transports his characters into the Kingdom of Narnia in a different way in each of the seven books in his *Chronicles of Narnia* (16). Students can brainstorm for other ways of reaching Narnia or some other world. They can then list the features of Narnia and compare them with those of our world. Creating a new world and choosing a different way of reaching it would require synthesis thinking.

One of the most difficult tasks that both the prince and Tom Canty have in Mark Twain's *The Prince and the Pauper* (28) is convincing people of their true identity. Students can work in small groups to prepare skits in which either Tom or the Prince finds an original way to prove who he is. They can begin this task by brainstorming for as many possible solutions as they can think of. The process of taking the existing characters and writing a new dialogue would likewise involve synthesis thinking.

The last kind of thinking listed by Sanders is *evaluation*. Evaluative thinking involves two steps: setting up standards or values, and determining how well various alternatives fulfill these criteria. Good decision-making depends upon clear thinking at each of the other levels. It requires that one recognize relationships, understand cause and effect, be able to predict outcomes, and think of important, useful alternatives.

This two-step process of evaluation can be used to judge a character in literature, an exercise that both enhances a student's decision-making ability and deepens his understanding of the character. Katherine Paterson's *The Master Puppeteer* (22) describes a period in Japan when there was widespread hunger. Saburo steals from the rich—to give to the poor. The young boy Jiro says, "Then he is not really bad, is he? Even if he is a thief?" His father replies, "It is always bad to be a thief. . ." (22, p. 7).

Students can draw up lists of the traits of a good man and those of a bad man, and then match Saburo's characteristics with those on the lists. Just counting the characteristics that match is not a valid basis for judging. Students can debate the relative importance of the various traits. The group frequently will not agree on a decision; students can learn that it is all right to have different views, provided they have sound reasons for their conclusions.

Later in the book Jiro is faced with a vitally important decision. He thinks he knows who Saburo is and could win a large reward by revealing him to the authorities. On the other hand, there are strong reasons for not making his identity known. Teachers can encourage students to make this decision for Jiro. The ability to predict outcomes is most important here. Students can list all the consequences that might happen and all the people who would be affected by each of the choices. Individual items listed can then be categorized as positive or negative and their relative importance weighted. Possibly a third choice—perhaps some sort of compromise—will be suggested, and if so it also should be evaluated.

Manos, the dying king in *First to Ride* (9), has the right to name his successor. Instead, he says that the next king will be the one who comes riding on the back of a Fleet One, one of the untamed horses. After reading the book, students can decide on reasons why they think this method of choosing a king was wise or unwise. Expanding the problem, the teacher can ask small groups of students to decide on a method of choosing a king in a particular circumstance. The total group can then decide on criteria by which to evaluate the plans and consider each of the methods suggested.

In *The Big Wave* by Pearl Buck (7) Jiya loses his whole family in a tidal wave. A rich old gentleman offers to take him as his son. He is also offered a place in the home of his best friend, whose father is a poor farmer. Which offer should he accept? Students, trying to make this decision, will determine what they consider to be the most important values in life. They then should describe the quality of life Jiya would expect to have as a consequence of each of the possible decisions. A decision can be made by comparing these descriptions.

CONCLUSIONS

Strategies designed to teach thinking—translation, interpretation, application, analysis, synthesis, and evaluation—have been combined with the teaching of literature in this discussion. Literature has been utilized to provide stimulating and enjoyable content for exercises designed to develop thinking skills, while at the same time thinking activities have enhanced the study of literature. This presentation has dealt with levels of thinking in the cognitive domain only, but it is evident that frequently the suggested strategies will have positive effects upon students' attitudes, sensitivities, and values.

REFERENCES

1. Alexander, Lloyd. *The Book of Three.* New York: Dell Publishing Co., 1964.
2. _____. *The First Two Lives of Lukas-Kasha.* New York: Dell Publishing Co., 1978.

3. _____. *The High King.* New York: Dell Publishing Co., 1968.

4. _____. *Time Cat.* New York: Avon Books, 1968.

5. Baker, Betty. *Walk the World's Rim.* New York: Harper & Row, 1965.

6. Bloom, Benjamin S., ed. *Taxonomy of Educational Objectives. Handbook I: Cognitive Domain.* New York: Longmans, Green, 1961.

7. Buck, Pearl. *The Big Wave.* New York: Scholastic Book Services, 1960.

8. De Saint-Exupery, Antoine. *The Little Prince.* Translated by Katherine Woods. New York: Reynal & Hitchcock, 1943.

9. Crowell, Pers. *First to Ride.* New York: Scholastic Book Services, 1959.

10. Hoberman, Mary Ann. *A House Is a House for Me.* New York: Viking Press, 1978.

11. Hunt, Irene. *No Promises in the Wind.* New York: Berkeley Publishing Group, 1983.

12. Kendall, Carol. *Gammage Cup.* New York: Harcourt, Brace & World, 1959.

13. Lawson, Robert. *Ben and Me.* New York: Dell Publishing Co., 1939.

14. _____. *Mr. Revere and I.* New York: Dell Publishing Co., 1953.

15. L'Engle, Madeleine. *A Swiftly Tilting Planet.* New York: Dell Publishing Co., 1979.

16. Lewis, C.S. *The Chronicles of Narnia.* 7 books. New York: Macmillan Publishing Co., 1970.

17. McCollum, John A. *Ah Hah! The Inquiry Process of Generating and Testing Knowledge.* Santa Monica, Calif.: Goodyear Publishing Co., 1978.

18. Mirsky, Reba Paeff. *Thirty-One Brothers and Sisters.* New York: Dell Publishing Co., 1952.

19. Nostlinger, Christine. *Konrad.* Translated by Anthea Bell. New York: Franklin Watts, 1977.

20. O'Dell, Scott. *Island of the Blue Dolphins.* New York: Dell Publishing Co., 1960.

21. Parish, Peggy. *Key to the Treasure.* New York: Dell Publishing Co., 1966.

22. Paterson, Katherine. *The Master Puppeteer.* New York: Harper & Row, 1981.

23. Sanders, Norris. *Classroom Questions: What Kinds?* New York: Harper & Row, 1966.

24. Serraillier, Ian. *Escape from Warsaw.* New York: Scholastic, n.d.

25. Taba, Hilda. *Teachers' Handbook for Elementary Social Studies.* Palo Alto, Calif.: Addison-Wesley Publishing Co., 1967.

26. Taylor, Theodore. *The Cay.* New York: Avon Books, 1969.

27. Torrance, E. Paul. *Guiding Creative Talent.* Englewood Cliffs, N. J.: Prentice-Hall, 1962.

28. Twain, Mark. *The Prince and the Pauper.* New York: Scholastic Book Services, 1958.

29. Winocur, S. Lee. "Developing Lesson Plans with Cognitive Objectives." In *Developing Minds: A Resource Book for Teaching Thinking,* edited by Arthur L. Costa. Alexandria, Va.: Association for Supervision and Curriculum Development, 1985.

USING THINKING SKILLS
IN MODIFIED ESL

by Patsy A. Jaynes

In her description of a thinking skills program in a modified ESL classroom, Patsy A. Jaynes suggests how to use Bloom's taxonomy to teach basic skills in courses across the curriculum. She outlines the structure and content of the program, and presents data on its effectiveness. The teaching/learning process that teachers incorporated into their classrooms included clustering (a non-linear way of organizing information), student assignment contracts, grouping students by reading level, dialogue journals, and reading logs. In addition, different levels of Bloom's taxonomy of thinking skills were used in daily lesson assignments. Students were encouraged to go beyond factual knowledge to analysis, synthesis, and evaluation of new information. Jaynes reports that the project improved students' scores on standardized reading and language proficiency tests, as well as their mastery of content course material.

The author is Program Evaluation Specialist in the Department of Second Language Education, Jefferson County Public Schools, Lakewood, Colorado.

Arvada Senior High School in Arvada, Colorado, is one of Jefferson County Public School District's thirteen comprehensive high schools. The total enrollment for Arvada High is approximately 2,000 students with English as a Second Language (ESL) students comprising only five percent of the total. However, as ESL students gain competence in the English language, they are mainstreamed into modified core-curriculum classrooms. The modified classrooms at Arvada Senior High School are designed to provide a positive learning experience for students who score at or below the 25th percentile on a grade-level standardized reading test. As the ESL students are scheduled into the modified classrooms (language arts, history, and biology), there is a definite impact on these classrooms. The impacted modified classrooms may have from one-third to fifty percent of limited-English-speaking students enrolled along with the regular modified students.

Many of the ESL students were from the pre-literate H'mong culture of rural Cambodia, precluding a history of educational opportunities. The regular modified students were coming into the project classrooms with a history of poor attendance, lack of reading ability, and general difficulties with school. Initially, this high concentration of ESL students in the modified classrooms was a cause of concern. Both the teachers and the regular modified students had difficulty in making adjustments to culturally and linguistically different students.

An interdisciplinary/critical thinking pilot project was created to assist the mainstreamed ESL students, the regular modified students, and their teachers. The modified teachers were assisted in developing skills in team teaching and restructuring content materials to teach basic skills within the context of Bloom's Taxonomy. Curriculum was coordinated across the disciplines of language arts, history, biology, and English as a Second Language.

Project teachers planned coordinated units for each semester using the language arts and ESL classes as content reinforcement of social studies while the students were learning the required language skills. The teachers also met on a weekly basis as a commitment to communication for continued cooperation and coordination.

Concurrently with common subject/content planning, all participating teachers were trained to use the same teaching/learning processes. Bloom's model of cognitive objectives was used for all lessons and assignments.

By having project teachers use the same common teaching techniques, there was a framework of consistency as students went from one class to another in their school day. Participating teachers also shared their high expectations for student production and achievement, and their organization, standardized requirements, and Bloom's Taxonomy as the common basis for their planning.

The teaching/learning processes that teachers jointly incorporated into their daily lessons were as follows:

1. *Clustering (Mapping):* This non-linear way of organizing information has also been called *webbing*. It is a process for integrating information that forms the base for many theories of conceptual thinking. It is a visual display of categories and their relationships. It is used by teachers to organize materials and concepts for teaching and by students to integrate concepts for meaning. These clusters can be used as a pre-reading activity, study guides, or basic outlines for written composition. Clustering is used in all project classes: language arts, ESL, biology, and history.

2. *Student Contracts:* The weekly student contracts organize the daily assignments for project students. These contracts are kept in a three-ring looseleaf notebook and keep track of weekly reading, writing, and other assignments. Students know their status each week and are cognizant of their earned grade on a regular basis.

3. *Grouping:* Long a standard at the elementary level, adult and peer tutors have been made available to the project teachers so that they

146

can group their students into higher and lower groups, based on an informal reading inventory. Keeping in mind all students were reading below the twenty-fifth percentile, teachers were able to sort them into two groups: those reading at a higher or intermediate level (grades six to nine) and those reading at primary levels (grades three to five). Teachers use differentiated lessons for each group based on students' ability to read materials and accomplish written assignments.

4. *Word of the Day:* All project teachers emphasize the same vocabulary word each day. These words are taken from the content area lessons and are assessed at the end of each week by the language arts teacher and the ESL teacher. These words are defined, are used in the classrooms, and are an integral part of a student's day.

5. *Completed Sentences:* All teachers—science, history, ESL, and language arts—remind students to produce all work, either written or spoken, in complete sentences.

6. *Dialogue Journals:* Students are required to write daily in their journals. These are read by the language arts and ESL teachers. This activity is a conversation in writing between the students and teachers. It provides a meaningful natural experience in both reading and writing. This also gives the teacher a chance to develop a personal relationship with each student.

7. *SSR/Reading Logs:* There are two times during the school day that are set aside for SSR. Additionally, students are required to keep a weekly log of the number of pages read and the time spent reading books other than texts.

8. *Bloom's Taxonomy:* Teachers incorporate the different levels of Bloom's critical thinking skills into their daily assignments. They encourage students to go beyond the knowledge/comprehension levels to work with analysis, synthesis, and evaluative efforts. Teachers work with the students and take them in a systematic way from the pragmatic lower levels of Bloom to the higher levels of synthesis and evaluation.

This project was studied intensively in its first semester of operation. The purposes of the study were to (a) identify growth in reading by the ESL project students, (b) show all students' (both ESL and modified) increased ability to achieve content area objectives, and (c) show improvement in all students' total academic functioning.

The general approach used in this study was to collect data from the following evaluation instruments: *Secondary Level English Proficiency* (SLEP), Test Forms 1 and 2; *Language Assessment Scale* (LAS), Forms

A–B; an *Individual Reading Inventory* (IRI); Level 19 of the *California Achievement Test* (CAT), Reading Subtest; and third and fourth quarter, spring 1985 grades.

The subjects were seventy-two high-school-age students enrolled in modified core-curriculum classes during the spring semester of 1985. Seven teachers provided the instruction for the project classrooms.

The data collection instruments used in the study collected pre/post information on the participants.

The SLEP is a 150-item, four-option multiple choice test of English language proficiency. It provides a total score and diagnostic subscores that measure ability in (1) understanding spoken English and (2) understanding written English. It is designed as a placement instrument by public secondary schools. It is considered highly reliable and "the content validity of the [SLEP] test is good, particularly for English as a second language students enrolled in grades seven through twelve. The construct validity also appears to be good..." (Charles Stansfield, "Reliability and Validity of the Secondary Level English Proficiency Test," *System* 12 [1984]: 1–2).

The LAS is a standardized convergent oral language measure that consists of (1) phonemic, (2) lexical, and (3) syntactical subtests. These subtests measure general language ability and may be used for diagnostic purposes. Pre- and posttest scores were both available for this study.

The Reading Subtest of Level 19 of the CAT was also used for the ESL participants. This standardized test of general reading ability was routinely used by the Jefferson County School District's Office of Second Language Education to qualify students for inclusion into their state-funded English Language Proficiency Program. For those students whose productive language levels were higher (an LAS of 3 or higher), both pre- and posttest CAT scores were available.

Third quarter and fourth quarter grades in academic subjects were recorded for all student participants. Grades for such classes as art, vocational education, music, and student assistant were not considered in this study.

Data were collected from approximately February to June of 1985. Grades were recorded from the central office's computer bank. The results of the initial study show that students met the pilot project's objectives in the abbreviated time of one semester.

Students' growth objectives included the following:

A. Growth in Reading

Thirty-nine of the ESL project students had pre/posttest scores on an IRI. The ESL students showed the most improvement as forty-nine percent of the project ESL students improved one grade level or more on the pre/post IRI. Even though two different *Individual Reading Inventories* were used, invalidating these results, both IRI's were graded material from 3rd grade reading level to 11th grade reading level, giving some credibility to the improvement in scores. (The SRA copy of a secondary IRI has been perceived as superior to the original Jefferson County IRI and will be used hereafter.) The mainstreamed students showed little gain. The teachers saw this as a result of an accumulation of 10 years of negative experience in school environments, lack of attendance, and lack of seriousness while taking the inventory. Quite possibly, the ESL students were spared this background and approached the task with the proper attitude.

B. Increase in Ability to Achieve Content Area Objectives

The basic method to assess the ability to achieve content area objectives was to compare student achievement grades in academic subjects from halfway through the spring semester (3rd quarter grades) to the end of the semester (4th quarter grades and/or semester grades).

The ESL students showed slightly better success in grade improvement. Of the forty-five ESL project students, nineteen showed grade improvement by one letter grade from the third to fourth quarter in one or more academic classes. Ten of the twenty-seven modified students showed the same gain. Of those nineteen ESL project students with improved grades, forty-two percent showed improvement in two or more academic classes by raising their grades from third to fourth quarter by one letter grade. This shows an expansion of the ability to meet content area objectives across classes and subjects. Thirty percent of the modified project students achieved the same intra-subject improvement.

Overall, forty percent of all project students were able to meet content area objectives in academic classes. A critical look at those improved grades, however, shows them to be at the lower end of the scale. Forty-six percent of the improved grades were either a "D" or "F" to "C," while thirty-one percent were from "F" to "D"—i.e., from failing to passing. This is important to a high school student needing a certain number of credit hours to meet graduation requirements.

C. Improvement in ESL Students' Total Academic Functioning

The SLEP Test Manual indicates that ESL students who score at the seventieth percentile (scaled score of fifty to fifty-one) or above on the SLEP are at the advanced proficiency level where students speak and understand English.

The SLEP provides fine discrimination for the lower end of the language assessment scale and provides for charting growth of students who have a pre/post position, the goal being one of mainstreaming without the continuing aid of ESL special instruction.

Of the thirty-four project ESL students with pre/post SLEP scaled scores, seventy-nine percent improved their scores. Fifty percent of the ESL project students improved their scores by three levels or more.

The potential for the project students to continue to show growth in their ability to function successfully within academic classes is great. The seventy-nine percent improved SLEP score rate of Arvada's project ESL students shows positive growth toward total mainstreaming.

D. Individual Growth in English Skills by ESL Project Students

Along with the gains shown on the SLEP, an analysis of the LAS, Level II Test, found a forty-four percent growth factor. Of the thirty-nine project ESL students who have both pre- and posttest scores, seventeen improved one or more levels. More than one-half (66.7 percent) of the ESL project students passed their language arts class. This is a higher success rate than for the modified students in the same project language arts class. Only 43.5 percent of the modified project students passed their semester course.

A survey completed in August 1983 by Jefferson County's Office of Program Evaluation showed that at the secondary level, fifty-seven percent of the regular secondary teachers teaching at ESL-impacted schools seldom had adequate communication with the ESL staff. The efforts of this project reversed this noncommunication factor, as ESL and content area teachers met and planned together on a weekly basis.

The majority of the project teachers came into the pilot program as master teachers with a background in team teaching; therefore, only a small amount of project effort was spent in learning how to teach as a team. However, in this project, this was the first time a major effort was undertaken to promote teaming combined with communication between the ESL teachers and regular classroom teachers. The teachers were allowed latitude to expand their skills, with very positive results. It was documented at the final workshop that the teachers found the teaming effort to be the best achieved objective and they celebrated the true interdisciplinary effects. They genuinely supported being able to share the same students for approximately eighty percent of their teaching day. This resulted in a continuance and consistency of processes that left the students knowing that their collective group of teachers cared about their education and left the teachers knowing the students better.

The staff felt that a real strength of the program was the consistency of processes. The modified mainstreamed students liked the structure and the consistent set of standards from class to class; ESL students benefited from the repetitions. The teachers enjoyed the challenge of using Bloom's Taxonomy and the innovative ways of making lesson plans. The clustering activities helped students read and study for content area lessons. More student language was produced and students became actively engaged in the Bloom model of critical thinking processes.

The joint curricular efforts made lesson objectives coherent and clear, and teachers felt that their lessons were of higher quality than before. The use of reading logs, journals, and weekly contracts in all classes gave the students a more tangible way of seeing their progress and evaluation.

The most successful staffing technique was the support to each content area project classroom with a tutor as paraprofessional. The initial IRI test was given for grouping purposes. Once each classroom was divided into two groups by reading ability, differentiated lessons, objectives, and materials were planned for each group. The tutor managed one group under the supervision of the teacher, thus maintaining a ten or twelve to one ratio in each project classroom. The second most significant achievement reported by project teachers was the improved relationship between the ESL and the modified students. In a school that had seeds of cultural conflict three years ago, this change is to be celebrated. The joint classroom activities gave insight and empathy to staff and students alike.

To summarize, principal findings from this descriptive study indicated that student objectives were met. Major characteristics included the following:

- Approximately one-half of the ESL project students with pre/posttest data available improved one grade level or more on the IRI.
- Forty-two percent of the ESL project students improved their content area grades by one letter grade from third to fourth quarter. Thirty-seven percent of the modified students showed the same improvement.
- Fifty-eight percent of the ESL project students and fifty-nine percent of the modified students passed their second semester academic classes.
- Seventy-nine percent of the ESL project students showed a gain on their SLEP test scores.
- Forty-four percent of the ESL project students showed improvement on the LAS, Level II, by one or more levels.

The positive intersupport and intercommunication between ESL staff and impacted content area teachers, combined with an interdisciplinary equal process approach, helped all students to grow and achieve.

THE DIRECT TEACHING OF ANALYSIS

by Ronald E. Charlton

Ronald E. Charlton writes that it is not enough to ask students to analyze materials: they must be instructed in how to go about the process of analysis. Charlton outlines a method of teaching analysis skills that is based on Bloom's taxonomy and Beyer's teaching framework. Students begin by defining their goals; they then break down material into its component parts, and look for relationships between these parts; finally they identify the organizing principles of the parts to the whole. Combining practice in these skills with the modeling and guided practice suggested by Beyer, Charlton finds that the students can improve their analytic skills in all areas—from biology through woodshop.

The author is Science Coordinator for Mt. Lebanon School District, Pittsburgh, Pennsylvania.

Analysis is a basic thinking skill which we expect students to be able to perform. We often ask students to analyze materials. Sometimes they accomplish the analysis to their own and our satisfaction. Sometimes they do not. Some students can analyze effectively. Some students cannot. The problem seems to be that we really do not explicitly teach students the skill of analysis, but rather we give them practice doing analysis. Those who can analyze do it. Those who cannot either soak it up to some extent by virtue of being in the class where analysis is being practiced, or they fall by the wayside, never really learning the skill.

In order to explicitly teach analysis we have developed a generic skill model of analysis that can be modified to any content area. Our model is based upon Bloom's taxonomy and the explicit teaching framework of Beyer.

Bloom recognizes three levels of analysis. At the first level the student is expected to break down material into its constituent parts and to identify or classify the elements. At the second level the student is required to find the relationships among the elements and to determine their connections and interactions. At the third level the student is required to identify the organizational principles that unify the whole. Not every situation lends itself to all three levels of analysis. The teacher must determine the goal(s) of the analysis and the levels of analysis that will be used.

ANALYSIS—A GENERIC SKILL MODEL

1. State the reason for the analysis. What are you trying to find out?
2. Break down the material into the elements.

   a. Identify the clues to look for.

   b. Search the material piece by piece.

3. Define the relationship (s) of the elements to one another.
4. Identify the organizational principles of the elements to the whole.
5. State what you have found.

This model is designed for teaching all three levels of analysis. Students expected to analyze at the first level would use steps 1, 2, and 5. Students expected to analyze at the second level would use steps 1, 2, 3, and 5. Students expected to analyze at the third level would use all the steps.

To the generic skill model of analysis we can apply Beyer's framework for the explicit teaching of a skill. Beyer's review of the research on skill learning indicates that skills should be taught continuously using a framework of six stages: readiness, introduction, guided practice, expansion/broadening, guided practice, and application (to autonomous use).

We can look at a specific example to see how this might operate. Suppose the teacher's objective was to have students analyze line graphs to interpret data, a common type of analysis in science. In many cases students are given the graphs and told to analyze them. Student performance of the task is often less than adequate. We ask ourselves, "What went wrong?" The answer is twofold. First, we made assumptions about the students' skill level. We assumed that they were at the level of application. Second, we did not directly teach them how to analyze line graphs.

Let's try it another way. Let's teach the skill before we expect students to apply it. Begin by introducing analysis in general. Define it. Explain it. Have students explain it. When you are satisfied that the students have a general idea of the concept, give them the generic skill model for analysis and explain the model. Let the students know what is expected at each level of analysis. The defining, explaining, and model presentation should only take ten or fifteen minutes, and it is time well spent.

The next step is an important one. Have the students analyze something they are familiar with in their everyday life. Work through this analysis with the students. At this time we want the focus to be on the skill, not on the subject matter content. We have used the analysis of a stereo system with our students (Figure 1). You may find examples even more appropriate for your students. Make sure the students understand the skill by giving them at least one more guided practice—more if necessary. The guided practice can occur during the same class period as the introduction of the skill. Additional guided practice could take the form of homework assignments that are reviewed the next day in class.

Figure 1. The Analysis of a Stereo System

ELEMENTS. What are the individual parts of a stereo system?

Power supply	Amplifier
Speakers	Radio tuner
Tape deck	Turntable

RELATIONSHIPS. How do the elements interact with each other?

Power supply—amplifier	Power supply—turntable
Power supply—radio tuner	Amplifier—tape deck
Amplifier—speakers	Tape deck—speakers

Many other relationships are not included to save space.

ORGANIZATIONAL PRINCIPLES. How do the relationships among the elements go together to make the system work?

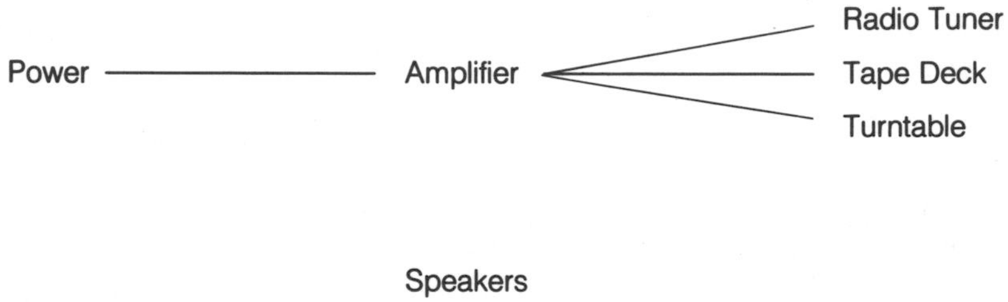

Speakers

When you are sure the students have a good understanding of the general skill of analysis, you can then apply the skill to more specific subject matter content. We now return to the analysis of line graphs introduced above. The students now have a model to use for analysis. The teacher builds upon the model by briefly reviewing and reinforcing it every time the students engage in analysis. The teacher should prepare a planning guide to focus the analysis on the task at hand (Figure 2). The planning guide helps to keep the lesson going by suggesting questions for the teacher to ask. It also identifies the three levels of analysis and how they relate to the specific content.

Figure 2. Teacher Planning Guide

SKILL: Analysis

SUBJECT AREA: Science (Biology)

GOAL: Analysis of line graphs to interpret data

I. IDENTIFY THE ELEMENTS OF THE GRAPH.
- A. Does the graph have a title? If so, what is the title?
- B. What is the label of the variable indicated by the horizontal (X) axis?
- C. What is the label of the variable indicated by the vertical (Y) axis?
- D. What are the units of the graph?
- E. How many lines are on the graph?
- F. What does each line represent?

II. SEARCH THE GRAPH TO FIND THE ELEMENTS.

III. IDENTIFY THE RELATIONSHIPS AMONG THE ELEMENTS.
- A. What is the value of Y for each X location?
- B. How do the two variables (X, Y) influence each other?
- C. Where does each line go on the graph?

IV. IDENTIFY THE ORGANIZATIONAL PRINCIPLES.
- A. Is there a pattern?
  - 1. For a single line?
  - 2. For all the lines?
- B. What does the whole graph indicate?
- C. Can any inferences be drawn based on the graph?

V. STATE WHAT WAS FOUND.

The teacher may also want to make a student guide sheet for student use with specific questions that correlate the skill model with the subject matter content (Figure 3). As the students become more proficient in the skill of analysis, after several guided practices, the questions may become less directive and fewer in number.

An ideal situation would be to have reinforcement and guided practice of the skill in other courses and in other grade levels, but even within

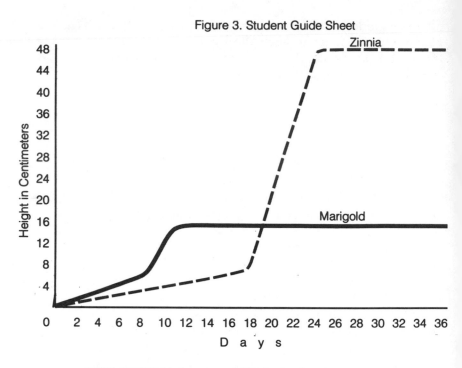

Figure 3. Student Guide Sheet

STEM GROWTH. Average of 20 plants of each type.

DIRECTIONS: Analyze the graph above using the analysis skill model and answer the questions below.

(Answers provided for teacher use)

1. What is the title of the graph?
   (Stem Growth)

2. What is the label of the X axis?
   (Days)

3. What is the label of the Y axis?
   (Height in Centimeters)

4. What are the units of the graph?
   (Days, Centimeters)

5. What does each unit represent?
   (2 days, 4 centimeters)

6. How many lines are on the graph?
   (Two)

7. What does each line represent?
   (Marigolds, Zinnias)

8. Which plants had the most rapid growth during the first 12 days?
   (Marigolds)

9. What is the period of the most rapid growth for the marigolds? (Day 9 through Day 11)

10. What is the pattern of growth for the marigolds?
    (Slow but steady growth for the first 8 days; rapid growth for Days 9 through 11; no additional growth for the rest of the time)

11. What is the pattern of growth for the zinnias?
    (Slow but steady growth for the first 15 days; rapid growth for Days 16 through 24; no additional growth for the rest of the time)

12. What does the graph indicate about the growth of marigolds as compared to zinnias?
    (Marigolds grow faster for the first 11 days to reach a final height of 16 centimeters. Zinnias grow slowly for the first 15 days, but then grow rapidly until Day 24 to reach a final height of 48 centimeters.)

the confines of a single course, teachers may be able to make significant improvements in students' ability to analyze.

The skill of analysis may be approached in a slightly different manner depending upon the content and the goals of the teacher. The important thing is to explicitly teach the skill before it is to be used and to review the steps of the skill when it is used. The examples that follow illustrate some different approaches.

A history teacher might use the skill of analysis when teaching about the American Civil War. The teacher may want to have students analyze the causes of the war. Students would need to consult source materials: students could be given copies of primary sources, or they could go to the library to find sources on their own. Students would be directed to search the source materials piece by piece for any evidence of issues of strife between the northern states and the southern states. They would be asked to write down the issue and the dates of concern. For example, from 1816 to 1857 there was a see-sawed battle in Congress over tariffs with the northern states generally favoring high protective tariffs and the southern states favoring low tariffs and free trade. Even this first level of analysis, identifying the elements, would give students a better understanding of the multiple causes of the American Civil War.

The teacher could move to the second level of analysis, relationships. Students would be required to determine if there were any relationships among the issues identified in the first level. A major example of such a relationship is the free homestead issue entangled with the slavery question. This relationship led to the Missouri Compromise in 1820, the Compromise of 1850, and the problems involved with these compromises.

If desired, the third level of analysis, organizational principles, could be pursued at a basic level by having students write a comprehensive paper on their findings from the first two levels. At an advanced level we have the makings of a doctoral dissertation in history.

The use of analysis is not confined to academic areas. Teachers in the fine arts and in the practical arts also need to teach and use the skill of analysis.

An art teacher might be teaching a lesson on the use of color. One of the basic ideas in this type of lesson is the organization of the color wheel. The teacher could introduce the students to the three primary colors of red, blue, and yellow. This could be followed by giving the students a color wheel with the primary and secondary colors and asking them analysis questions at the three levels.

A woodshop teacher might have students analyze the requirements for their projects before they begin to work. Analysis at the first level might include the type of wood to be used, the type of hardware to be used, and the tools to be used. Second-level analysis might include how each piece of wood joins to another piece, whether the joints will be nailed or glued or both, and whether power tools or hand tools will be used for each of the operations. Third-level analysis would have students plan all of the construction sequences and visualize the finished project.

The skill of analysis can and should be used in all content areas. You can explicitly teach the generic skill model and then use it at whatever level meets your learning objectives.

REFERENCES

Beyer, Barry K. "Practical Strategies for the Direct Teaching of Thinking Skills." In *Developing Minds: A Resource Book for Teaching Thinking*, edited by Arthur L. Costa. Alexandria, Va.: Association for Supervision and Curriculum Development, 1985.

Bloom, Benjamin S. *Taxonomy of Educational Objectives. Handbook I: Cognitive Domain*. New York: David McKay Company, 1956.

CONVERSATION WITH
ARTHUR WHIMBEY

Arthur Whimbey maintains that early verbal give-and-take between parent and child develops the kind of intelligence that leads to academic success. He discusses research showing the distinctions between successful and unsuccessful learners: good students think systematically, draw on information they bring to a problem, and work carefully and deliberately toward problem solution. In contrast, poor students attack problems unsystematically and superficially; they are indifferent toward accuracy, and are generally careless in their problem solving. Whimbey maintains that good thinking, like golf, involves a set of skills that can be demonstrated and practiced. If they practice consciously, responding to guidance and feedback, students can significantly improve their thinking skills.

In this chapter the initials JLS identify the name of the publication where it appeared originally: The Journal of Learning Skills, *Winter 1982.* Reprinted with permission.

Arthur Whimbey is the author of Intelligence Can Be Taught *and the coauthor of* Problem Solving and Comprehension.

JLS: Why have past experimental studies failed to show that intelligence can be improved by training?

WHIMBEY: I think the reason is that psychology and the study of intelligence are very young sciences. We're only gradually coming to understand what it is that intelligence tests measure and how this can be improved through training. Some of the early attempts to improve intelligence—pre-school programs that were run during the early sixties—began with the notion that low intelligence resulted from sensory deprivation, and that intelligence could be improved through the enrichment of sensory input. This was translated into providing students with clay and paint and trips, mobiles for the young infant, and other things that would provide sensory stimulation. However, more recent studies indicate that it isn't just raw sensory stimulation that's needed, but instead a particular type of verbal interaction with an adult that produces the pattern of thinking that's called academic intelligence.

JLS: What type of interaction is that? What kinds of early experiences develop intelligence in children?

WHIMBEY: Intelligence develops through a type of verbal interaction that teaches the child to make discriminations and to keep track of rela-

160

tionships. Developmental psychologists tell us that without educational intervention, higher levels of intelligence tend to arise from a distinctive type of verbal interaction in the pre-schooler's home. In the lower-income home, where children are closely spaced and the mother doesn't have too much time for each child, if a child comes to his mother and asks to buy a candy bar, the mother may answer, "Here's some money. Bring back the change." In the upper-income home, the children are more widely spaced, and the mother often has a richer educational background and may be more interested in the child's education. A mother in this environment might say, "Here's 25¢. The candy bar's a dime and you'll get 15¢ change. That's a nickel and a dime, or three nickels. When you come back, we'll count the change." And when the child comes back, they do count the change together. This teaches the child the mental pattern of analyzing a complex entity into relevant parts. It teaches the child to systematically make discriminations and classifications which are meaningful with respect to some goal. And it isn't just this one type of pedantic situation—it's a verbal interaction all along the way. An eight-year-old telling a four-year-old, "Put on your boots 'cause mommy said so," is different from the mother telling the child, "You have to put on your boots because it's raining outside, and you don't want your feet to get wet. If you get wet you'll get a cold and have to stay in bed." The mother is explaining the cause-and-effect relationship. This kind of continual asking and answering questions develops the type of intelligence needed for academic success.

JLS: Much of your work is based on an early study by Bloom and Broder. Tell us about this study. What did it show about cognitive learning?

WHIMBEY: In 1950 Benjamin Bloom and Lois Broder published a monograph entitled "Problem-solving Process of College Students". The Bloom and Broder study had diagnostic and remedial components. First, they asked students with both high and low scores on aptitude tests to think aloud while solving academic reasoning problems. They found that the problem-solving behavior of low-aptitude college students was characteristically different from that of high-aptitude students.

The cognitive profile of low-aptitude college students had two prominent features. First, there was one-shot thinking, rather than extended, sequential construction of understanding. Second, there was a willingness to allow gaps of knowledge to exist, an attitude of indifference towards achieving an accurate and complete comprehension of situations and relations. These students were mentally careless and superficial in solving problems. They often rushed through instructions or even skipped them, and selected a wrong answer on the basis of a feeling or a guess. They were almost completely passive in their thinking, taking little time to consider a question or break it down into its component parts.

High-aptitude students, by contrast, made an active attack on problems. When a question was initially unclear, they employed a lengthy sequential analysis in arriving at an answer. They began with what they understood of the problem, drew on other information, and carefully proceeded through a series of steps that brought them to a conclusion.

Having isolated the habitual thinking deficiencies of low-aptitude students, Bloom and Broder undertook to develop a remedial training program. This was only a pilot project, but the method they developed may find wide application. A set of problems was selected on which the contrasting approaches of good and poor students were clearly evident. Introspective reports of extremely capable students were then collected, and these model solutions served as the primary teaching material. Students were trained individually in the procedure of thinking aloud while solving sample reasoning problems. During a typical training session, the student attempted to solve a problem while thinking aloud. His verbalizing was reviewed and discussed by the instructor, and he was then given the protocol of model solutions to the problem. With the assistance of the instructor, the student made a list of differences and similarities between his solution and that of the model. The instructor emphasized that the student should look for differences that occurred regularly, rather than those that were unique to individual problems.

In the sessions that followed, time was divided between practice in acquiring the approach used by the model and comparison and analysis of solution protocols. When solving problems, the student attempted to apply the general principles derived from his list.

JLS: How well did the program work?

WHIMBEY: No standardized test was used to evaluate program success. School grades were taken as a criterion of gain. Comparison with various control groups indicated that grades on comprehensive examinations increased to a significant degree—enough to allow the experimental students, who had been failing and on probation, to continue in college. In addition, there were marked changes in the students' problem solving in training sessions. They approached problems more actively, began with what they understood, set up hypotheses, reasoned sequentially in steps and so on. Students reported a carry-over effect to all their thinking. For example, they reported taking a more analytical approach to the arguments of others, and thinking twice before making comments in class discussion.

162

JLS: If this work was done in 1950, why hasn't it surfaced until recently? Didn't Bloom and Broder follow up on their work?

WHIMBEY: It's kind of interesting that Bloom, after the publication of the 1950 monograph, did not pursue this research, but instead got into mastery learning. The reason was that, in the pilot project with college students, academic reasoning problems from various content areas were used. These problems, from disciplines such as physics and political science, required both reasoning and subject-area knowledge. Bloom and Broder found that there was often a gap in the students' knowledge that interfered with the development of critical reading and reasoning. So Bloom got more concerned with ensuring that students had the foundation in knowledge. With thirty years of hindsight, we see that the problem with the standard mastery learning method is that it doesn't teach students *how* to master the material. We now realize that many students need courses focussing on teaching students how to learn.

JLS: You have been using a method similar to Bloom and Broder's for some years now. What do you feel is the most critical problem in teaching improved thinking?

WHIMBEY: Teaching thinking runs into a peculiar difficulty. Generally there are two phases to teaching any skill. The skill is explained and demonstrated to the student. The student practices the skill with guidance and feedback. For example, golf is taught by showing the novice how to grasp the club, place his feet, and how to move his arms and body as he swings. The novice watches the pro, he can even watch a slow-motion film of the pro in action, and in this way he can learn the pro's technique. The pro observes the pupil as he practices, he points out his flaws and he shows him how to improve.

In contrast to playing golf, the activities of reasoning are generally carried on inside one's head. This makes it difficult for a teacher to teach and for a learner to learn. To teach something, we would like it out in the open where both teacher and student can see it. As it is, a beginner cannot observe how an expert thinks in analyzing complex ideas. And the expert has trouble demonstrating his technique to a beginning student.

JLS: How do you solve that problem? What instructional strategies appear effective in helping students to improve their thinking?

WHIMBEY: One solution to this dilemma is to have both teachers and students think aloud as they work through ideas. Have them vocalize their thoughts as they analyze relationships, sort concepts, and form generalizations. If both students and experts vocalize their thoughts as they work through complex ideas and relationships, the steps that they take are open to view, and their activities can be observed and communicated. Naturally a person cannot put all the motions of his mind into words, any more than a map-maker can show every bend and hill along the road. But research shows that he can exhibit enough of his thinking for someone else to follow his path through a problem or complex concept.

JLS: What kinds of problems are most suitable for cognitive training?

WHIMBEY: I believe the most crucial characteristic is that all of the information that a student needs to solve the problem should be available to him. That is, the problem should not be unsolvable because of lack of knowledge. On the contrary, the problem acquires difficulty from the necessity of careful, thorough sequential processing. For example, take a problem like this: Cross out the letter after the letter in the word "pardon" which is in the same position in the word as it is in the alphabet.

Let's look at how a good problem solver would approach this problem. When he reads "Cross out the letter after the letter", he may stop and say, "This is confusing." Reading a little further he'll say to himself, "Okay, so I have to cross out a letter which is in the same position in the word as it is in the alphabet. 'P' is in the first position in the word 'pardon'. But 'a' is in the first position in the alphabet. In the word 'pardon', 'a' is in the second position, 'r' is in the third position. Okay, 'd' is in the fourth position in the word and it's also in the fourth position in the alphabet. But now in the beginning of the problem, there was something confusing. Let me go back to it. I have to cross out the letter *after* the letter in the word 'pardon'. So I have to cross out the letter after the 'd'—cross out the letter 'o'."

You can see how solving this problem is a step-by-step process. Even the good problem solver initially finds it confusing. But he starts with something that he can get a grip on and then gradually works through it and eventually works back to the more complicated part. Now, in contrast, the poor problem solver, who does badly on IQ tests or the S.A.T., will very often just cross out the "d". He'll just lose the initial section of information. He kind of blurs over it in his mind. And sometimes he may even cross out the "d" in the word "word". He hasn't isolated that he has to cross out a letter in the word "pardon". He isn't that careful in his interpretation of the sentence. We find that this kind of approach—teaching content-free problem-solving techniques—is highly effective in helping students develop analytical thinking skills.

JLS: You have also suggested ways of teaching thinking skills in the content areas. Could you give us an idea of how this can be done?

WHIMBEY: Well, Jack Lochhead, at the University of Massachusetts,

Amherst, is teaching kids thinking skills as part of their learning physics and engineering. First students work through content-free problems of the kind I just discussed. Then he has them shift over to problems in physics. Here's the kind of problem that's used—simple, but one that's often deceptive to students: A bicyclist sets out on a ten-mile trip. The first half of the trip is level. But on the second half, he must go up and down two hills. Sketch a distance vs. time graph that is consistent with the above information.

JW Carmichael, at Xavier University, has a similar training program. Proposed science majors spend a pre-college summer in a cognitive training program; these skills are later reinforced through cognitive training with chemistry problems, an integral part of the introductory chemistry course. It's been three or four years since the program has been instituted at Xavier, and it does seem to be effective. There's been a whole standard deviation increase in students' performance on a standardized test of introductory chemistry published by the American Chemical Society.

Another example is Bloomfield College, where the approach is being used in a remedial math course. There, our approach was used in two sections of remedial math along with the remedial math text. For comparison, another two sections used just the remedial math course in the conventional method. A standardized test of remedial math showed significantly larger gains by students using the cognitive training methods and thinking aloud in the solution of math problems.

JLS: Bloom and Broder used one-to-one instruction. That's not very practical for wide use. What do you suggest as an alternative?

WHIMBEY: What seems to be a reasonable compromise is to have students work in pairs and take turns as problem solver and listener. The student who's designated as the problem solver reads the problem out loud and does all his thinking out loud. He may make diagrams to supplement the exhibition of his thinking. In general, he externalizes his own thinking. The listener is asked to listen for the strategies that the problem solver is using in order to learn the strategies and also to listen for errors. If the listener catches an error, he points it out to the problem solver, saying, "Now, listen, read that over a little more carefully; perform that computation a little more carefully; count that a little more carefully." Or the listener may ask, "What exactly is that relationship?" When students take turns in this way, on one problem, one student is the problem solver, the other's the listener. On the next problem, they switch roles.

JLS: What role do you think the *Journal of Learning Skills* can play in improving instruction in thinking skills?

WHIMBEY: I think we're just starting to get an understanding of how students who score well on IQ tests and who are academically successful differ in their thinking from students who have academic difficulties. We're also beginning to get an understanding of how to teach this academic thinking skill. It's in this regard that I'm happy to see the publication of the new *Journal of Learning Skills*, a journal which will allow communication among practitioners who are actually in the field teaching students to think more effectively—practitioners who are seeking improved methods and who also have a theoretical orientation—developing procedures which make sense and are effective.

Recently a number of prominent psychologists, such as Hilgard and Cronbach, have been critical of psychology, acknowledging that traditional psychology and traditional psych journals have focussed on learning problems that are remote from the classroom, and haven't really contributed to the improvement of academic competence. On the other hand, a number of the applied journals describe procedures without any real theoretical rationale. And in some cases these journals have perpetuated notions that really don't contribute to the improvement of learning. I believe that the *Journal of Learning Skills* will fill the gap between theory and practice by being a clearinghouse and forum for the dissemination of studies focussing on cognitive aspects of real academic learning.

TEACHING PRECISE PROCESSING THROUGH WRITING INSTRUCTION

by Kendall Didsbury

Kendall Didsbury has developed a writing program that focuses on Arthur Whimbey's "precise processing." This is a method where students are asked to identify and "precisely spell out the series of operations" they use in solving an academic problem; they are then asked to apply these operations in solving an academic problem; they are then asked to apply these operations in solving new problems. An important classroom assignment in Didsbury's program is students' written responses to a collection of essay questions. Students are then asked to carry out a series of pre-writing activities that help them break the assignment into component parts.

The author teaches English at Tilton School, New Hampshire.

Without having to restructure our junior English classes, we have improved our students' expository writing skills while teaching them to be more perceptive and analytical in their thinking. We found Arthur Whimbey's "precise processing" brought the objectives of Tilton School's conference-based writing program into sharper focus and gave us a new impetus to fine-tune our program.

In "The Key to Higher Order Thinking Is Precise Processing" [*Educational Leadership* 42 (September 1984): 66–70], Whimbey shows it is not necessary to "rearrange or restructure academic topics to exercise specific reasoning skills":

> All we need to modify is our pedagogy, shifting the emphasis to mental processing, with provisions made to observe and provide feedback on the processing. For example, if a student has difficulty following worked examples to solve new problems, a teacher might ask the student to explain the changes or operations occurring between the first and second step of the example, probe with helpful questions when the explanation is incomplete or erroneous and continue this until the student is able to precisely spell out the series of operations and apply them in solving new problems (Whimbey, p. 69).

We have learned that Whimbey's thinking strategy has been very helpful in our writing program. In its most recent revision this course builds on Whimbey's work by using three strategies to help students become precise sequential thinkers and more confident writers.

The central innovation of our program is the collection of essay questions that we assign. Each assignment consists of a specific problem and a body of detailed and proscribed data. By controlling the amount and type of information that each student has, the writing instructors can be more effective in addressing the intellectual stumbling blocks of the pre-writing process.

Take, for example, the following assignment. It demands that students classify information to solve a problem:

In one segment of "60 Minutes" Andy Rooney, a CBS commentator, talked about the words advertisers use. He reported that the ten most commonly used words were the following:

1. new
2. natural
3. light
4. save
5. free

6. rich
7. real
8. fresh
9. extra
10. discover/discovered

These words appear most frequently because they connect the product being advertised with values that are important to us. In a well-organized essay, identify the values that these words suggest.

In order for students to respond effectively to this problem, they must carry out the following pre-writing activities in sequence:

1. Turn the statement of the problem into a question. ("In a well-organized essay, identify the values that these words suggest" becomes "What are the values that these words suggest?")
2. Identify several connotations for each word.
3. Group words that share common meanings.
4. Determine the cultural values implied in each grouping.
5. Find advertising examples that demonstrate how the use of each of the 10 words implies the values hypothesized in step 4.
6. Write a one-sentence answer (a thesis statement) to the question posed in step 1.
7. Create a writing plan (an outline) that identifies the thesis statement and supports it with examples from each word grouping.

We do three things to help students become adept at using such a process. First, the students observe how another writer solved a similar problem. They read a description of a sample problem, study an explanation of the thought processes used in the pre-writing process, and analyze a model essay. Next, the instructor leads the students through the pre-writing process on their first essay. In the class discussion the students practice the sequential process about which they have just read. By the end of the class the students and teacher will have developed a writing plan that the students can use to complete their essays. As they write their essays, the teacher will check that the students employ the correct thinking process. Finally, the teacher will give the students a second writing assignment based on the original model. For this paper they will receive no help in processing the information because we assume that they have internalized the cognitive strategies sufficiently and will be able to work independently.

When creating these assignments, we look for subjects about which students have prior knowledge; we want them to recognize that they have something substantial to say. Consequently, many of the topics deal with popular culture. Among the more successful topics using classification skills have been those listed below:

Problem	*Data*
1. What personal characteristics do young Americans admire?	The results of a survey about American heroes
2. To whom does a particular magazine appeal?	A summary of articles in a magazine with a precise demographic focus
3. What are the programming tastes of the 1967–68 television audience?	A list of the top 10 prime-time TV shows for 1967–68
4. Describe the role of married women in 1845.	A list of rules for wives written in 1845
5. Explain how life will be different in 2000 A.D.	A list of predictions of scientific and technical innovations that will be made in the next 14 years

Students find these assignments challenging and informative. Generally they are surprised by how many insights they have; consequently, they gain confidence in their writing ability.

We also try to make the assignments as interdisciplinary as possible. During the twelve weeks of the course, we teach five types of writing problems:

1. Classifying Information
2. Comparison and Contrast
3. Analysis of Structure
4. Analysis of Character
5. Problem Solving

While some of the assignments are literature based, many come from a variety of subject areas. For example, one of the traditional comparison-/contrast assignments asks students to compare two short stories having similar themes. In our program, on the other hand, we include two social studies assignments: one using paired statements from the Republican and Democratic Party platforms, and another pairing statements from the USSR constitution with reports by foreign correspondents. Both assignments ask the students to contrast points of view. Likewise for the third type of writing problem, analysis of structure, we not only present several poems for analysis but also provide a diagram of a complex piece of machinery and ask that students describe the purposes of the mechanical components.

We have found that the diversity of topics encourages the transference of writing and thinking skills to essays assigned in other courses. After doing a social studies assignment in English class, students are less likely to ask their history teachers if the next papers will be graded for form as well as content. They know that good writing follows from clear and precise thinking.

The use of these assigned topics makes possible a second innovation: the opportunity to provide feedback on mental processing. When the students prepare their first essay for each type of writing problem, the teachers monitor their students' performance in a workshop/conference setting. Students write every day, and the teachers use most classes to read the newest drafts. Because the teachers are familiar with the data in each assignment, they can not only make comments on the sentence style, grammar, and general organization; they can also respond to the analytical processing in the essay. For instance, if a student has drawn a faulty inference, the teacher can ask the youngster to explain the sequential steps used to analyze the data and then help the student re-analyze the information correctly.

A side benefit of observing how students respond to thinking problems is a new approach for teaching how to correct errors in sentence mechanics. One of the most common grammatical mistakes is to use the pronoun *it* or *this* to refer to a concept described in a prior noun clause. Previously we had corrected this error by showing our students that the pronoun referred too broadly to all or part of the last sentence. To rectify the error we told our students to replace the pronoun with a word that renames the antecedent concept. Now we not only teach the grammatical concept of broad reference but also address the underlying difficulty of abstractions by asking students to describe how they arrived at the faulty statement. Thus we deal with the cause of the problem and not just its symptoms.

Another good example of how cognitive skills can prevent usage errors appears when we correct a student's misuse of the verb *to be*. Our students frequently write sentences in which the subject and complement are falsely coordinated (i.e.,"Physically attractive women are Mike's bad points," instead of "His infatuation with physically attractive women is Mike's weakness."). Before we incorporated cognitive skills in the curriculum, we prevented this error by mandating that students avoid the use of *to be* as much as possible. Now we let them use linking verbs freely, and when they write a sentence equating unlike things (as in our example), we ask them to review with the teacher how they developed the idea. They quickly recognize that they mean "weakness" when the say "bad points" and that women are not the character's weakness but rather his infatuation with them is. Using this process, we show them why the verb *to be* is difficult to use, and we suggest the context in which it can be used correctly. Most importantly, we enlarge their repertoire of sentence styles rather than diminishing it, while, at the same time, improving the quality of their thinking.

Our third innovation occurs in our instruction of the editing process. We place great emphasis on editing for two reasons. First we want our students to learn to revise their own work and to outgrow the need for writing conferences—to become independent writers. We also want our students to become self-critical thinkers. Whereas the pre-writing lectures and the writing conferences taught our students how to think about a problem, our discussions about editing concentrate on teaching students how to stand at a distance from their writing and think about thinking, a skill called metacognition. Specifically, we teach our students how to identify whether and how fully their thinking has served their writing.

We initially teach our students metacognitive skills by showing them how other writers' thinking resulted in a particular essay structure. As our students read and analyze model essays, they learn why the particular thinking processes are appropriate to that assignment. Moreover, later in class discussions, the students evaluate different thinking strategies to determine which one will be more successful under a given set of conditions. Through this process the students learn to be more self-conscious and thus more effective in their planning.

We complement this critical editing process with a second technique. Early in the course students receive an evaluation sheet of 33 questions listed under four headings: organization, mechanics and grammar, content, and style. We review each of these questions with the students when we teach the particular concept. Furthermore, every time students prepare their final drafts they are expected to use the questions to review their work, and when the teachers grade the essays, they also use the evaluation sheet as a grading criterion. Thus, the application of these questions by both students and faculty reminds the students of their writing goals and reinforces the desired impression that good writing can be achieved, not magically, but one step at time.

Those questions appearing under the organization and content headings have proved to be especially effective in helping students recognize sloppy thinking. These questions read as follows:

Organization

1. Does the paper have a clearly defined introduction, middle, and conclusion?
2. Does the introductory paragraph contain a thesis statement that expresses the central idea of the paper?
3. Is the thesis statement followed by a statement of organization that signals how the paper will be developed?
4. Does each body paragraph contain a single topic sentence which supports, explains, or otherwise reinforces the idea expressed in the thesis?
5. Does each sentence in each paragraph elaborate on the topic sentence of the paragraph?
6. Does the concluding paragraph begin with a restatement of the thesis?

Content

1. Does the thesis statement effectively respond to the writing problem as presented?
2. Does each paragraph provide appropriate supporting details, evidence, and information in sufficient quantities to be effective?
3. Does each topic sentence serve as more than a label for a group of similar sentences? Does every topic sentence imaginatively and perceptively show the relationships between the supporting details?
4. Does the introduction grab the reader's attention and focus it on the thesis?
5. Does the conclusion convey a sense of completeness, of loose ends tied up?

These questions listed under the organizational heading remind students that thinking involves sequential steps. Students quickly learn that factual evidence supports topic sentences and that topic sentences serve a thesis. Similarly, the questions related to content evaluate the depth of thinking in an essay; they help a student distinguish between shallow and insightful ideas. Together the two sets of questions hold students accountable for their work and encourage them to be their own most severe critic.

Because this writing program is so time consuming, it is a separate semester course. We limit the discussion of literature to the second semester because we have found that the intensive aspect of the writing has several advantages. First, the students incorporate new writing skills more consistently into each paper. Because success in the program depends on reaching competency in writing, we also find it possible to guarantee a higher minimum level of writing proficiency. Finally, the extensive time commitment that the English department has made to composition work reminds the students of the importance that the school places on writing and thinking skills.

Unfortunately, the program's chief asset creates its greatest problem. How does the average high school English teacher with a pupil load of 120 to 160 find time for a conference-based writing course? Here are some suggestions. First of all, so that work load is shared, the school should require each of its English faculty to teach this course. In schools where teachers must teach more than one section of writing, the program should be staggered so that some students take the course each semester. Secondly, the administration should limit the class size to twenty or twenty-five students. To be effective, this course demands that students write daily; therefore, teachers can expect to correct a theme per student each week. Schools that have a large enrollment and have flexibility might increase the size of literature classes to compensate for the small writing sections. Thirdly, the faculty should plan on fewer writing assignments during the rest of the year.

Under these conditions a conference-based program can probably work. Our experience has been that on the workshop days (class periods when students revise their writing) most students have only a couple of paragraphs prepared for a critique. The conferences tend to be short because the teacher knows the potential thinking/writing problems implicit in each assignment and can quickly identify a student's errors. Our teachers have found that they develop a repertoire of questions appropriate for each stage of the writing process; therefore, they can help as many as ten or twelve students in a period. During the waiting time the other students work on their papers or work on some self-teaching grammar exercises that are also assigned each week.

By attacking writing problems through sequential thinking, we have begun to show students that the composing process is not an occult art but rather a practical craft. They no longer see writing as a monumental and intimidating endeavor; writing problems become manageable because the students know how to approach each task in the composing process. At the same time the nature of the material and the emphasis on thinking skills fosters the students' self-image because they recognize that they have something intelligent to say and that exploring ideas can be fun.

THINKING ABOUT LEARNING: AN ANARCHISTIC APPROACH TO TEACHING PROBLEM SOLVING

by Jack Lochhead

Jack Lochhead maintains that scientific progress is not the result of strict adherence to a set of rigid logical procedures. Rather, "good science is a search for methods that have the widest conceivable application." Good scientists do not follow a prescribed method; they "discover methods that work."

However, when we teach students science we behave as if there were one problem-solving methodology that all students should adopt. Lochhead maintains that instruction of this kind prevents students from examining problem-solving options and critically evaluating their own attempts at problem solution. Since science is distinguished "not by its method, but... by self-awareness of method," in effect we are preventing students from practicing science when we insist that they use a particular problem-solving approach.

This chapter is reprinted with permission from The Journal of Learning Skills, *Winter 1982.*

The author is Director of the Cognitive Development Project at the University of Massachusetts, Amherst.

Most philosophers of science claim that science progresses because its practitioners follow a set of logical procedures known as the scientific method. They acknowledge that individual scientists lapse occasionally from this strict discipline, but they see these lapses as either detrimental to the progress of science or at best lucky breaks which must eventually be reexamined. There is considerable debate about the precise structural details of the "scientific method", but few philosophers doubt it exists.

In his book *Against Method* (1975), Feyerabend sees no such method.

> ... the idea of a fixed method, or a fixed theory of rationality, rests on too naive a view of man and his social surroundings .... there is only *one* principle that can be defended under *all* circumstances and in *all* stages of human development. It is the principle: *anything goes.* (pp. 27–28)

To Feyerabend "lapses" in scientific discipline are essential for "progress". In addition to the standard techniques of logical argument, he sees propaganda, rhetoric and the exercise of raw power as tools which the successful scientist must use to "advance" knowledge.

Support for the anarchist position can also be found by studying the history of science. Kuhn (1962) has shown that new scientific theories often cannot be logically evaluated within the context of the theories that preceded them. Thus scientists who want to break new ground afford to restrict themselves to any arbitrary set of methodological techniques. The only rule which can guide the selection of a new technique is that it work. A new method must first of all convince the investigator and second be convincing to other scientists. Thus the good scientist does not *follow* a prescribed method, but on the contrary discovers methods that work.

This view of science is not a rejection of all methodology in favor of totally unstructured investigation. It simply states that scientists should learn many methodologies and use each as a tool rather than as a religion. For Feyerabend, the practice of science is an art requiring the exercise of many skills, rather than the methodical application of techniques. The genius of the successful scientist is in the art of inventing and selecting appropriate tools.

By now the reader may well wonder what all this has to do with teaching problem solving. Novice problem solvers scarcely need instruction in anarchy. According to Bloom and Broder (1950) they:

1. . . . have great difficulty in ascertaining what they are required to do.
2. . . . (demonstrate a) lack of objectivity in dealing with problems.
3. . . . seem to grope blindly toward a solution. Their problem-solving is characterized by feelings, hunches and guesses.
4. . . . (have an) inability to complete a chain of reasoning.
5. . . . lack necessary subject-matter knowledge. (pp. 38–39)

Clearly these students need to be taught a specific method for systematic thought.

THE PROBLEM-SOLVING DILEMMA

But problems arise as soon as one tries to define a problem-solving methodology that ought to be taught to all students. While experts can agree on the merits of various special techniques (e.g. breaking problems into parts, examining special cases, or making linear approximations), there is no consensus as to the best overall strategy. Some people advocate starting every problem by drawing a picture, others prefer a list of known facts, still others demand a statement of goals. The choice between these general strategies seems (and is) arbitrary.

If we ignore the selection dilemma and, blessed with immaculate insight, impose some procedure upon our students, then we face yet another difficulty. Many students will stubbornly ignore our advice; others will follow it for a time before giving up. Unless we are willing to impose severe grading penalities, few seem to benefit from our wisdom. A colleague once required his students to lay out a complete solution plan before solving any problem. During the final exam he walked around the room and noted that over half the class left blank spaces before each solution to be filled in as a final step. My experience has been similar. I start each semester with a strict policy on exactly what each solution must include, but as the semester wears on the policy wears down. I always feel guilty about letting students off the hook, but I never have the energy to impose the required discipline.

RESOLVING THE DILEMMA

Epistemological anarchism offers an explanation for both of the above difficulties. Experts cannot agree on the best overall strategy because there is none. Students, and teachers, will not conform to any one strategy because to do so would be ineffective and unwise. Man's special genius is not as the user of tools—virtually any life form[1] can do that; it is as the inventor of tools. Seen from this perspective, drilling students in a particular methodology for problem solving actually denies them the opportunity to learn, because the key to problem solving lies in *finding* an appropriate method. But then where are we? The students described by Bloom and Broder surely need to learn something; they definitely lack discipline and a sense of systematic method. What can be done to help them?

An answer to the above questions lies in a more careful analysis of the anarchist position. When Feyerabend states "anything goes" he only tells part of the tale. Science is distinguished from other endeavors not by its method but rather by self-awareness of method. Scientists keep track of *both* their conclusions and their methods. Feyerabend should perhaps have said "anything goes provided one knows what one is doing." Novice students, particularly poor ones, haven't the vaguest notion of how they solve or fail to solve problems; and it is this single weakness that makes learning almost impossible. They do not need to be taught methods which they can only follow in a mindless fashion, *rather they need to be taught to think about whatever method they happen to choose.* A problem solver who reflects upon his method can learn from mistakes and will make progress even when guided by faulty intuitions. I should also point out a second necessary restriction on anarchism. In order to keep track of one's method, one must apply it consistently. Many low aptitude students view each new situation as distinct from everything else; they make no attempt to find methods that work in as many different situations as possible. *Good science is a search for methods that have the widest conceivable application.*

DEVELOPING AN AWARENESS OF
THOUGHT PROCESSES

Making students conscious of their own reasoning has long been a central concern in education. Dewey (1933) saw the fostering of reflective thought as a key element in higher education. Today most courses in problem solving stress the importance that awareness has in:

1. allowing students to be in control of their own thoughts.
2. permitting students to refine effective techniques and reject ineffective ones.

The standard method for promoting such awareness is to present and discuss a variety of problem-solving techniques. Several variants of this approach are discussed by Hayes (1976), Larkin (1975), Norman (1977), Rubinstein (1975), Schoenfeld (1979) and Wickelgren (1974). While this approach has often been effective, it has rarely been anarchistic. Although it does teach a diversity of approaches, it nonetheless specifies the rules and acceptability of each. In so doing it does not develop as fully as it might the students' skills in inventing and evaluating their own strategies. The need for this latter kind of training is perhaps greatest among the low achieving students described by Bloom and Broder. These students are unprepared for the sophistication of a course on comparative methodology because they have not yet learned to examine even a single strategy.

In working with such students, there is a danger of assuming that, because they invent ineffective strategies, those strategies are not worthy of examination. We may feel it necessary to first teach them a good strategy and then show them how to examine it. This view is based on the erroneous assumption that the process of invention may be separated from the process of evaluation. It is only through constructing a strategy that one can become aware of the components to be examined; but it is only through self-reflection on these components that one understands how to construct them.

A true anarchist's approach to teaching problem-solving would not show students how to solve problems, but would instead force them to consider whatever solutions they chose to use. Such a process has been developed by Arthur Whimbey.[2] In his approach students are asked to work in pairs. They are given a series of relatively easy problems which they must work according to the following rules. For each problem one student takes on the role of problem solver and the other the role of listener; they then switch roles for the subsequent problem. The problem solver's role is to read the problem aloud and to continue talking throughout the entire solution process. The listener's role is to keep the problem solver talking and to continually probe for more detailed descriptions of the problem solver's thought process. A good listener will ask for clarification of even the most trivial steps. These are often the most difficult to explain, since they have become automatic and were probably learned when we were too young to grasp their meaning. The listener must *not* solve the problem or give hints to the problem solver; his function is solely to demand greater clarity.

The above process is described in greater detail in a problem solving workbook (Whimbey and Lochhead, 1979) which includes a series of simple problems, each accompanied by one or more solutions. These solutions contain an outline of key steps; some are verbatim transcripts from a model problem solver's thinking aloud protocol. However, the solutions are not presented as optimal. In fact, students refer to them only when their own methods fail. They are told that there is nothing special about the book's solutions; any procedure is equally good provided it works and provided they understand why it works.

Solving problems according to Whimbey's rules is a demanding and rewarding task even for college faculty. Few of us have ever been conscious of our own thinking at the level of detail this exercise demands. Yet the method has also proved useful for high school remedial programs. Because this material meets the needs of so divergent a population, I feel it is tapping important fundamental skills. Furthermore the approach demonstrates the power of appropriately controlled anarchy. By allowing each student to find his own way, all students can learn effectively, even when there is a wide range of talent.

I would now like to contrast the structure and the anarchy in Whimbey's approach. Problems in the workbook are simple and they have one right answer. The role of each student is well-defined and it is important for the teacher to insist that all participants adhere to their roles. Students are sometimes asked to hand in a written record of their thoughts while working a problem. In many cases this exercise does not produce acceptable results until students have been threatened with grading penalties. But within the variety of solution methods students produce, anything goes. The only criteria imposed on a solution are that it work and that it can be explained. Teachers must resist the temptation to show off by demonstrating a "better" method. This display can only curb the student's confidence; it discourages inventions, risk-taking and self reflection, while promoting only imitation.

Although the Whimbey method does not teach a method for solving problems, it does stress certain attitudes. These include:

1. a faith in persistent systematic analysis

2. concern for accuracy
3. the patience to employ a step-by-step procedure
4. avoidance of wild guessing
5. a determination to remain actively involved with the problem.

It is these general characteristics that describe the differences between good and poor problem solvers, not knowledge of some list of techniques.

The approach described above can be applied to almost any of the conventional disciplines. Introductory physics is one example. I have found that by using appropriately selected problems, it is possible to move students through physics with very little direct instruction on how to work problems. Traditional physics exercises can be used, but they are improved by the following changes. Most textbook problems stress the algebraic or formula-related perspective on physics. To the expert such problems also suggest graphical, pictorial and even verbal images. Unfortunately, as Perry (1968) has shown, undergraduates tend to see things only as they are presented, and they have great difficulty translating between different perspectives. It is therefore highly instructive to give students problems that require translation between different representations,[3] for example, a problem with an algebraic statement that requests a graphical answer. This mixing of traditional modes is highly challenging and helps students understand the role of symbolization in their own thought processes.

In making students, and ourselves, more conscious of how symbolization schemes affect our thinking, we also open up the possibility of pushing anarchism one step further. Why restrict students to the symbolization conventions of the past? Why not allow them to experiment with their own idiosyncratic systems? Faced with the image of Babel my own interest in anarchism wanes, but there are specific instances where the idea does work. Perhaps the most striking example concerns angular motion. The current fashion in physics is to use axial vectors to represent torques and angular velocities. This use of vectors is conceptually quite different from their use in representing linear velocities, but students fail to notice the distinction (and we usually do a terrible job of pointing it out to them). I have found it useful to ask students how they would represent the orientation of a plane in three dimensional space. Their answers rarely involve axial vectors, but the exercise of considering the difficulties involved in creating such a representation allows them to appreciate the axial system when it is presented to them.

Another application of anarchism to the physics classroom concerns the construction of formulas. Clement, Lochhead and Soloway (1979) have shown that science students have great difficulty in translating English statements into mathematics. For this reason, I do not give students the formulas of physics. Rather I ask them to construct these formulas out of what they already know. For example, one question I have used is the following:

> An object that is high off the floor has potentially recoverable energy that can be obtained by dropping it. That energy is related to the height off the floor, the strength of gravity, and the mass of the object. Write a formula that is consistent with this information.

There are an infinite number of possible answers, and the students learn a great deal by considering the alternatives. In grading these problems I allow any answer that is consistent with the English statement, whether or not it is "correct" physics. Even after the students do learn the "correct" formula an element of anarchy remains. Students from my course are as likely to use $E = ghm$ as the more conventional $E = mgh$.

These last two examples are helpful in demonstrating the advantages of epistemological anarchism. By taking the position "anything goes", one is freed from the blinders imposed by our methodological habits. This is particularly important in teaching, where we are often blind to the students' difficulty because we are unaware of the peculiarities of a system in which we are too thoroughly enmeshed. Of course, after we study alternatives we are always free to return to the old system; but we do so by choice and with greater understanding.

EVALUATION

Because the above approach is relatively new, there is no objective evidence for its effectiveness. Students and faculty often make strong statements in its support, but data from large statistically meaningful samples has not yet been gathered. However, the method shares much in common with the Guided Design[4] system developed by Charles Wales. A recent review of Guided Design (Wales, 1979) shows that a single course can have measurable impact on college students' four year grade point average. A much greater impact would likely be possible from a series of these courses.

CONCLUSION

Although the tenets of epistemological anarchism may at first seem absurd, particularly as applied to the low achieving student, they are both reasonable and practical. Feyerabend claims that the key to scientific progress has not been adherence to a well defined methodology. This paper suggests that students can be taught to become effective problem solvers without being programmed to execute specific problem-solving techniques. If this view is correct, the key to successful problem solving lies not so much in the mastery of techniques as in the art of inventing and selecting appropriate strategies.[5]

NOTES

[1] I may for example consider myself to be merely the tool of a virus.

[2] Arthur Whimbey is not to my knowledge an anarchist. His approach developed out of his experience as a teacher, not from theoretical musings.

[3] Excellent work in this area has been done by George S. Monk.

[4] Guided Design was not developed from anarchist principles and many of its advocates would take strong exception to the views expressed in this paper.

[5] Larkin (1978) provides empirical evidence for this conclusion. Her analysis of the problem-solving protocols of both experts and novices shows clear differences in the ability to select strategies.

REFERENCES

Bloom, B.S., and Broder, L.J. *Problem-solving Processes of College Students: An Exploratory Investigation.* Chicago: The University of Chicago Press, 1950.

Dewey, J. *How We Think.* New York: Heath Books, 1933.

Feyerabend, P. *Against Method.* Atlantic Highlands, N.J.: Humanities Press, 1975.

Hayes, J.R. "It's the Thought That Counts: New Approaches to Educational Theory" in D. Klahr (ed.), *Cognition and Instruction.* Hillsdale, N. J.: Lawrence Erlbaum Assoc., 1976.

Kuhn, T.S. *The Structure of Scientific Revolutions.* Chicago: The University of Chicago Press, 1962.

Larkin, J. "Developing Useful Instruction in General Thinking Skills" in SESAME Report. University of California, Berkeley, 1975.

Larkin, J. "Processing Information for Effective Problem Solving" in SESAME Report. University of California, Berkeley, 1977.

Monk, G.S. *Constructive Calculus.* University of Washington, 1978.

Norman, D.A. "Teaching Learning Strategies", mimeo. University of California, San Diego, 1977.

Perry, W. G., Jr. *Forms of Intellectual and Ethical Development in the College Years: A Scheme.* New York: Holt, Rinehart and Winston, 1970.

Piaget, J. *Biology and Knowledge.* Chicago: The University of Chicago Press, 1971.

Polya, G. *How to Solve It.* Princeton, N.J.: Princeton University Press, 1948.

Rubinstein, M.F. *Patterns of Problem Solving.* Englewood Cliffs, N.J.: Prentice-Hall, 1975.

Schoenfeld, A.H. "Can Heuristics Be Taught? The Elements of a Theory and a

Report on the Teaching of General Mathematical Problem-Solving Skills." In *Introduction to Cognitive Process Instruction*. Philadelphia: Franklin Institute Press, 1979.

von Glasersfeld, E. "Cybernetics, Experience, and the Concept of Self" in Ozer, M.N. (ed.), *A Cybernetic Approach to the Assessment of Children: Toward a More Humane Use of Human Beings*. Boulder, Colo.: Westview Press, 1979.

Wales, C.E. "Does How You Teach Make a Difference?" *Engineering Education* (February 1979.

Whimbey, A., and Lochhead, J. *Problem Solving and Comprehension: A Short Course in Analytical Reasoning*. Philadelphia: Franklin Institute Press, 1979.

Wickelgren, W.A. *How to Solve Problems: Elements of a Theory of Problems and Problems Solving*. San Francisco: W.H. Freeman, 1974.

HOLISTIC THINKING SKILLS INSTRUCTION: AN INTERDISCIPLINARY APPROACH TO IMPROVING INTELLECTUAL PERFORMANCE

by William A. Sadler, Jr.

William A. Sadler, Jr., discusses a holistic approach to learning that combines the teaching of analytical thinking with communication to improve students' intellectual skills. The program, which is in use at Bloomfield College, in New Jersey, and at Paul Robeson High School, in Chicago, integrates analytical skills instruction into every content course in the program; further, skills acquired in one course are reinforced in another—across such different academic disciplines as the humanities and the sciences.

Like Arthur Whimbey, Sadler views intelligence as a set of identifiable behaviors, and sets about finding ways to help students apply analytic and problem-solving skills to their academic tasks.

The author is Dean of the College of Arts and Sciences at Lock Haven University, Pennsylvania.

A number of cognitive development programs emphasize teaching from a taxonomy of thinking skills. While such taxonomies may be helpful in diagnosis, interventions are likely to be more successful if they are holistic. As Arthur Whimbey has suggested, teaching thinking is like teaching a sport: the teacher is a coach, modeling actions, calling students' attention to effective and ineffective strategies. The tennis coach knows that a new player must get the feel of the entire action in swinging a tennis racket; attempting to help the player string together a series of component behaviors comprising the swing will not get the ball over the net. Similarly, instruction in thinking skills is most effective if it is holistic, combining analytical thinking practice with communication to improve students' general intellectual abilities.

Such a program is in use at Bloomfield College, in New Jersey, and at Paul Robeson High and Middle School, in Chicago. First developed by my colleagues and me as a two-year core freshman program at Bloomfield College, and later extended for four years, the program has been adapted for middle through high school use at the Robeson school. At both sites, the program focuses upon developing cognitive skills. These include basic processes of reading, writing, and computation for many students; but the major skills aimed for are those of analytical thinking and communication. Whether in math, natural science, social science, humanities, career planning, or human development classes, students are directed toward the improvement of *communication* and *analytical thinking skills*. Analytical skills learned in one course, such as humanities, are reinforced in others, such as science. Thus, these skills have a better chance of becoming a permanent part of a student's behavioral repertoire. We chose these two cognitive skills because we believe they are of fundamental importance to our students' successful achievement in both their college and later careers.

With these two skills as primary goals, a new, more difficult problem arose. What does analytical thinking mean? Teachers in the sciences were more comfortable with the concept of analysis than were those in the humanities; the latter had to develop their own definition and model for teaching analytical thinking. After several years of trying to teach it, most program teachers concluded that we were talking about reading and solving problems intelligently. But had we reduced program classes to a basic, remedial level? Reading physics, Freud, Orwell, and Kafka in required program courses (as our Bloomfield College students did) hardly seemed remedial. Then what were we doing? Regardless of discipline, our common aim was to improve students' intellectual performance—to help them read with more intelligence and understanding. But what does that involve?

As a first step in improving students' analytical abilities, we had to specify our understanding of intelligence in terms of behaviors that could be identified, taught, and assessed. We came to see intelligence, at least in terms of our course aims, as a complex set of behaviors, involving attention, selection, analysis (breaking something down into constituent parts), formulating an idea, testing it (with experience and logic), and applying it (in a practical way or through an enlargement of understanding). In effect, we were constructing a model of analytical, problem-solving intelligence, similar to that underlying IQ and Scholastic Aptitude Tests.

We learned three important lessons from implementing a skills-oriented learning program at the college level. First, it is crucial to articulate a set of primary goals, such as the development of basic and higher-level cognitive skills. Second, it is essential to specify these goals precisely, so that teachers can tailor instruction and assignments to meet these goals, and monitor students' and their own progress in attaining them. In other words, we needed to know exactly what we wanted students to do and then to make that objective clear to them. Third—also a principle—pedagogy is more important than content. As Kierkegaard put it, the *how* is more important than the *what*. Until teachers assimilate that principle, they will find teaching skills an unsatisfying, nearly impossible task.

PROGRAM IMPLEMENTATION: HOW TO DO IT

How is such a program set in motion? Most teachers found that students had trouble getting the main point of written material. To help them develop both communication and analytical skills, we decided our first target would be to require them to get the point. Our search for suitable materials lasted several years; in fact it is continuing. One of the books that worked for us at Bloomfield College was a collection of short essays in natural science by Steven Gould, *Ever Since Darwin*. Most of its chapters are tightly structured arguments that explode previous assumptions through careful reasoning and evidence. Students are assigned a chapter and then asked to compose an essay on their own, often in class, to demonstrate that they got the point. They can state it in their own words, and they can cite evidence from the chapter supporting their idea. When we first used this method, two grades were possible: Yes or No. Students either got the point or they did not. Most received a No on their first few papers. After several attempts teachers began asking, "Can I give a No +? A Yes −?".

Eventually we reverted to letter grades. But the lesson had been learned effectively by both teachers and students. An author had communicated a message; students could take definite, teachable steps to receive that message. But the most important aspect was that students had to take those steps *on their own,* receiving feedback after they had first tried without help to get the message.

This kind of experience confirmed another principle for us: to make students work on their own. It was a particularly hard lesson to learn. Most teachers have developed an inclination to help students through material with lectures, supplemental readings, recitation sections, illustrations, outlines, and other teaching aids. At Bloomfield College and Paul Robeson High, the faculty has learned to resist that inclination. Students are forced to ask their own questions in order to analyze and understand the material. *Students need to learn to question the material, because the questioning process is basic to intelligent understanding.* Once they learn to question, to carry on a dialogue with the material, they are well on the way to comprehension.

That phase has some cost factors, however; it requires much feedback. In one course, our workload amounted to 27 papers per student per semester, or 54 papers per student per year. In other words, a social science or humanities teacher with a class of 20 grades over 1,000 papers each

185

year for one class. Science classes developed their own version of this active principle. Using this "discovery method" students do experiments, form their hypotheses, and test them against experience and logic. Teachers act as resource persons, consultants, and feedback experts. Math and human development courses use a similar model.

Wherever this approach is used, teachers are more like coaches, eliciting improved performance, rather than being didactic imparters of information. Coaching has become a model for many of us who are pursuing the task of improving cognitive skills.

We discovered that an effective educational program must focus on students in the process of developing competencies. That is, we needed to create an environment that not only reinforced generic skills but also permitted a clearly delineated developmental model to operate. Whatever their placement in the program then, students follow a sequential learning pattern. One step leads to another; students must demonstrate a satisfactory degree of mastery with each step before progressing to another part of the program. This results in a more complex analysis of arguments and then in the more demanding task of applying one major idea to another in doing a comparative assessment. By the time students finish the program, they have demonstrated their capacity to follow a book-length argument in discussions and papers; they can also apply a set of major ideas (such as Freud's notion of internal conflict) to a historical event (such as the Salem witch trials). In science, students move from simple experiments determining the properties of space to calculations about the movements and phases of stars.

Here again the analogy with sports is appropriate. The teaching of skills works when a carefully structured series of actions builds upon each other. A beginning or intermediate skier does not start on a tough expert trail. But in high school and college classes something like that may happen. Consider the common general education course in Western civilization given to college freshmen. Such a course often proposes to provide students with information about history, to help them understand and critique both historical events and major ideas, compare the values of one person or era with another, and use these insights to prepare for both careers and life. The kinds of cognitive skills needed for such a task, not to mention the requisite level of maturity, far exceed the developed capacities of most students. Educational programs often push too much on students too soon, forcing them into survival strategies rather than fostering growth. In teaching skiing, for example, if students want to use advanced trails with expertise and enjoyment, they must first learn the necessary maneuvers and be able to integrate them easily in a variety of challenging situations. The same principle applies when teaching intellectual skills.

By trying to teach cognitive skills effectively, we learned from our experience, which was later clarified through reading about human development. These ideas can lead to some fundamental policies. Underlying these policies are some basic assumptions that should be made explicit: (1) intelligence is a complex of skills that can be developed; (2) a focus on student activity, especially questioning and a verbalization of thinking, is an important method to develop intelligence; (3) the provision of regular, appropriate feedback is equally important; (4) the use of a sequential learning pattern that requires mastery at each stage promotes this development; (5) an environment that is conducive to cognitive development and promotes student/teacher interaction is most desirable; and (6) teachers need training to provide this kind of instruction effectively. These assumptions have been articulated into the following policies that we believe to be most important:

- Develop a clear, consistent focus on cognitive development.
- Identify specific objectives so that both teachers and students know what is expected.
- Determine the levels and abilities of students and keep a close watch on their progress.
- Make students learn to question the material.
- Develop a sequential learning pattern that starts with what students need to learn first in order to move toward the stated objective.
- Require students to demonstrate a mastery of each behavior before allowing them to move to more advanced tasks.
- Construct active learning experiences that require students to develop and test their competencies.
- Provide regular, careful, sensitive feedback so that students have a good idea about what they are doing right as well as what they need to correct.
- Construct an environment that constantly reinforces cognitive development, promotes student initiative and faculty/student interaction, and provides support, encouragement, and rewards for both faculty and students.

Strong faculty involvement made the program possible. Although the program is completely interdisciplinary, courses are broken down according to general academic divisions. Faculty responsible for a course meet together on a regular weekly basis, not only for course planning and monitoring, but also for teacher training. Teachers share critical incidents with the group regularly. All classes are observed; nearly everyone has a class taped, which is then observed with several other teachers, who help select portions to be shown to the entire faculty group for analysis and discussion. Consultants have been used to provide specific instruction on new methods; and faculty have learned from them to continue to instruct and coach themselves. Most teachers attend *educational conferences* on a variety of issues. Faculty continue to read about human development, learning, and education—topics that most had not explored earlier. In short, the discovery method has been applied to the development of the faculty as educators. What sustains the process is the emergent, closely knit groups of teachers. What threatens the teamwork principle is the tendency to break from the group and revert to covering content. One way to prevent that is to establish some criteria by which faculty can assess their own development; the best context for this is a supportive group, which helps individuals in self-assessment and growth.

What kind of results can be expected from this program? Perhaps the first indication is a change within faculty. There is often a notable rise in morale, a recovery of a sense of excitement that comes from meaningful interaction and mutual learning with peers. This leads to a heightened sense of collegiality. A danger here is that if only one group has formed to teach skills, it may become a clique. If there is an overall attempt to redefine learning in terms of cognitive development, however, then there is the possibility for a sense of shared purpose among faculty, administration, and students. Another result is the undeniable improvement in students. They develop competencies; they learn to deal more effectively with increasingly difficult material; they question more and become more curious; their grades improve; they realize, often for the first time, that teachers care about them and want to help them develop. For faculty, there is the recovery of a sense of mission for higher education. Indeed, this educational experience is liberating for students and faculty, and it serves real needs.

COGNITIVE MODIFIABILITY IN ADOLESCENCE: COGNITIVE STRUCTURE AND THE EFFECTS OF INTERVENTION

by Reuven Feuerstein, Ronald Miller, Mildred B. Hoffman, Ya'acov Rand, Yael Mintzker, and Mogens Reimer Jensen

Reuven Feuerstein and his colleagues focus on the learning abilities of culturally deprived adolescents. Their definition of deprivation does not connote culturally different, but rather the learners' inability to learn from their environment. According to Feuerstein, this inability stems from an early, deprived Mediated Learning Experience.

Feuerstein has designed an intervention program, Instrumental Enrichment (IE), to address the needs of adolescents with such environmentally induced learning disabilities. The IE system, first developed in Israel and now in use in the United States, is a set of content-free exercises intended to improve these students' intellectual functioning. In this chapter, Feuerstein and his colleagues provide examples of IE exercises and discuss how the exercises are incorporated into a structured mediated learning experience. Finally, they present data on Instrumental Enrichment's effects on various cognitive and intelligence measures.

This chapter is reprinted with permission from The Journal of Special Education *(Summer 1981): 269–87. Copyright © 1986 The Journal of Special Education.*

Difficulties in learning occur at many levels and range from very specific to more generalized problems, as the conditions we call learning disability and mental retardation, respectively, tend to suggest. Perhaps the most pervasive problem confronted by education is the difficulty for some in learning to learn, whether in a narrow field or in the broader sense of a reduced ability to adapt to novel events and situations.

Increasing numbers of children who experience difficulties in learning are being called learning disabled. Presumably the ability, or some part of it, that facilitates learning in so-called normal individuals is absent or deficient in the learning-disabled person. In this sense, special education means education for special or disabled people. This approach to the problem of the nonlearner or low-functioning individual has been criticized (for example, see Dunn [2]) because it places the locus of the problem within the individual. In other words, it is not the individual's performance that is low; rather, it is his/her competence to learn that is impaired. It has been suggested that learning disability might be more appropriately called teaching disability. Clearly, the implication is that we require special kinds of education for children with learning difficulties. The locus of the problem does not lie with the child; it lies with the teacher who is unable to impart learning to the child.

The problem with both of these approaches is that although they both contain elements of truth, neither includes the whole truth. A more plausible explanation may emerge if the two approaches are combined or reconciled to include and account for both sides of the coin. The first step in this direction is the recognition that learning, or at least some part of it, is a product of the interaction between the teacher and learner. If so, a disability may reside in the nature of the interaction. A second and related step is to distinguish between the phenomenon of learning (or nonlearning) and the learner. Consequently, it is not the learner who is special but his condition or state. In similar vein, a distinction may be drawn between the teacher and the curriculum; that is, it is not necessarily the teacher who is disabled but the curriculum that is disabling under certain circumstances. Thus, what is required is a special kind of educational curriculum to satisfy the needs of a special kind of nonlearning phenomenon. In the sections that follow an attempt is made to develop these points. The etiology of low cognitive performance is discussed and the nature of the nonlearning phenomenon is described. This is followed by a brief description of an intervention program designed to reverse low cognitive performance and some relevant empirical findings.

MEDIATED LEARNING EXPERIENCE

Our concern in the field of educational intervention has been directed not to special children but to an understanding of and remedy for a syndrome that we refer to as cultural deprivation. By this term we do not refer to an individual from a culture that is deprived or depriving but rather to an individual deprived of his/her own culture, whatever that culture may be. Defined operationally, cultural deprivation refers to a state of low modifiability; that is, an inability or reduced ability to learn by direct exposure to environmental events. This condition finds expression in poor cognitive performance. Unlike the phenomenon of cultural difference, however, cultural deprivation is exemplified not by failure in certain restricted fields of knowledge because of a lack of familiarity, but by a generalized reduced propensity to learn and become modified even under apparently conducive learning conditions. In order to understand and subsequently reverse the syndrome of cultural deprivation, it is necessary to consider the etiology of low cognitive performance and inadequate cognitive modifiability.

We argue that human intelligence is an expression of two distinct kinds of learning. As with learning in other living organisms, human

190

learning may occur as a result of direct exposure to the environment. Most psychological theories, such as the stimulus-response learning theory and the stimulus-organism-response Piagetian approach, are concerned with how the individual learns in reaction to or in interaction with the environment of objects and events. In addition to this universal kind of learning, we maintain that human learning involves a qualitatively different kind of learning with respect to its end product. Learning how to learn (or, in our terms, cognitive modifiability) is a direct function of what we refer to as Mediated Learning Experience (MLE). In contrast to learning by direct exposure, mediated learning occurs when a mediator interposes himself between the learner and the environment and interprets the world to the learner. Thus MLE is not necessarily synonymous with social interaction. The issue is not whether the individual receives stimulus information from inanimate or animate sources but the kind of information that is received. The essence of a mediated interaction is that in the process of mediating information, a transformation occurs that facilitates the transmission of meaning not inherent in the raw stimulus or sensory information impinging on the organism. Typically mother-infant interactions abound with instances of mediated learning. For example, the mother selects certain stimuli for presentation and ignores others. She frames, filters, schedules, and provides a sequence for the stimuli presented. She attributes specific meanings to objects and events. Thus, temporal, spatial, causal, and other relationships not inherent either in the objects or in the child's actions are mediated by the mother and other significant caretaking figures. In addition to transmitting all kinds of specific information that is simply not available via direct exposure, such as a knowledge of the past, mediated learning provides the kind of experience necessary for the building of cognitive structure.

It would appear that the need to impose order on the world, and the cognitive tools required to achieve this, are not readily available from either environmental or constitutional sources. Instead, it is that collective human activity that is referred to as culture that elicits the need and provides the tools for the imposition of order and understanding on the world. In its broadest sense, MLE may be understood as the psychological component of cultural transmission. The universal phenomenon of cultural transmission from generation to generation has tended to be taken for granted by psychologists (a noteworthy exception is Bruner [1]), not only with respect to the psychological processes involved but also with respect to their psychological products. Apart from their specific contents, different cultures all provide a structure within which the direct exposure to and experience of objects and events may be organized, interpreted, and understood. Appreciation of the past and anticipation of the future are cultural imperatives that render the human organism adaptable by invoking representational processes that enable the individual to project himself beyond the immediate world of direct observation and action. Although language is a powerful medium for cultural transmission, MLE may be provided in modalities other than language; furthermore, not all language use has a necessary mediating function. The defining characteristics of MLE are (a) an intention, not necessarily conscious, on the part of the mediator to interpret to the child the experienced world and (b) to transcend the experience and the needs of the immediate here and now by the mediated learning. The language of instruction and the level of technological sophistication of a given culture are not determinants of effective mediated learning. Whether a child learns to construct a canoe or a transistor radio, he/she must simultaneously learn to plan ahead, employ appropriate strategies, understand how the parts are related to the whole, draw logical inferences, and so on. Over and above the specific contents of any task or skill, whether writing a computer program or tracking an animal, information must be organized, operations performed, and an entire set of complex activities integrated into a purposeful and meaningful system of action. Thus, MLE may be understood as the transmission of universal cognitive structures by the initiated to the uninitiated and immature members of society. It is the acquisition of structure that renders the individual adaptable or modifiable.

ETIOLOGY OF LOW COGNITIVE PERFORMANCE AND MLE

The significance of the MLE concept as a crucial component of the development of intelligence becomes evident when the relation between it and learning by direct exposure is considered. We contend that the more and the earlier an individual is provided with MLEs, the greater will be his/her ability to benefit from direct exposure. Therefore, culturally deprived individuals (that is, individuals deprived of MLE) have difficulty in learning because they lack the cognitive structures that serve to connect, organize, integrate, and relate stimulus information. In short, such individuals do not have the cognitive equipment with which to adapt to new and novel events in a manner that would deepen their understanding and render them increasingly modifiable.

In addition to the MLE emphasis on the structural components of mental activity, it also has important etiological implications. Low cognitive performance is usually attributed to either environmental or constitutional factors. Arguments supporting socioeconomic factors such as poverty, class, and education are intended to counter claims that the basis of low cognitive performance is either of a genetic or cogenital nature. In terms of MLE theory, neither environmental nor constitutional factors may be regarded as direct causal factors that inevitably produce low cognitive performance. The direct or *proximal* etiology of low performance is a lack of MLE. Genetic, socioeconomic, and environmental conditions are only indirectly implicated in the sense of being *distal* factors that may, but do not necessarily, trigger conditions that impede the provision of MLE. Thus, sensory and organic impairments of various kinds as well as psychological conditions may render an individual less receptive to MLE. Alternatively, various social and psychological conditions such as poverty or emotional disturbance may prevent the mediator from providing adequate MLE. Whatever the distal condition that results in low cognitive performance, the proximal or necessary condition is inadequate MLE. The educational implications of conceptualizing the etiology of low cognitive performance in the above way are of both theoretical and practical importance. By locating the cause of low cognitive performance in either the socioeconomic conditions of the students' parents or in genetic/organic disorders, or even in developmental disorders that may arise during critical periods in the preschool years, the educator is confronted with conditions over which he/she has no control. If, however, low cognitive performance is directly attributable to a lack of MLE, irrespective of any associated distal conditions, then the problem falls squarely within the educator's domain. Furthermore, and of even more fundamental significance, there is no reason to believe that the syndrome of cultural deprivation—as reflected in low cognitive performance—is an irreversible or immutable condition. Although it must be acknowledged that certain extreme distal conditions may set practical limits to both the provision and reception of MLE, in principle a state of low cognitive performance may be reversed by the provision of appropriate MLE. The point that must be emphasized is that this theory of cognitive modifiability does not necessarily imply that there are no limits to an individual's cognitive functioning. What the educator may extract from the theory is that there are no *preconceived* limits, and that the extent of cognitive modifiability is a function of the investment the educator is willing or able to make. In practical terms this means that the responsibility for educational decisions must be returned to the educator. Although psychologists, sociologists, and medical practitioners may provide information concerning manifest performance levels, organic conditions, and socioeconomic conditions, all of which may help in indicating the extent and nature of the investment required, it is the educator who is responsible for teaching and who must decide whether or not to make the investment.

COGNITIVE MODIFIABILITY

From an educational perspective, the explanatory value of any psychological theory is a function of its power to serve as a blueprint for cognitive change. A theory of cognitive modifiability that describes the phenomenon of low cognitive performance and explains its etiology must also incorporate the two additional and related components of assessment and intervention if it is to have any real significance for education. Within the context of cognitive modifiability the goal of both assessment and intervention is the production of meaningful structural cognitive change. In the assessment situation, the purpose is not to produce long-term changes but to assess the potential of the individual's structural modifiability and to diagnose any specific difficulties that individual may encounter in the process. The goal of intervention is to bring about long-term changes of a kind that will render the individual modifiable. In terms of our definition of the syndrome of cultural deprivation, intervention must be directed at the production of structural changes that will transform the individual into an autonomous learner. The term *structure* is not lightly employed, and neither are the implications for intervention minimized or overlooked. The essence of a structural change is that its effects should show an increment over time, as opposed to the simple accumulation of specific information that is subject to a gradual process of fading, forgetting, or extinction.

Given, on the one hand, an etiology based on a lack of MLE and, on the other hand, a goal of producing structural changes, intervention procedures must be designed to provide a link in the causal chain of events. Clearly, intervention must take the form of providing the kinds of MLEs that for a host of reasons the individual has missed. But in addition, intervention must be directed at those cognitive processes whose malfunction or failure to function adequately have prevented the construction of requisite structure by the low-performing individual. Thus, intervention procedures must be developed with the goal of correcting deficient cognitive functions in order to produce changes in the cognitive structure. The point should be made, [however,] that cognitive structures cannot simply be implanted directly by training or intervention. The focus of intervention, in terms of our approach, is to provide the individual with the functional prerequisites that will enable him/her to construct the cognitive structures that will enhance modifiability—that is, learning through direct exposure to impinging stimuli.

INTERVENTION: INSTRUMENTAL ENRICHMENT

To meet the above requirements, an intervention program called Instrumental Enrichment has been designed primarily for use with culturally deprived young adolescents. The program is intended as a phase-specific substitute for MLE. Traditionally, adolescence has not been the focus of cognitive intervention efforts, although it is typically the period at which low cognitive performance can no longer be ignored or glossed over by either the educational authorities or the individuals concerned. In the present forum, a complete description of the program, didactic methods, and supporting theory and research is not possible (see Feuerstein, and others [4]. For the present purposes, the more salient theoretical and conceptual characteristics of the program are emphasized, while those reflecting technique and classroom application will not be discussed. The program consists of 15 instruments containing pencil-and-paper exercises as follows: Organization of Dots; Analytic Perception; Orientation in Space I, II, and III; Comparisons; Categorization; Instructions; Family Relations; Illustrations; Numerical Progressions; Temporal Relations; Stencil Design; and Transitive Relations and Syllogisms. The program is integrated into the regular school curriculum and extends over a 2- to 3-year period, with a minimum of three sessions per week devoted to work on the instruments. While the names of the individual instruments indicate the dimensions of the program, in another sense the program is intended to be content-free.

The term *content-free* is intended to convey that the contents of any particular exercise are merely a vehicle, or instrument, to achieve the overall goals of the program. The major goal of Instrumental Enrichment is to enhance the cognitive modifiability of the individual, and this is achieved by the implementation of six subgoals as follows:

(a) The correction of deficient cognitive functions;

(b) The teaching of specific concepts, operations, and vocabulary required by the Instrumental Enrichment exercises;

(c) The development of an intrinsic need for adequate cognitive functioning and the spontaneous use of operational thinking by the production of crystallized schema and habit formation;

(d) The production of insight and understanding of one's own thought processes, in particular those processes that produce success and are responsible for failure;

(e) The production of task-intrinsic motivation that is reinforced by the meaning of the program in a broader social context; and

(f) A change in orientation towards oneself from passive recipient and reproducer to active generator of information.

Although the achievement of all the subgoals of the program depend on an active interaction between the three elements of student, teacher, and instruments, subgoals (b) and (d) rely heavily on the teacher's contribution. The remaining subgoals are achieved by the nature of the instruments themselves with the exception of the last subgoal, which is a product of all the others together. In general, each instrument focuses on a particular or small set of deficient functions, while incorporating most of them in a more diffuse fashion. Depending on the nature of the instrument and the students involved, specific contents may have to be taught and different kinds of insight and understanding encouraged and elicited. The exercises are designed to capture the interest of the students and to enhance task-intrinsic motivation by being graded in difficulty and balanced with respect to the effort required and challenge presented. Constant repetition is used to achieve crystallization and automatization of schema, not by monotonously repeating the same task but by holding constant the same principle while varying the kinds of exercises and applications. In this way schema become more fluid as well as more spontaneous.

ILLUSTRATION: ORGANIZATION OF DOTS AND SYLLOGISMS

The actual implementation of the subgoals may be illustrated with reference to two instruments, Organization of Dots and Syllogisms, the first and last instruments, respectively. Examples from these instruments are provided in Figures 1 and 2. Organization of Dots is a nonverbal instrument in which the task throughout is to organize an amorphous cloud of dots by projecting into it the virtual relationships (that is, relationships that are potential but not yet actualized) required for the identification of a given standard figure. The student has to join the dots pertaining to the model figure while bearing in mind that the orientation of the model may change and that one form may be superimposed on the other. The logico-verbal reasoning tasks in Syllogisms involve the application of set theory to the understanding and solution of syllogisms. Although apparently very different in nature, both instruments remediate similar deficient functions, albeit at a different level. Organization of Dots focuses primarily on the difficulty in projecting virtual relations. Thus the student must project onto a random set of dots a structure of relationships that matches a given model. In the case of Syllogisms, although the focus is on formal operations, relations must be imposed on a set of elements according to a model—not a concrete form but an abstract logical model. In a broad sense, then, both instruments deal with the need to impose order on the world. Deficient functions that may impede successful performance include impulsivity, a lack of spontaneous comparison between the model and the solution, a lack of precision, and an inability to consider two sources of information simultaneously. All these deficiencies are challenged in both Organization of Dots and Syllogisms, despite the very different nature of their content and tasks. To correctly find the shapes in the clouds of dots or to solve the class-inclusion tasks, the learner must gather the data by sharp and precise perception of the

The student must perceive the dots in an amorphous, irregular cloud so as to project figures identical in form and size to those in the given models. The task becomes more complicated by density of the dots, overlapping, increasing complexity of the figures, and changes in their orientation. Successful completion demands segregation and articulation of the field.

Among the cognitive functions involved are:

Projection of virtual relationships	Use of relevant information
Discrimination of form and size	Discovery of strategies
Constancy of form and size across changes in orientation	Perspective
	Restraint of impulsivity

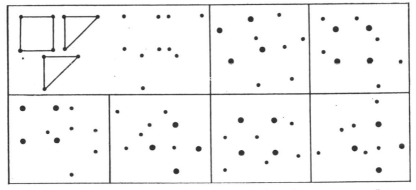

The thickened dots aid in projecting the square, but also serve as a distractor and prevent the perception of similarities between frames. In addition to the functions and operations listed on the title page (above), the tasks involve labeling, precision and accuracy, planning, determination of starting point, systematic search, and comparison to model. Successful completion aids in creation and maintenance of motivation.

Figure 1. Example from Organization of Dots

components of the task, must compare in a precise manner his/her production with that of the model, and must recognize that some elements have properties that require simultaneous consideration.

With respect to the second (b) subgoal, it is clear from Figures 1 and 2 that the contents, operations, and vocabulary involved in the tasks are different for each instrument. Nevertheless, the need for labeling and defining the task elements and applying strategies in the solution of a problem remain invariant across all instruments. The third (c) subgoal of producing crystallized and flexible schema that are spontaneously activated is difficult to illustrate without exposure to an entire instrument. However, it should be fairly obvious from the examples provided in Figures 1 and 2 how these tasks may be varied with respect to complexity, novelty, and variety while keeping constant a set of prerequisite func-

Each one of the shapes below represents a set. Every set has a name.

The names of the sets are: salt, spices, food, ice-cream, dessert, cake, pepper, vinegar.

Fill in the name of the set.

Fill in the names of the sets in the correct places.

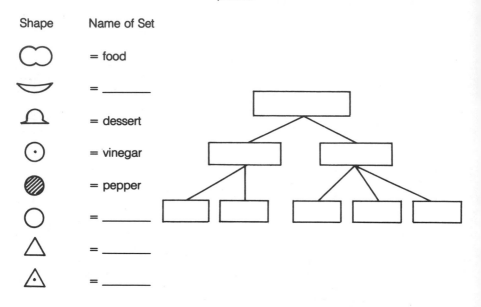

Shape	Name of Set
CO	= food
▽	= _____
⌂	= dessert
⊙	= vinegar
◉	= pepper
○	= _____
△	= _____
△	= _____

Logico-verbal reasoning becomes highly abstract. Meaning is based on the rules, which have been acquired regarding members of sets and sub-sets. The task involves encoding and decoding, use of signs, finding relationships, discovering the principle upon which categories have been formed, choosing and processing relevant data, and thinking logically.

Figure 2. Example from Syllogisms

tions, strategies, and operations. In this way the dual aim of crystallization and flexibility is achieved by repetition through variation. The fourth (d) subgoal of creating insight is accomplished by pointing out to the student the reasons for specific failures or difficulties, such as failure to apply a learned strategy, and also by group discussions of what is required for successful performance. The kinds of tasks represented in Figures 1 and 2 are designed to be intrinsically motivating, the fifth (e) subgoal. They are not derived from regular school subject matter, which often carries with it associations of failure, boredom, and monotony. Perhaps most important is that the tasks are difficult and represent an intellectual challenge without requiring a great deal of prior content knowledge. The discovery by the low performer that he/she is able to successfully solve tasks for which his/her peers and even the teacher do not have ready answers is a powerful motivational incentive that may be used to break the vicious circle of self-fulfilling negative expectations. Even the limited illustration provided by the examples in Figures 1 and 2 is sufficient to indicate how the sixth (f) subgoal is achieved. The tasks from the first to last instrument require the generation of information by the student, not the passive registration and reproduction of facts. The common thread running through all the instruments is that understanding and our ability to adapt depend on the manner and extent to which we are able to impose structure on objects and events in the environment. Space does not permit a discussion of the role of the cognitive map in the underlying conception and design of Instrumental Enrichment, but it should be mentioned that the above account is incomplete for this reason.

EMPIRICAL SUPPORT

The question of whether Instrumental Enrichment works will be directed primarily to three aspects: long-term effects, differential effects, and theoretical issues concerning the nature of the effects. Although the basic evaluation research studies on the immediate short-term effects following the completion of the Instrumental Enrichment program have been reported in detail elsewhere (4, 5, Notes 1 and 2), a brief descriptive statement of the general findings here provides a background against which the long-term, differential, and theoretical aspects of the program may be viewed.

The original research was conducted in Israel (see Feuerstein and others [4]) on a total sample of 218 retarded adolescents between the ages of 12 and 15 years. Results of IQ tests indicated that the subjects ranged from borderline to educable mentally retarded, and their general level of scholastic achievement was about 3 to 4 years behind their school peers. Three major findings emerged from the research findings. First, immediately following the completion of the program, significant gains on various cognitive and intelligence measures were obtained by groups that received Instrumental Enrichment (IE) with respect to comparison groups that received a general enrichment program (GE). Second, despite the fact that the IE groups received less instruction in formal school subjects, amounting to + 300 hours over a 2-year period, the comparison groups did not perform significantly better than the IE groups on any of the school achievement tests. Not only were initial pretest significant differences in favor of the comparison groups eliminated on the posttests, but the IE groups performed significantly better than the comparison groups on a few of the achievement tests. Third, no significant differences between the IE and comparison groups were obtained on measures of self-image. Essentially similar findings have been reported in the United States (Note 1) and Canada (Note 2), although research in North America has not yet been completed.

The above research findings indicate that Instrumental Enrichment produces fairly substantial gains in performance on cognitive and intellective tasks. A follow-up study was conducted to test the extent to which the short-term gains of the groups were sustained over time. Approximately 2 years after the completion of the program, the students in both the IE and GE groups were drafted into the Israeli Army and 184 subjects (IE = 95, GE = 89) were tested on an Army intelligence test called the DAPAR. The DAPAR test yields a stanine score (10 to 90).

In the initial stage of the evaluation research, the Primary Mental Abilities test (PMA) was used as a pre- and postintervention criterion measure. For the follow-up study, the DAPAR scores were analyzed using analysis of covariance with the initial PMA pretest scores as the covariate. The analysis yielded a highly significant difference between the DAPAR scores for the IE ($M = 52.52$) and GE ($M = 45.28$) groups ($F = 28.8, p < .001$). These results indicate that the gains achieved by the IE groups on the posttests (immediately following the intervention) were sustained and continued to differentiate between the groups even after about 2 years.

Educational research, especially of an innovative nature, does not permit the kind of precision or control afforded by the laboratory. The results presented are not intended to provide conclusive answers to any of the questions posed. They do suggest that valuable information may be derived by going beyond the question of whether an intervention program works. Taken as a whole, the data appear to support the general conclusion that low-functioning adolescents benefit from intervention and that meaningful cognitive changes are possible beyond the early years of life. Although a single measure of intelligence may represent meager research evidence of cognitive change, such measures carry considerable weight in determining life opportunities. In the case of the IE subjects, their scores on the DAPAR test placed them within the normal IQ range, and consequently they were eligible for opportunities that are closed to the low-functioning individual. All are agreed that the ultimate test of intervention is adaptation to life. Today, perhaps more than ever before, education is the key to successful adaptation. Instrumental Enrichment in both its didactic and material aspects represents an application of a general theory of cognitive modifiability. The theory attempts to explain and thereby to lay the foundation for the production of cognitive changes that will enable individuals to become increasingly modified as a result of their encounters with educational and life experiences.

REFERENCES

1. Bruner, J.; Oliver, R.; and Greenfield, P. M. *Studies in Cognitive Growth.* New York: Wiley, 1966.
2. Dunn, L. M. "Special Education for the Mildly Retarded—Is Much of It Justifiable?" *Exceptional Children* 1 (1968): 5–22.
3. Feuerstein, R.; Rand, Y.; and Hoffman, M. B. *The Dynamic Assessment of Retarded Performers.* Baltimore: University Park Press, 1979.
4. Feuerstein, R.; Rand, Y.; Hoffman, M. B.; and Miller, R. *Instrumental Enrichment.* Baltimore: University Park Press, 1980.
5. Feuerstein, R.; Rand, Y.; Hoffman, M. B.; Hoffman, M.; and Miller, R. "Cognitive Modifiability in Retarded Adolescents: Effects of Instrumental Enrichment." *American Journal of Mental Deficiency* 6 (1979): 539–50.

NOTES

1. Haywood, H. C. "Modification of Cognitive Functions in Slow-Learning Adolescents." Paper presented at the 5th International Congress of the International Association for the Scientific Study of Mental Deficiency (IASSMD), Jerusalem, Israel, August 1979.
2. Narro, H.; Silverman, H.; and Waksman, M. "Assessing and Developing Cognitive Potential in Vocational High School Students." Paper presented at the 5th International Congress of the International Association for the Scientific Study of Mental Deficiency (IASSMD), Jerusalem, Israel, August 1979.

USING VOCABULARY STUDY TO GENERATE THINKING

by Ernestine W. Roberts

Ernestine W. Roberts discusses ways of facilitating critical thinking through vocabulary development. She notes that vocabulary, like thinking skills themselves, "transcends all disciplines, even though there is vocabulary that is unique to each discipline." She suggests that vocabulary study be used as a means to teach thinking skills in all academic disciplines, and provides a series of vocabulary development exercises. Some of the exercises can be used in all academic fields, others are content-area specific. These include crossword puzzles that reinforce word skills, practicing with synonyms, analyzing the relationships between sets of words, categorizing lists of words, and evaluating math facts while working toward problem solution.

The author is a Reading Specialist, Pine Bluff Schools, Arkansas.

With the emphasis on reform of public schools, there has been a gradual shift away from teaching higher-level cognitive skills. This is a serious trend. If we are to educate a population which is capable of solving problems and taking positions in today's complex job market, it is obvious that thinking skills should be taught to students. The formal instruction should be followed by ample time allotted for practicing and perfecting these skills.

Thinking transcends all disciplines. Vocabulary study is also an area which transcends all disciplines, even though there is vocabulary that is unique to each discipline and is best learned in that setting. Vocabulary skills and thinking skills may at first appear to be incongruent, but Barry Beyer in "Common Sense About Teaching Thinking Skills" gives a clear definition of critical thinking which helps clarify the relationship.

> Critical thinking has been defined in various ways: careful and exact evaluation and judgment; subjecting a topic to severe criticism; thoughtful consideration about issues of great import, issues that imply considerable risk or danger; range of very specific analytical or evaluative skills such as identifying bias in a statement, judging the logic of an argument, or evaluating the accuracy of a given factual claim (1).

It is reasonable to conclude that if the activity includes areas such as categorizing, problem solving, analyzing, generalizing, and evaluating, it becomes a critical thinking activity.

Because introducing new vocabulary is one of the prerequisites of good teaching, vocabulary study provides an outlet through which all secondary education disciplines can teach thinking skills. This chapter provides a group of unrelated vocabulary exercises that can be used in the various disciplines to provide vocabulary enrichment and practice in thinking.

SYLLACROSTIC (ALL AREAS)

The syllacrostic is a variation of the crossword puzzle and can be used to reinforce a wide variety of word skills including syllabication, synonyms, antonyms, homonyms, and vocabulary. In order to solve the puzzle, students will have to analyze the data given. The material for this activity can be drawn from any of the content areas.

It is simple to construct a syllacrostic. First choose a general topic. Then decide on the terms you want to use. Next take a sheet of paper and draw a box at the top. This is the syllabox.

Below the box and to the left of the page, list definitions for the terms you've chosen. To the right of each definition, draw a line. Students will write the word that fits the definition on this line. Inside the syllabox, write all your terms in syllable form, listing each syllable separately and alphabetically. Students must read the definitions and then attempt to construct the right answer from the syllables provided. The number of syllables in each term can be written in parentheses.

Mathematics Syllacrostic

a	er	oc	ri
al	ge	om	ta
an	gle	pen	tan
cir	gon	quad	tri
cle	hex	rec	try
e	lat		

---

1. A set of points, all equally distant from one certain point.
   (2) _____
2. The space between two lines of surfaces that meet.
   (2) _____
3. A figure having six sides and six angles. (3) _____
4. A figure having eight sides and eight angles. (3) _____

5. A figure having five sides and five angles. (3) _____
6. A figure having four sides and four angles. (5) _____
7. A figure having four sides and four right angles.
   (3) _____
8. A figure having three sides and three angles.
   (3) _____
9. The study that measures and compares lines, angles, surfaces, and solids. (4) _____

Answers: 1. circle 2. angle 3. hexagon 4. octagon 5. pentagon
6. quadrilateral 7. rectangle 8. triangle 9. geometry

SMASHING TV SYNONYMS (Reading, English)

The purpose of this activity is to give students practice in working with synonyms through creative thinking and use of a thesaurus. Learners need to be aware that there are many ways of stating ideas. This exercise will show learners that the television shows they watch could have been called by other words which retain the same meaning. This activity is a vocabulary building exercise. It also causes students to think creatively as they try to figure out names for popular shows.

Student Directions: On this sheet you will find the names of ten popular television shows. The titles do not look familiar because they are synonyms for the shows' real titles. Your job is to figure out what the real titles are. You may use your dictionary or thesaurus to help figure out the real titles.

1. Administration of Justice in Darkness
2. The Power Clan
3. Unlike Blows
4. The U.S. Stationary Musical Performers
5. Household Knots
6. The Lady Records Homicides
7. Which Person Is in Charge?
8. Astounding Tales
9. Acclaim
10. Events in Existence

Answers:
1. Night Court
2. Dynasty
3. Different Strokes
4. American Bandstand
5. Family Ties
6. Murder She Wrote
7. Who's the Boss?
8. Amazing Stories
9. Fame
10. Facts of Life

A variation of this activity would be to give students a list of current television shows or song titles and have them create alternative titles.

CATCH THE CONNECTION (English, Social Studies, Reading)

This activity is designed to provide an opportunity for students to analyze the relationship between sets of words and to produce a word that corresponds to the given set in the same way.

Student Directions: In each set of words given below, you will find two words that have a definite relationship. Choose from the vocabulary list one of the words that fits the single word in the same way as the paired words. Insert this word where the ? appears.

1. dim	jump	4. lake	paddle
fade	?	?	row
2. mask	geese	5. chimpanzee	apple
hide	?	ape	?
3. find	dirt	6. sink	reward
?	filth	rise	?

Vocabulary words: leap   discover   fowl   lagoon   fruit   punish
Answers: 1. leap   2. fowl   3. discover   4. lagoon   5. fruit   6. punish

CREATE A CATEGORY (All Areas)

The purpose of this activity is to provide students with an opportunity to analyze a list and to come up with a category that relates to the words in the list. This can be done in most content areas including science, math, English, social studies, and home economics.

Student Directions: In each of the sets below, three of the words are related. Circle the word that is unrelated. On the line at the top of the set, write the word or phrase that explains the relationship existing among the remaining three words.

1. _____

    pennies
    nickels
    dimes
    squirrels

2. _____

    polygon
    quadrilateral
    circle
    hexagon

3. _____

    iris
    grass
    petunia
    daisy

4. _____

    snake
    sparrow
    crow
    eagle

5. _____

    wok
    counter
    electric fry pan
    microwave

6. _____

    educational
    enormous
    comedy
    adventure

Answers: 1. *coins*, squirrels 2. *figures with straight edges*, circle 3. *flowers*, grass 4. *birds*, snake 5. *things that cook*, counter 6. *kinds of TV programs*, enormous

THINKING IN MATH

This activity gives students an opportunity to evaluate the facts that are given and to come up with a solution to the problem.

Student Directions: Tina just got four new stamps for her collection. She is confused about which stamp comes from which country. Can you sort out the stamps?

Country   _____   _____   _____   _____

Color   _____   _____   _____   _____

Picture   _____   _____   _____   _____

1. The stamp with the train on it is pink.
2. The German stamp has a picture of a runner.
3. The flower is not on the French stamp.
4. The Swedish stamp is not pink.
5. The plane is not on a yellow stamp.
6. The United States stamp is blue.
7. The flower is on a violet stamp.

Answers:

Country	France	Germany	U.S.	Sweden
Color	pink	yellow	blue	violet
Picture	train	runner	plane	flower

SUMMARY

To obtain a well-rounded education, a student has to be taught more than just the basics. He or she needs to be taught to think. Through the preceding vocabulary activities, students will be challenged to use key thinking skills. They will be given an opportunity to analyze data and relationships between words. They will categorize words with commonalities. They will evaluate facts and create solutions. In short, by engaging in these activities, students will take a positive step toward becoming the thinkers and problem solvers they will need to be to take positions in today's complex world.

REFERENCES

1. Beyer, Barry K. "Common Sense About Teaching Thinking Skills." *Educational Leadership* (November 1983): 41–49.
2. Robertson, Judy, and Strange, Vonna. "Principles of Compagination: A Critical Analysis/Process Approach." *The Reader IRA in Arkansas* 9, no. 1 (October 1985): 4–7.

TEACHING CRITICAL THINKING: ARE WE MAKING CRITICAL MISTAKES? POSSIBLE SOLUTIONS

by Robert J. Sternberg

Robert J. Sternberg *argues that conventional thinking skills programs present problems unlike those that students will encounter as adults: there is often not a "best possible" solution, problems are complicated and intractable, and important consequences result from whatever solutions are chosen. He has devised a thinking skills program to train students for real-life types of problems. This program,* Intelligence Applied, *teaches general intellectual skills and critical thinking skills to high school and college students. The program uses a wide range of problems— from "neat academic ones to messy practical ones"—many of which have no "right" answers. Sternberg describes several aspects of the program, and shows how they deal with a range of problem types. He feels strongly that students will not be able to transfer thinking skills into everyday life unless "programs designed to teach thinking skills reflect the realities of everyday problem solving and decision making."*

This chapter is condensed from a two-part version that appeared in Phi Delta Kappan, *November and December 1985. Reprinted with permission.*

The author is Associate Professor, Department of Psychology, at Yale University, New Haven, Connecticut.

Probably never before in the history of educational practice has there been a greater push to teach children to think critically. The signs are everywhere: multiple alternative programs to teach critical thinking at a variety of ages (1), tomes that review in some detail the numerous programs available (2), workshops for teachers and administrators sponsored by prestigious educational organizations, and an outpouring of journal articles on teaching critical thinking.

However, what is required for critical thinking in adulthood and what school programs are doing to develop critical thinking have little relation to one another. In the real world, problems are not easily defined, information needed to solve a problem is often not readily available, solutions are context-related, and a "best possible" solution is not often clear. Moreover, the problems—and their possible solutions—have important consequences, and many problems are complicated, messy, and stubbornly persistent.

What's to be done? If current approaches to teaching critical thinking do not deal adequately with the demands of critical thinking in everyday life, then how are we to train students for the demands that life will present them?

I do not believe that the problem we face is insoluble—though it is complicated, and, like most real-life problems, there is no one right solution. One possible solution is to supplement the kinds of training in critical thinking that we are now giving students with training that involves solving real-life problems. In my own theory of intelligence (3), I have distinguished between the more academic and the more practical applications of thinking skills, and I have found in my research that the skillful application of thinking skills to one of these domains in no way insures their skillful application to the other. Moreover, good thinking in one academic or practical area of endeavor does not guarantee good thinking in another. So programs need to sample a variety of content domains and a variety of thinking skills—and to sample them in ways that are true to the way problems appear in our everyday lives.

In my own program for training thinking skills (4), I have attempted to address some of the problems I have noted in conventional thinking skills programs by including a range of problems—from neat academic ones to messy practical ones. When I have presented a précis of the program to audiences and have described some of the practical problems, I have been challenged on several occasions with regard to my wisdom in including problems that have no "right" answers. After all, how can solutions to such problems be objectively scored? They can't be, of course, any more than solutions to any of life's significant problems can be objectively scored.

Teachers and students are often less comfortable with these less academic problems in the program—resolving conflicts, using informal knowledge to reach complex decisions, deciding what kinds of responses are adaptive or maladaptive in given situations, and so on. But comfort at the cost of reality is no virtue. If we wish to prepare students to solve the problems they will confront in their lives, then we must present them with realistic simulations of real problems, not merely with problems that are tailored to our convenience because they are objectively scorable or have been removed from context.

The time has come to be critical of critical-thinking programs. But I do not believe that we need to throw away what we have. Much of what we have is quite good (5). Moreover, there are even a handful of programs, such as Philosophy for Children, that take into account at least some of the issues I have raised. What we must do is supplement what we have and make it better. And we can start right now. Do you have a real problem you are having trouble solving? Present it to your class. They may not solve it, but they'll learn something from trying.

We need not continue to make the mistakes we have been making, and some programs are less susceptible to these mistakes than others. In the remainder of this article, I describe my new program, *Intelligence Applied*, which was designed to avoid as many of these mistakes as possible.

Intelligence Applied is a yearlong course that trains intellectual skills in general and critical-thinking skills in particular. It is intended for students in high school or college. Students may be of any socioeconomic level, although, in order to profit fully, high school students using the program should be of at least average ability.

The program is divided into five parts. The first provides some historical background on theories of intelligence and on attempts to increase intelligence. It also describes the "triarchic" theory of human intelligence on which the program is based (6). According to this theory, intelligence must be understood in its relation to the internal, mental world of the individual; to the external, environmental world of the individual; and to the individual's experience as it relates to the internal and external worlds.

The second part of the program contains training material relevant to intellectual skills that deal with the internal world of the individual. This training material is directed at three kinds of mental processes: 1) metacomponents, or the executive processes used to plan, monitor, and evaluate problem solving; 2) performance components, or the nonexecutive processes used to carry out the instructions of the metacomponents; and 3) knowledge-acquisition components, or the nonexecutive processes used to learn how to solve the problems that are then controlled by the metacomponents and solved by the performance components.

For example, consider a problem of analogical reasoning: WASHINGTON : 1 : : LINCOLN : (a. 5, b. 10, c. 15, d. 20). Metacomponents are used to judge the nature of the problem (that it is an analogy), to decide on the steps that are needed to solve the problem (e.g., understanding each of the terms of the analogy, inferring the relation between WASHINGTON and 1, applying this relation from LINCOLN to each of the possible answers, and so on), to decide the order in which these steps should be executed, to monitor whether the steps one has chosen are really leading to a solution, and the like. Performance components are used to actually execute the steps in solving the problem. Knowledge-acquisition components were used at some time in the past to learn how to solve analogies of this sort. The three kinds of components are used interactively to figure out that the analogy deals with the faces of Presidents that appear on currency.

The third part of the program contains material relevant to the experience of the individual in solving problems presented by various kinds of tasks and situations. In particular, individuals receive instruction and practice in how to deal with novel kinds of problems and situations and in how to automatize (make subconscious) various aspects of information processing.

For example, in the section on dealing with novelty, one might be presented with a counterfactual analogy that is a modification of the one presented above. It might read: Suppose that the denominations of all currency were doubled in value. Then what would be the completion of WASHINGTON : 2 : : LINCOLN : (a. 10, b. 20, c. 25, d. 40)? The solution now becomes 10. In this problem and others in the section dealing with novelty, students must learn to think in new ways and to deal with problems that differ in kind or in content from those to which they are accustomed.

The fourth part of the program contains training and exercises in intelligence as it is applied to everyday life. In this part of the program, students face everyday problems: resolving conflicts, making decisions about relationships with other people, decoding nonverbal cues, and so on. The idea is to train and encourage students to apply the mental processes of intelligence to everyday life, not merely to academic situations.

The fifth and final part of the program deals with the emotional and motivational blocks that prevent students from applying their intelligence to everyday living—blocks such as lack of motivation, lack of perseverance, inability to translate thought into action, fear of failure, and spreading oneself too thin.

Now, just how does this program circumvent the pitfalls described earlier? Consider each of the "critical mistakes" and how the program responds to it.

1. and 2. *Problems of recognition and definition.* Recognizing the existence and nature of a problem are metacomponents of the process of solving problems. Consider, for example, the part of the program that deals with "defining the nature of a problem." This section opens with some real-life illustrations of inadequate definitions of problems, including people unable to meet their expenses who define the problem as underearning rather than overspending; a political leader who defined a problem as one of covering up the events surrounding a politically motivated burglary rather than one of minimizing the damages of full disclosure; and second-graders at a Hebrew day school who, when given an ability test in English in the afternoon, read it right to left because they believed that material presented in the afternoon—their normal time for learning Hebrew—should always be read from right to left. The program then contains tips on improving one's definition of problems, such as reread or reconsider the question, redefine goals, and ask whether the goal

toward which one is striving is realistic. Finally, students are presented with a series of problems that develop skills in defining problems.

An example of a problem that develops skills in defining problems is the nine-dot problem. In this problem the student is presented with three aligned rows of three dots each and is instructed to connect the dots with straight lines, without lifting the pencil from the paper and without drawing more than four lines. Most students fail to solve the problem without guidance, in part because they assume that the pencil must stay within the implicit perimeter defined by the nine dots. In fact, the problem can be solved only if the pencil goes outside that assumed perimeter. After students have tried the problem on their own, the text makes the point that we often introduce constraints into the definition of a problem that are not actually there in the first place.

3. *Ill-structured problems.* Many of the problems in the training program are ill-structured. That is, there is no crystal-clear, step-by-step path to a solution. The nine-dot problem is one example of such an ill-structured problem.

The hatrack problem is another. In it, students are told to use a variety of prespecified items to construct a hatrack. The critical elements that students must somehow recognize are that two poles can be bound together with a C-clamp and can be supported by wedging them, like a pole lamp, against the floor and ceiling of a room and that the clamp can be used as a hook for the hat. There is no clear path to attaining these two insights in this ill-structured problem.

Finally, consider one of the mathematical insight problems included in the text: "A man was putting some finishing touches on his house and realized that he needed one thing that he did not have. He went to the hardware store and asked the clerk, 'How much will 150 cost me?' The clerk in the hardware store answered, 'They are 75 cents apiece, so 150 will cost you $2.25.' What did the man buy?" Treating this as a well-structured problem will lead only to failure. None of the routine algorithms that students might readily apply to this problem will work. Rather, students must look at the problem in a new way in order to realize that the man bought house numbers. Again, no clear path to this insight exists, and one must often realize that problems that appear to be well-structured may in fact be ill-structured.

4. through 6. *The solution of everyday problems depends on context, and there is no one best solution to such problems.* Unlike many other programs, *Intelligence Applied* emphasizes everyday problem solving in everyday contexts, both in a special chapter on practical intelligence and in numerous illustrations and practice exercises throughout the book. For example, a problem on resource allocation requires the student to imagine that he or she is the campaign manager for a senatorial candidate

and has $100,000 to spend on a political campaign. The student must decide how to allocate the funds. In another problem on resource allocation, the student has to decide what kinds of tests should be conducted before a new product, the widget, is introduced to the market. In a problem on solution monitoring, the student must consider what kinds of steps could be taken to monitor adherence to an arms-reduction treaty, given the possible tendency of the parties to such an agreement to cheat. Thus the program contains not only the usual kinds of highly structured problems whose solutions are unique and independent of context, but also problems that have no unique solution and whose solutions depend on context.

The role of everyday context is emphasized throughout the program because most problems that an individual faces must take account of such context. When students are instructed in the components of thinking, they are usually given a set of fairly academic kinds of problems. For example, the performance component of inference is taught, in part, in the context of test-like analogies, both verbal and nonverbal.

But in *Intelligence Applied* this component of thinking is also taught through everyday inferences and the fallacies that accompany them. For example, one inferential-fallacy problem tells students that "Josh and Sandy were discussing the Reds and the Blues, two baseball teams. Sandy asked Josh why he thought the Reds had a better chance of winning the pennant this year than did the Blues; Josh replied, 'If every man on the Red team is better than every man on the Blue team, then the Reds must be the better team.' " The inferential fallacy of "composition" in this example is not uncommon. Any number of "blue-ribbon" commissions consist of sets of experts who, individually, are among the best in their fields but who, collectively, prove unable to work together.

The role of context is so central to the *Intelligence Applied* program that students are taught explicitly how to use context in their learning and problem solving. The section of the program that deals with learning vocabulary, for example, does not merely present lists of words to be memorized, nor does it concentrate merely on learning specific words from context. Rather, it sharpens the general learning-to-learn skills that students will need to figure out the meanings of words from context. The emphasis is not on specific word knowledge (there are too many words to make such training very useful) but on teaching students how to use context to acquire word knowledge.

7. *The role of informal knowledge in problem solving*. Everyday problem solving depends on informal knowledge at least as much as it depends on formal knowledge, and the *Intelligence Applied* program recognizes this fact. One kind of problem from the chapter on practical intelligence, for example, shows students pictures of two people interacting and tells them that one of the people is the other's supervi-

sor. Students must decode nonverbal cues to determine which individual is the supervisor. When students first encounter such problems, it is unlikely that they have ever been formally taught what kinds of cues to look for. Hence they must rely on informal knowledge. The program actually teaches students to look for such nonverbal cues as direction of gaze, relative formality of dress, age, tenseness of hands, and socioeconomic class.

Take an example in a lighter vein. Students are shown pictures of couples, half of which are genuine (they are involved in a close relationship) and half of which are fake (the couples were posed by a photographer to look as if they were involved in a close relationship). Once again, students are asked to use informal knowledge to decide which couples are real and which are fake. Later, the students are taught to look for such clues as relaxation, body lean, positioning of arms and legs, tenseness of hands, match in socioeconomic class, distance between the bodies, and amount of physical contact.

In another section of the same chapter, students are presented with this problem: "Rate the following strategies of working according to how important you believe them to be for doing well at the day-to-day work of a business manager: a) think in terms of tasks accomplished rather than hours spent working, b) be in charge of all phases of every task or project you are involved with, c) use a daily list of goals arranged according to your priorities, d) carefully consider the optimal strategy before beginning a task, e) reward yourself upon completion of important tasks." Students give their ratings on a scale of 1 to 7. Once again, their ability to make sensible ratings depends on informal rather than on formal knowledge.

8. *Consequentiality of solutions.* Although the *Intelligence Applied* program contains its share of academic kinds of problems, it also introduces problems in which the solutions matter, either to the student or to others. For example, one insight problem in the text asks the student to figure out from given information how Napoleon died. The answer, though still disputed in some quarters, is from arsenic poisoning caused by arsenic present in wallpaper. Just as death from lead poisoning is not uncommon in our own times, death from arsenic poisoning was not an uncommon cause of death in the past, and Napoleon's death and how he died certainly had an impact on the world.

Students are encouraged to think about problems relevant to their own lives as well as to the lives of others. For example, in a kind of problem that recurs throughout the text, students are asked to think of an instance in their own lives in which the better use of a given component of information processing, such as the metacomponent of strategy selection, might have resulted in better problem-solving performance. Or students might be given a problem and asked how conscious and deliberate application of a component of information processing might improve problem solving or decision making. In one such problem for strategy selection, students are asked to "list some of the steps [they] would take in order to help [them] decide among colleges and choose the best one."

9. *Group problem solving.* The training program discusses some of the problems associated with group problem solving, especially the problem of "groupthink," in which the efforts of a group of thinkers are much less than the sum of their individual efforts. But the role of group problem solving in the program does not end with the text itself. The text of the *Intelligence Applied* program is accompanied by an instructor's manual that suggests many opportunities for group problem solving. For example, each chapter in the manual has a list of individual and group projects that can be done by members of the class.

10. *The complication, messiness, and stubbornness of everyday problems.* The text contains problems that reflect these unpleasant attributes of everyday problems. For example, in conflict-resolution problems, students are given case studies of conflicts that need to be resolved. The problems may be interpersonal, interorganizational, or international. The students must decide on the merits of the alternative ways of resolving the conflicts. In one such conflict, a family is deciding whether or not the wife's mother should move in with them. In another problem, two nations depend on water from a single river, and the nation upstream is unintentionally polluting the water through the generation of hydroelectric power. These scenarios are constructed so that the case for each party to the conflict is rated roughly equal in merit. The resolution of the conflicts is thus by no means a routine affair. In these problems students must face the complication, messiness, and stubbornness of the problems that confront them in their daily lives.

I have tried to show that the critical mistakes we make in the teaching of critical thinking are not inevitable, nor are they irremediable. Rather, programs can be constructed that reflect the realities of critical thinking in everyday life. *Intelligence Applied* is one example, but the possibilities abound for constructing other valuable programs.

Still, unless programs designed to teach thinking skills reflect the realities of everyday problem solving and decision making, it is doubtful that students will be able to apply what they have learned from these programs to their everyday lives. The only way to insure the transfer of training from thinking-skills programs to everyday lives is to teach for that transfer, and, at a minimum, such teaching involves avoiding the critical mistakes I cited above. We must teach students to solve problems

215

as they occur in the real world, not as they appear in the simple, orderly world of courses in critical thinking—a world in which, unfortunately, none of us lives.

REFERENCES

1. Martin V. Covington and others, *The Productive Thinking Program: A Course in Learning to Think* (Columbus, O.: Charles Merrill, 1974); Reuven Feuerstein and others, *Instrumental Enrichment: An Intervention Program for Cognitive Modifiability* (Baltimore: University Park Press, 1980); Matthew Lipman, Ann M. Sharp, and Frederick S. Oscanyan, *Philosophy in the Classroom*, 2d ed. (Philadelphia: Temple University Press, 1980); and Arthur Whimbey, with Linda S. Whimbey, *Intelligence Can Be Taught* (New York: E. P. Dutton, 1975).

2. Susan Chipman, Judith Siegel, and Robert Glaser, eds., *Thinking and Learning Skills: Current Research and Open Questions,* 2 vols. (Hillsdale, N.J.: Erlbaum, 1985); and Raymond S. Nickerson, David N. Perkins, and Edward E. Smith, *Teaching Thinking* (New York: Academic Press, forthcoming.)

3. Robert J. Sternberg, *Beyond I.Q.: A Triarchic Theory of Human Intelligence* (New York: Cambridge University Press, 1985).

4. Robert J. Sternberg, *Intelligence Applied: Understanding and Increasing Intellectual Skills* (San Diego, Calif.: Harcourt Brace Jovanovich, forthcoming).

5. For a discussion of what is good in what we now have, see Robert J. Sternberg, "How Can We Teach Intelligence?" *Educational Leadership* 42 (1984): 38–50.

6. Sternberg, *Beyond I.Q.*

THE DIRECT TEACHING OF THINKING AS A SKILL

by Edward de Bono

Edward de Bono discusses his view of the thinking process and the best means of teaching thinking as a skill. He defines thinking as "the operating skill with which intelligence acts upon experience," and finds that perception and thinking have a crucial relationship, which is infrequently and insufficiently explored. Human beings have active, self-organizing systems. They arrange incoming information into patterns that allow complex tasks such as crossing a road and recognizing friends to become apparently simple. A pattern-making system has its disadvantages, however: the point-to-point thinking underlying it can lead to an inappropriate focus on details. This, in turn, can lead one away from finding solutions to problems.

de Bono feels that teaching thinking as part of content area instruction is ineffective, since "attending to content distracts from attending to the thinking tools being used." His CoRT system is not taught as part of content; it teaches students to use a set of thinking "tools" that can be transferred to different academic areas and to real-life situations.

This chapter is reprinted with permission from Phi Delta Kappan *(June 1983): 703–8. Copyright © 1983 by Edward de Bono.*

The author is director of the Cognitive Research Trust in Cambridge, England, and of the Edward de Bono Resource Center, 56 Harrison Street, New Rochelle, NY 10801.

A major trend may be developing in education toward the direct teaching of thinking as a skill. I intend in this article to answer two basic questions related to this trend. First, what is thinking? And second, how can we teach thinking directly? My answers spring from 16 years of experience in the field. During this time I developed an instructional program on thinking skills that is now used by several million schoolchildren in many different countries and cultures.

Of course, some educators believe that thinking is simply a matter of innate intelligence. Two corollaries follow from this belief: (1) we do not have to do anything specific to help highly intelligent individuals learn how to think, and (2) there is little we can do to help less intelligent individuals learn how to think. Thus those who hold this belief rest content. Yet many highly intelligent individuals often seem to be rather ineffective thinkers. Such people are often good at reactive thinking and puzzle solving—but less able to think about topics that require a broader view. They may show cleverness, but not wisdom.

I prefer to see the relationship between intelligence and thinking as similar to the relationship between a car and its driver. Engineering determines the innate potential of the car, but the skill with which the car is driven must be learned and practiced. Thus I would define thinking as "the operating skill with which intelligence acts upon experience."

What, then, is the relationship of information to thinking? It seems obvious to me that God can neither think nor have a sense of humor. Perfect knowledge precludes the need to move from one arrangement of knowledge to a better one. Thus perfect knowledge makes thinking unnecessary. Nonetheless, educators often seem to believe that we can attain such perfect knowledge. However, even if it were possible to absorb perfect knowledge about the past, we can only have very partial knowledge about the future. Yet, as soon as a youngster leaves school, he or she will be operating in the future. Every initiative, decision, or plan will be carried out in the future and thus will require thinking, not just the sorting and re-sorting of knowledge. I have coined the term "operacy" to stand alongside literacy and numeracy as a primary goal of education. Operacy is the skill of doing things, of making things happen. The type of thinking that my program (which I will describe later) teaches is very much concerned with operacy.

In short, information is no substitute for thinking, and thinking is no substitute for information. The dilemma is that there is never enough time to teach all the information that could usefully be taught. Yet we may have to reduce the time we spend teaching information, in order to focus instead on the direct teaching of thinking skills.

The relationship between logic and thinking is likewise not a linear one. The computer world has a saying, "Garbage in—garbage out." In other words, even if the computer is working flawlessly, this will not validate a given outcome. Bad logic makes for bad thinking, but good logic (like the flawless computer) does not insure good thinking. Every logician knows that a conclusion is only as good as the premises. Mathematics, logic (of various sorts), and—increasingly—data processing are excellent service tools. But the deeper we advance into the computer age, the greater the need to emphasize the perceptual side of thinking, which these tools serve.

Meanwhile, emotions, values, and feelings influence thinking at three stages. We may feel a strong emotion (e.g., fear, anger, hatred) even before we encounter a situation. That emotion channels our perceptions. More usually, there is a brief period of undirected perception, until we recognize the situation. This recognition triggers emotion, which thereafter channels perception. The trained thinker should be operating in the third mode: perception explores the situation as broadly as possible, and, in the end, emotions determine the decision. There is no contradiction at all between emotions and thinking. The purpose of thinking is to arrange the world so that our emotions can be applied in a valuable manner.

The relationship of perception to thinking is, to my mind, the crucial area. In the past, far too many of our approaches to thinking (e.g., mathematics, logic) have concerned themselves with the "processing" aspect. We are rather good at processing but poor in the perceptual area.

What do I mean by perception? Quite simply, the way our minds make sense of the world around us. Language is a reflection of our traditional perceptions (as distinct from the moment-to-moment ones). Understanding how perception works is not so easy. But this is a crucial point—one that has a direct effect on the way we teach thinking.

Imagine a man holding a small block of wood. He releases the wood, and it falls to the ground. When he releases it a second time, the wood moves upward. This is strange and mysterious behavior. The third time he releases the wood, it remains exactly where it is—suspended in space. This is also mysterious behavior. If I were now to reveal that, in the second instance, the man was standing at the bottom of a swimming pool, then it seems perfectly natural for the wood to float upward. In the third instance, the man is an astronaut in orbit; thus it is perfectly natural for wood to remain suspended, since it is weightless. Behavior that seemed strange and unaccountable suddenly seems normal and logical—once we have defined the "universe" in which it is taking place.

The traditional universe of information handling is a "passive" one. We record information through marks on paper or marks on magnetic tape. We can handle and process that information. The marks on the surface of the paper or tape and the information itself do not alter, unless we alter them.

An "active" system is totally different; here, the information actually organizes itself into patterns. We human beings have self-organizing information systems. I first wrote about them in 1969 in my book, *The Mechanism of Mind* (1). I showed then how such systems work, and I suggested how the structure of a nerve network would produce such pattern-making effects. My hypothesis has since been simulated by computer, and the nerve network functions substantially as I had suggested (2). In the world of information handling, the concept of self-organizing information systems is now coming to the fore (3). Such systems are quite different from our usual computers.

Once we enter the "universe" of active, self-organizing systems, then the behavior of such things as perception and creativity becomes quite clear. The processes are no longer mysterious. Just as happened with the block of wood, phenomena that seemed to be unaccountable are suddenly seen to be explicable—once we have identified the appropriate universe.

The function of a self-organizing system is to allow incoming experience to organize itself into patterns. We could loosely compare these patterns to the streets in a town. The self-organizing system is immensely efficient; it allows us to get up in the morning, cross a road, recognize friends, read and write. Without such a pattern-making and pattern-using system, we would spend about a month just in crossing a road.

However, the advantages of a patterning system are also its disadvantages. "Point-to-point thinking" is a good example. In this kind of thinking, we follow a pattern from one point to the next—and then follow the dominant pattern from that next point onward. In an experiment that I conducted jointly with the Inner London Education Authority (4), I asked 24 groups of 11-year-olds to discuss the suggestion that "bread, fish, and milk should be free." Although many of the children came from deprived backgrounds, 23 of the 24 groups opposed the idea of free bread, fish, and milk. The point-to-point thinking that led to this stand went as follows: (1) the shops would be crowded; (2) the buses going to the shops would be crowded; (3) the bus drivers would demand more money; (4) the drivers would not get more money, and they would go on strike; (5) other people would go on strike as well; and (6) there would be chaos—so giving away bread, fish, and milk is a bad idea. Thus can point-to-point thinking lead us astray, as we miss the forest while fixating on the trees.

However, direct teaching of thinking can offset the disadvantages of a patterning system. At the end of a pilot project on the teaching of thinking in Venezuelan schools, for example, we held a press conference. A journalist attending that conference claimed that all attempts to teach thinking are really a form of brainwashing in western capitalist values. The journalist happened to be wearing spectacles. So I removed her spectacles and asked what she used them for. She told me that she used the spectacles in order to see things more clearly. I then explained that the perceptual tools we were teaching in the lessons on thinking served the same purpose. The tools enable youngsters to scan their experiences so that they can see things more clearly and more broadly. A better map of the world is the result. These thinkers can still retain their original values and choices, however. Giving spectacles to nearsighted individuals enables them to see three glasses on a table—containing wine, orange juice, and milk. The individuals still exercise choice as to which drink each prefers. In the same way, our instructional program cuts across cultures and ideologies. The program is used in industrialized nations, such as Canada and Great Britain, and in developing nations, such as Venezuela and Malaysia; it will soon be used in Cuba, China, and Bulgaria—as well as in Catholic Ireland.

My point is that, in terms of perception we need to achieve two things: (1) the ability to see things more clearly and more broadly and (2) the ability to see things differently (i.e., creativity or "lateral thinking" [5]). As I have said, perception takes place in an "active" information system. Such systems allow experience to organize itself into immensely useful patterns, without which life would be impossible. But, as I said above, the very advantages of the patterning system are also its disadvantages. We must overcome these disadvantages and improve perception in two ways: in breadth and in creativity or lateral thinking (both of which fall under the heading of "change").

Let me turn now to the second question that I posed at the beginning of this article. How can we teach thinking as a skill? Such teaching is going on right now; it is not tomorrow's dream, but today's reality. Millions of children are involved. In Venezuela, for example, 106,000 teachers have been trained to use my program, and every schoolchild takes a course in thinking. By law, Venezuelan schoolchildren in every grade must have two hours of direct instruction per week in thinking skills. The contracts of some labor union members in Venezuela specify that their employers must make provisions to teach them thinking skills. My program is also in use in many other countries—including Australia, the U.S., and Israel, as well as those nations I have mentioned previously.

The program of which I speak is called CoRT. (The acronym stands for Cognitive Research Trust, located in Cambridge, England.) I have already outlined the theoretical foundation for the design of this program. The lessons themselves focus on the perceptual aspect of thinking. The design of the tools takes into account the behavior of self-organizing patterning systems.

The design criteria for a practical instructional program should include the following elements.

- The program should be usable by teachers who represent a wide range of teaching talents, not just by the highly gifted or the highly qualified. (The 106,000 Venezuelan teachers were not all geniuses.)
- The program should not require complicated teacher training, since it is difficult to generalize such programs. (The CoRT program can be used by teachers with no special training or with only simple training.)
- The program should be robust enough to resist damage as it is passed along from trainer to trainer—and thence from new trainer to teachers and, finally, to pupils.

221

- The program should employ parallel design so that, if some parts of the program are badly taught and other parts are skipped or later forgotten, what remains is usable and valuable in its own right. (This contrasts with hierarchical design, in which a student must grasp a basic concept before moving on to the next concept layer; failure at any concept layer in a program of this type makes the whole system unworkable.)
- The program should be enjoyable for both teachers and youngsters.
- The program should focus on thinking skills that help a learner to function better in his or her life outside of school, not merely to become more proficient at solving puzzles or playing games.

Before considering ways of teaching thinking, we must confront a prior question: Should thinking be taught in its own right? Certain practical considerations affect the answer to this question. For example, there are no gaps in the school schedule as it now exists. Thus it seems to make more sense to insert thinking skills into an existing subject area. English makes a good home, because a natural synergy exists between thinking and the expression of thought in language. In addition, the teaching style is often more open-ended in English classes than in some other subject areas. However, the CoRT program has been used effectively by science teachers, by music teachers, and even by physical education teachers.

Despite these practical considerations, I believe that we should have a specific place in the curriculum that is set aside for the teaching of thinking skills. This formal recognition is essential so that pupils, teachers, and parents all recognize that thinking skills are being taught directly. In time, I would certainly hope that the skills taught in the "thinking lessons" would find their ways into such subject areas as geography, history, social studies, and science. However, the first step is to establish "thinking" as a subject in its own right.

Having dealt with this question, we can now look at some of the traditional approaches to the teaching of thinking:

- *Logic, mathematics, and data processing.* These are very important subjects, but they concern themselves with processing, not with the perceptual side of thinking. The better that students become at processing, the more they need to strengthen their perception.
- *Critical thinking.* This is a popular approach because it is traditional. It also employs a relatively easy teaching method (the spotting of faults). This approach has only limited value, however. The spotting of faults—regardless of its usefulness in debate or argument—is only one aspect of thinking. The approach includes no generative, constructive, or creative elements. The avoidance of faults does not improve one's ability

to plan or to make decisions. The avoidance of faults is, to my mind, an aspect of thinking that has traditionally been overvalued.

• *Discussion.* Directly or indirectly, discussion must be the most widely used method of teaching thinking. Youngsters are asked to discuss (or write essays on) a subject. The aim is to provide practice in thinking. The teacher notes and comments on faults and inappropriate uses of evidence, hoping that students will extract from these clues some general principles of thinking, which they will then use in future, unrelated situations. In reality, relatively little transfer of thinking skills from one situation to another takes place.

• *Puzzles, games, and simulations.* I have used games and problems as motivators, to get people interested in thinking. However, because of the difficulty of transfer, I do not believe that such devices have much teaching value. A skillful chess player does not transfer to his or her everyday life the fine sense of strategy developed through playing this game. A youngster may develop a puzzle-solving method, but thinking does not seem to proceed in that same fashion in real life. I have grave reservations about the traditional information-processing model of thinking, which seems more a description than a system of operating.

This brings me to the central problem: transfer and content. Does a generalizable skill of thinking exist? Many theorists think not. They believe instead that there is thinking in mathematics, thinking in science, and thinking in history—but that in each case the rules are different, just as the rules for Monopoly differ from those for chess. I do not see this as a point of view with which I must either agree or disagree totally. Clearly, subject idioms exist. Nevertheless, it is possible to establish both habits of mind and specific thinking techniques that can be applied in any subject area. For example, the willingness to look for alternatives is a generalizable thinking habit. And deliberate provocation is a technique that can be applied to generate ideas in any situation.

Because we cannot succeed in teaching generalizable thinking skills through the use of specific content materials, some theorists believe that such skills cannot exist. But there is another way of looking at this situation: the view that generalizable thinking skills exist but cannot be taught using specific content. My experience has led me to the latter view. As I have already noted with regard to the "discussion method" of teaching thinking skills, little transfer of such skills seems to take place from one situation to another. Given the mechanics of perception and attention, this is hardly surprising. If the subject of a discussion is interesting, then—by definition—attention follows this interest. But this attention is not focused on the metacognitive level; that is, participants are not thinking about the *thinking* that they are using to discuss the subject. Moreover, it is very difficult to transfer a complex action sequence from one situation to another. That is why the CoRT program deliberately focuses on "tools" that can be transferred.

I have noticed among U.S. educators a tendency to try to teach thinking through content materials. This approach seems—to its proponents—to have two merits. First, this approach makes it easier to introduce thinking into the curriculum, because the material must be covered anyway (and it is already familiar to the teacher). Second, this approach seems to be killing two birds with one stone: teaching thinking *and* teaching content. But this approach is not effective. I am afraid that the nettle must be grasped. Either one wishes to teach thinking effectively or merely to make a token gesture. Attending to content distracts from attending to the thinking tools being used. Theory predicts this outcome: you cannot build meta-patterns on one level and experience patterns on another level at the same time. Experience backs up this expectation. Wherever there has been an attempt to teach thinking skills and content together, the training in thinking seems to be weaker than when those skills are taught in isolation.

So what is the CoRT method? It is best to illustrate this method with an example.

I was teaching a class of 30 boys, all 11 years of age, in Sydney, Australia. I asked if they would each like to be given $5 a week for coming to school. All 30 thought this was a fine idea. "We could buy sweets or chewing gum. . . . We could buy comics. . . . We could get toys without having to ask Mum or Dad."

I then introduced and explained a simple tool called the PMI (which I will describe later). The explanation took about four minutes. In groups of five, the boys applied the PMI tool to the suggestion that they should be given $5 a week for coming to school. For three to four minutes they talked and thought on their own. At no time did I interfere. I never discussed the $5 suggestion, other than to state it. I did not suggest that the youngsters consider this, think of that, and so forth. At the end of their thinking time, the groups reported back to me: "The bigger boys would beat us up and take the money. . . . The school would raise its charges for meals. . . . Our parents would not buy us presents. . . . Who would decide how much money different ages received? . . . There would be less money to pay teachers. . . . There would be less money for a school minibus."

When they had finished their reports, I again asked the boys to express their views on the suggestion of pay for attending school. This time, 29 of the 30 had completely reversed their opinion and thought it a bad idea. We subsequently learned that the one holdout received *no* pocket money at home. The important point is that my contribution was minimal. I did not interact with the boys. I simply explained the PMI tool, and the boys then used it on their own—as *their* tool. My "superior" intelligence and broader experiences were not influences. The boys did their own thinking.

The PMI is a simple scanning tool designed to avoid the point-to-point thinking that I mentioned earlier. The thinker looks first in the Plus direction (good points), and then in the Minus direction (bad points), and finally in the Interesting direction (interesting things that might arise or are worth noting, even if they are neither good nor bad). Each direction is scanned formally, one after another. This formal scan produces a better and broader map. Thinking is used to explore, not merely to back up a snap judgment. The thinker then applies judgment to the better map. The PMI is the first of the 60 CoRT lessons.

For the rest of this particular lesson on thinking, I might have asked the boys to apply the PMI in various ways (e.g., one group doing only "Plus" or "Minus" or "Interesting") to a number of thinking items, such as: Should all cars be colored yellow? Would it be a good idea for everyone to wear a badge showing his or her mood at the moment? Is homework a good idea? Note that the items are not related. Moreover, the groups would be allowed to spend only two to three minutes on each. This is quite deliberate and essential to the method.

The items are switched rapidly so that attention stays on the PMI tool and *not on the content*. Once skill in the use of the tool is developed, students can apply the PMI to other situations in other settings. One girl told us how she used the PMI at home to decide whether or not to have her long hair cut. Some children report that they have used the PMI with their parents, in discussing such major decisions as moving to a new town or buying a car. This is the sort of transfer that the CoRT program aims to achieve.

The PMI is a scanning tool, not a judgment tool. If a thinker spots 10 "Plus" points and only two "Minus" points, this does not necessarily mean that the idea is a good one. Like all scanning, the PMI is subjective, depending on the thinker's perspective. One boy said, as a "Plus" point, that yellow cars would be kept cleaner. Another boy slated this as a "Minus" point—because he had to clean his dad's car and would therefore have to perform this chore more often. Both were right.

The PMI is designed to be artificial, memorable, and easy to pronounce. At first, some teachers rejected "PMI" as pointless jargon. They preferred to encourage or exhort the youngsters to look at the good points and the bad points in any situation. The youngsters probably did so—at that moment. However, without the artificial term "PMI" to crystallize the process and to create a meta-pattern, the exhortation does not stick. One teacher told me how he had used the term "PMI" and how

225

his colleague, in a parallel lesson, had used exhortation. His colleague was soon convinced of the value of the term "PMI."

One girl said that she initially thought the PMI a rather silly device, since she knew how she felt about a subject. But she noted that, as she wrote things down under each letter (she was doing a written exercise instead of the usual oral approach), she became less certain. In the end, the points she had written down did cause her to change her mind. Yet *she* had written down the points. That is precisely the purpose of a scanning tool.

It is important to realize that the description of thinking and the design of tools are two totally different things. It is possible to describe the process of thinking and to break it into components. But then one is tempted to turn each component into a tool, on the premise that, if the components are taught, thinking skills must surely be enhanced. However, teaching someone how to describe a flower does not teach him or her how to grow a flower. The purpose of analysis and the purpose of an operating tool are separate and distinct.

The CoRT tools are designed specifically as operating tools. Such a design has two components: (1) the tool must be easy to use, and (2) it must have a useful effect. Abstract analyses and subdivisions of the thinking process may be intellectually neat, but this does not guarantee usability or effectiveness. My many years of experience, working with thousands of executives and organizations in different countries, have given me some insight into those aspects of thinking that have practical value. I have also worked with scientists, designers, lawyers, and many others who are involved in the "action world" of thinking, as distinct from the "contemplative world."

The CoRT program (6) has six sections, each consisting of 10 lessons: CoRT I (breadth), CoRT II (organization), CoRT III (interaction), CoRT IV (creativity), CoRT V (information and feeling), and CoRT VI (action). All teachers who use the program should teach CoRT I. (Some teachers use *only* the 10 lessons of CoRT I.) Thereafter, the sections can be used in any order. For example, a teacher might use CoRT I, CoRT IV, and CoRT V. The last section (CoRT VI) is somewhat different from the other sections, in that it provides a framework for a staged approach to thinking.

I believe that thinking is best taught to 9-, 10-, and 11-year-olds. Youngsters in the middle grades really enjoy thinking and motivation is very high. They have sufficient verbal fluency and experience to operate the thinking tools. The curriculum is more easily modified in the middle grades to include thinking as a basic subject. But the CoRT materials have also been used with children younger than 9 and with students ranging in age from 12 to adult.

So basic is thinking as a skill that the same CoRT lessons have been used by children in the jungles of South America and by top executives of the Ford Motor Company, United Kingdom. The lessons have been taught to students ranging in I.Q. from below 80 to above 140. The lessons have also been used with groups of mixed ability.

David Lane, at the Hungerford Guidance Centre in London, found that the teaching of thinking to delinquent and violent youngsters brought about an improvement in behavior, as measured by a sharp fall in the number of disciplinary encounters these youngsters had with supervisors (7). William Copley and Edna Copley, in preliminary work at an institution for young offenders, found similar changes (8). They recounted how one youth, on the verge of attacking an officer with a hammer, brought to mind a thinking lesson concerned with consequences—and quietly put the hammer down. I mention these changes in behavior for two reasons. First, I believe that the true test of teaching thinking is the effect of such teaching on behavior. Second, we do not really have any adequate way of measuring thinking performance. Standardized tests are largely irrelevant, because they do not allow us to observe the thinker's composite performance.

John Edwards taught the CoRT program in lieu of a portion of the science syllabus to a class in Australia. Using an analysis-of-discourse approach to measurement, he found that the trained students did significantly better at thinking than untrained peers; the trained students even seemed to do better in science, although they had had less instructional time devoted to that subject (9). It is not difficult to show that pupils who have had training in thinking produce a wider scan when they are asked to consider some subject. In Ireland, Liam Staunton found that, before CoRT training, individuals produced an average of four sentences on a topic, whereas after CoRT training they produced an average of 47 (10). We are currently analyzing data from the experiment in Venezuela and data from the Schools Council project in England.

I prefer that CoRT users carry out their own tests and pilot projects. Tests carried out by the designers of a program are of limited value for two reasons: (1) the conditions of teaching are ideal (and often far removed from those prevailing in schools where the program will be used), and (2) such studies always contain an element of bias.

It is impossible, however, to measure the soft data: the confidence of those who have had training in thinking, the focus of their thinking, their willingness to think about things, the effectiveness of their thinking, their structured approach and breadth of consideration. Teachers often sum up these factors as "maturity," in commenting about those children who come to their classrooms after some training in thinking.

I would expect four levels of achievement in the acquisition of thinking skills through use of the CoRT program:

- *Level 1.* A general awareness of thinking as a skill. A willingness to "think" about something. A willingness to explore around a subject. A willingness to listen to others. No recollection of any specific thinking tool.

- *Level 2.* A more structured approach to thinking, including better balance, looking at the consequences of an action or choice (taking other people's views into account), and a search for alternatives. Perhaps a mention of a few of the CoRT tools.

- *Level 3.* Focused and deliberate use of some of the CoRT tools. The organization of thinking as a series of steps. A sense of purpose in thinking.

- *Level 4.* Fluent and appropriate use of many CoRT tools. Definite consciousness of the metacognitive level of thinking. Observation of and comment on the thinker's own thinking. The designing of thinking tasks and strategies, followed by the carrying out of these tasks.

In most situations, I would expect average attainment to fall somewhere between levels 1 and 2. With a more definite emphasis on "thinking," this would rise to a point between levels 2 and 3. Only in exceptional groups with thorough training would I expect to find average attainment at level 4.

Perhaps the most important aspect of the direct teaching of thinking as a skill is the self-image of a youngster as a "thinker," however. This is an operational image. Thinking becomes a skill at which the youngster can improve. Such a self-image is different from the more usual "value" images: "I am intelligent" (I get on well at school) or "I am not intelligent" (I do not get on well at school, and school is a bore). Value images are self-reinforcing. So are operational images—but the reinforcement goes in opposite directions at the negative end. In other words, the less intelligent students find repeated evidence of their lack of intelligence, but they also notice those occasions when they do manage to come up with good ideas.

REFERENCES

1. Edward de Bono, *The Mechanism of Mind* (New York: Simon & Schuster, 1969).
2. M. H. Lee and A. R. Maradurajan, "A Computer Package of the Evaluation of Neuron Models Involving Large Uniform Networks," *International Journal of Man-Machine Studies* (1982): 189–210.

3. John Hopfield, "Brain, Computer, and Memory," *Engineering and Science* (September 1982).
4. Unpublished material, Cognitive Research Trust.
5. Edward de Bono, *Lateral Thinking* (New York: Harper and Row, 1970).
6. CoRT Thinking Program, Pergamon, Inc., Maxwell House, Fairview Park, Elmsford, N.Y. 10523.
7. Personal communication from David Lane.
8. William Copley and Edna Copley, *Practical Teaching of Thinking*, forthcoming.
9. Unpublished paper by John Edwards, James Cook University, Queensland, Australia.
10. Personal communication from Liam Staunton.

DEVELOPING STUDENTS' THINKING SKILLS THROUGH MULTIPLE PERSPECTIVES

by Ronald Lee Rubin

Ronald Lee Rubin teaches students to "appreciate and understand multiple perspectives" through methods of divergent questioning. Throughout his chapter, Rubin introduces a variety of techniques for encouraging divergent thinking. These include seeing different uses of common objects and different points of view on a given issue; playing different roles in a simulation; distinguishing between the letter and intent of a rule through discussion and mock trials; and defining concepts differently in different contexts. Rubin maintains that these activities promote better decision making and foster creativity in a wide range of areas, including social studies and language arts.

The author is Principal of Bingham Memorial School, Middlebury, Vermont.

The following learning activities are aimed at developing students' thinking skills as related to fostering an appreciation and understanding of multiple perspectives. The primary methodology involved utilizes divergent questioning. In turn, the activities have direct application to building students' ability to draw conclusions and make judgments and decisions in a fashion requiring the consideration of the total context affecting a particular judgment or decision.

These activities may be used as a unit of study concerning the development of attibutes that are essential to critical thinking or they may be incorporated into other units of study in the areas of social studies and language arts.

Although these activities are likely to be most useful in grades six through twelve, it is quite possible that instructor modifications would make them relevant to either younger or older students.

Activity 1: More Than One Way to See I

Objective: To help students to begin to be comfortable with the concept of multiple perspectives.

Method: The instructor asks students to define the purpose of common objects found in the classroom or at home (for example, a chair, desk, plate, bowl). S/he then turns the objects upside down or places them in some other unusual position and asks students to select one for which they are to imagine a purpose or purposes that might be served by the object in its changed position.

Students should be instructed not to be concerned with whether or not the defined purpose(s) is practical or real. They should be allowed to use other objects or constructs in developing a new purpose for the object.

For example, several chairs turned upside down might be used as a protective barrier or pen of some kind. Similarly, a bowl covered with aluminum foil might become a model of an unidentified flying object from a planet of Lilliputians.

Students should then be asked to draw or create clay replicas of the new object and to write a brief description of its function. Descriptions might be made more creative by fashioning them in the form of explanatory information cards commonly found in museums: to include statements regarding the period of time in which the object existed and was used, how it evolved, who invented it, why it was invented, and how it was used. Another approach might be to write descriptions as news reports which cite a new invention or discovery. Students should share their completed work with one another.

Activity 2: More Than One Way to See II

Objective: To help build and reinforce the concept of multiple perspectives.

Method: The instructor begins this activity by presenting students with a divergent question that represents two distinct points of view. S/he then asks students to consider both viewpoints. For example, the instructor asks:

- Which is more delicate, a snowflake or a person's self-esteem?
- Which is colder, a piece of ice or a cold heart?
- Which grows more quickly, a baby or self-confidence?

Students should then be instructed to argue both viewpoints by writing at least three supporting reasons for either position. Thereafter, they share these arguments with one another and may be involved in a series of classroom debates which provide experience relative to supporting both sides of the question posed and answered.

Activity 3: More Than One Way to See III

Objective: To help build and reinforce the concept of multiple perspectives.

Method: This activity may be conducted as a simulation, using role playing, or by the discussion of a real or imaginary event. For example, the instructor could present the following situation:

231

James is on the playground during morning recess and slaps Carla, a younger student, in the face. Carla runs to the teacher on duty (who did not actually observe the incident) and, with tears streaming down her face, informs the teacher of James' action.

The instructor then asks students to consider these questions:

1. What should the teacher on duty do?
2. Since the teacher on duty did not see the incident, how should s/he learn what actually occurred?
3. Are there any possible reasons that might have led James to strike Carla? What are they?
4. Do any of these reasons excuse or justify James's behavior or affect the manner in which the teacher should deal with James and Carla?
5. Are James and Carla bad people? Why or why not?
6. What might James and Carla do to avoid this situation in the future?

Students should write down their answers and share them with one another.

A variation of this activity would involve faculty members in the role playing of a similar situation that might occur between adults. In this instance, students write a brief narrative of what they witnessed occurring among faculty. These narratives are discussed and then students answer questions like those presented above, changing the names and roles of the actors as necessary.

Activity 4: *Distinguishing Between the Letter and Intent of a Rule*

Objective: To give practice in and therefore reinforce thinking skills.

Method: In this activity, the instructor presents a real or fabricated school rule. By offering successive illustrations of its apparent transgression, s/he leads students to distinguish between its literal interpretation and its intent or purpose. For example, the following situation might be used:

Hopeville Elementary School has recently adopted a new school rule which prohibits students from bringing any weapons or war-related toys to school. This rule was adopted to help lessen violent and aggressive play among students in the hope of establishing a more friendly, creative school atmosphere.

With this set of circumstances in mind, the students are then asked to determine whether or not the following student actions are contrary to the letter, the intent, or both the letter and the intent of the rule:

1. John brings his B-B gun and ammunition to school.
2. Sandy is making believe that a stick he found on the playground is

232

a sword and is chasing several classmates who are pretending to be dragons.

3. Emily brings in her father's hunting rifle for show and tell.
4. Paul brings a toy to school that can change from a robot into a rocket launcher.
5. Matthew brings a loud, battery-operated siren to school and wants to use it during indoor recess.
6. Michael and Nicole bring toy trucks to school and are playing a game they call "crash" during recess.

The instructor should feel free to elaborate on the above circumstances so as to enrich students' discussion.

A variation of the above activity would be to explore the principle of freedom of speech in various contexts as related to whether or not specific forms of speech are protected by the First Amendment to the Constitution. For example:

1. Jackie calls Louis a dummy.
2. Ian yells, "Fire, fire, fire," in a crowded movie theatre when there is really no fire.
3. Mary decides that to protest American involvement in El Salvador, she is going to burn the flag of the United States.
4. Workers at a local place of business put various posters around town, hand out leaflets, and take an ad in a newspaper, all of which express their discontent with what they believe to be unfair working conditions.
5. A newspaper reporter writes a story in which he accuses a government official of lying. The report indicates that the information cited came from a reliable source, but when asked to divulge the source of the information, the reporter refuses.

Elaboration of the above circumstances and the initiation of research are likely to make the activity more substantial and valuable.

Activity 5: Mock Trial

Objective: To extend and reinforce students' thinking skills by distinguishing between the letter and the intent of a law.

Method: This activity makes use of a well-known children's story as the basis for conducting a mock trial.

For example, the story of *Goldilocks and the Three Bears* might serve as a basis for examining the letter and the intent of the law as related to breaking and entering; the story of *Little Red Riding Hood* could be used to explore the legal concept of assault and battery; or *Jack and the*

233

Beanstalk could be used to study the concept of robbery. The latter would, of course, require the instructor to change the ending of the story such that the Giant lives and makes a complaint to the local police indicating that Jack robbed him of his possessions.

Whatever story is chosen, students should recreate a trial in its entirety. This entails selecting students to act as major protagonists from the story and choosing other children to participate as defense and prosecuting attorneys, witnesses, judge, jury, and police. Students must conduct various types of research relative to the legal principles involved in the particular story and those pertaining to more generalized legal concepts, such as preparation of briefs, admissable evidence, depositions, courtroom procedure, and role responsibilities. Additionally, they must carefully study the facts of the story in order to adapt it as a mock trial and to thoroughly prepare for participation in their particular roles. Following the accomplishment of these activities, students are ready to conduct the mock trial.

It should be noted that the mock trial is not a play. For example, although lawyers should prepare questions and review these questions with their teacher, the actual posing of such questions to witnesses should not be rehearsed. Instead, the simulation of the trial should occur as naturally as possible so that all participants are provided with the opportunity to act and react in a manner that encourages students to think on their feet.

Videotaping the mock trial will enable students to discuss the performance of their role responsibilities as they relate to both the process and the ultimate outcome expressed by the verdict.

Activity 6: Defining a Concept

Objective: To enable students to understand how variations in circumstances may affect the definition of a specific concept.

Method: The instructor begins this activity by placing the word "violence" on the chalkboard and asking students to define and brainstorm examples of violence. Thereafter, s/he offers the following situations and discusses each one with students relative to how they conform with or create differences in the meaning of the concept of violence.

Situation A: Brett doesn't like one of his classmates, Tyrone, because Tyrone comes from a wealthy family and Brett's family is poor. Brett waits after school for Tyrone and starts a fist fight with him.

Situation B: Marjorie is walking home from school after dance class and is tackled to the ground by two older boys who want to steal her money. Her friend Mark sees what is happening and shouts, "Leave her alone!" The two boys pay no attention to Mark, so he picks up a stick and uses it to beat the two boys off Marjorie until they, Marjorie and Mark, are able to run away.

Situation C: Carlos's mother, Virginia, is determined to do all that she can to prevent the spread of nuclear weapons. In her town there is a factory that manufactures the guidance systems for nuclear warheads. Carlos's mother has done everything possible to have the factory closed. She has written to her congressman, her state senators, and even the President. She has also submitted a petition to local and state officials with the signatures of over one thousand people who agree that the factory should be closed. In part, the petition states that by helping to produce nuclear weapons, the factory is threatening people throughout the country with grave danger and, in a sense, is holding people hostage as a result of that threat.

Virginia's efforts have no effect. She decides that the only way to close the factory is to use force to destroy the building. Virginia plants a time-bomb in the factory which is set to explode at a time when Virginia is certain that no one will be in or near the building. The bomb explodes as planned, destroying the building. No one is physically hurt, but obviously all the people who are employed in the factory lose their jobs.

Situation D: Barbara is a college student who is opposed to the denial of human rights in the Union of South Africa. The college she attends maintains a large number of investments in the Union of South Africa which help to support that country's economy and, in turn, support both the government and its policies. Barbara decides that one way to help change those policies is to protest economic support of the country and its government. Since her college provides such support through its investments, Barbara organizes and conducts a sit-down strike of students and faculty. The strike is so successful that no classes can be held and, as a result, non-striking students complain that their right to attend classes has been denied. Barbara explains that she and others involved in the strike are practicing passive resistance which she believes is protected by the Constitutional right of freedom of speech.

In summary, it should be noted that all of the above activities have been successfully used with students. Additionally, beyond the development of thinking skills, the learning experiences involved readily lend themselves to fostering creativity, research skills, and a wide variety of abilities that are ordinarily components of social studies and language arts curricula.

DEVELOPING THINKING SKILLS IN MUSIC REHEARSAL CLASS

by Douglas E. Reahm

As Douglas E. Reahm notes, music educators may at first find difficulties in introducing thinking skills into music education: performance classes, which emphasize ensemble playing, seem to run contrary to individual decision making. Students are asked to replicate a composer's music, not to think for themselves. However, Reahm maintains that "musicianship is largely a process of making decisions," and thinking skills instruction should be integral to the performance class. He suggests teaching students to think critically about the music they are playing, searching the best alternatives of tone and tempo, analyzing "what is not on paper"—the exact type of attack, a personal sound, the tone colors.

This chapter is reprinted by permission from Music Educators Journal. *Copyright © 1986 by Music Educators National Conference.*

The author is former Supervisor of Music, Grand Rapids Public Schools, Michigan.

School districts are searching for ways to teach students to think. The knowledge explosion has convinced us that the facts and figures we teach today will be less useful in the future than the skills of gathering, processing, and assessing information. What can music educators do to teach higher order thinking? Much of what we do runs contrary to individual decision making, especially in the performance classes where the ensemble is expected to play or sing as a group under the direction of the teacher. We teach students to replicate the music of the composer rather than to think for themselves. Is that our major goal? Are there alternatives to the lock-step rehearsal techniques which develop fine performers but do not teach students to be critical thinkers about the world of music?

Many of our secondary music performance classes do not encourage students to learn that musicianship is largely a process of making decisions. The more subtle the decisions, the less obtrusive the nuances of the music, and the more musical the performance. True musicianship is a melding of technical skills and decision making in how to image the music so the listener is not focused on the notes and the performance medium but drawn to the expressive thoughts which the music conveys.

Music educators have an obligation to teach higher order thinking in the performance class. The students need to know that many performance decisions are made consciously by the teacher and reflect both training and personal insight from years of performing, analyzing, comparing, and thinking about various styles of music.

Thinking is a process of reflecting upon, weighing, arguing, and supporting alternative points of view. In its technical definition it has a hierarchy of syntactical, logical, argumentative, and verbal principles to be mastered. It deals with inference, assumptions, and contradictions. In the educational setting the student can advance ideas, share reasoning, and hear the objections of other students. It is not necessarily focused on picking out errors, but is a search for the best alternatives through logical thought, sound argument, and perceptive insight. In order for this process to happen, the student must see that alternatives exist, know that decisions are being made, practice thinking skills, and be allowed to participate in some outcome.

Can we teach our students to think critically about the music they are performing? Yes, if we structure our classes to allow it to happen! This structure should involve the student in an analysis of performance options, experimentation, and conducting, as well as critical analysis of the teacher's interpretive decisions. In this way the students will become a thinking part of the class and be less like an organ pipe sounding at the touch of the organist. Instead of our being a conductor, we can assume the role of educator/conductor.

PERFORMANCE OPTIONS

The music that our secondary school bands, orchestras, and choirs perform is printed on paper and has visual symbols to direct both the player and the teacher in its interpretation. We should not only teach the symbols on the paper, but also analyze what is *not* on the paper. The crescendo and decrescendo markings are there, but the exact degree of amplitude is not there. A metric marking may be there, but the relative tempo changes are stated in broad terms and are left to the conductor's discretion. The notes are there, but the exact type of attack may be discretionary. The tone colors produced by the performing group are a combination of the teacher's personal sound preference and the group's playing or singing skill.

Teachers know that many of the symbols have relative meanings and that we make many decisions regarding their interpretation. Does the student know we are doing that? I think not. We instill our view of the performance options by repetitive drill until we are satisfied. We lead the students to believe in our finest autocratic tradition that there is but one way for the music to be performed. They perceive the teacher's direction as an attempt to achieve that single avenue to perfection. We pattern too many of our rehearsal techniques in the secondary school after the maestros of the symphony. Those techniques have a place in the education of young people, but they must be balanced by the broader perspective that only three percent of our students will become career musicians. The others will become amateur musicians and consumers.

We owe it to our students to let them know when we make critical and creative decisions about how the music will be performed. Tell the class the thoughts going through your mind during the rehearsal. "Band, that section was louder than I think it ought to be *because* I want to prepare for section B. How loud do you think A should be if there must be a contrast between the two sections?" "Choir, we can slow this to a crawl at measure 34, but I wonder if we can get it back to a run again. I would like three *suggestions* of possible ways to perform measures 34 through 55. What do we want to create here?" This should not imply that students will make the final selection of performance parameters, but they will learn that decision making is a part of rehearsing.

Some teachers may be concerned with the amount of time this routine would take away from the rehearsal. This is a part of the curriculum and therefore an integral part of the class time. We base confidence in the knowledge we gain largely on the attention we have given to alternatives. This process of alternative investigation will enhance the knowledge and thus the understanding of the students, leading them to better musicianship.

EXPERIMENTATION

In addition to investigating viable options, we should encourage bold experimentation in the music class. We should even make it possible for some nonmusical things to happen. We often leave the impression that there is one and only one way to perform the music. This short-changes the student. Time should be devoted to experimentation.

Each student in the class should believe that the music can be performed in a unique way according to his or her own specifications. Many of these performances will fall short of accepted musical standards, but we are teaching, not performing.

When the class has a good grasp of the notes and the basic interpretation of a section of music, ask that they each write ways they would change the dynamics, tempo, tone color, or phrasing of the section. The truly courageous teacher will let them alter notes both rhythmically and tonally. Select three or four students to share their concepts with the class. Discuss the students' ideas to help you and the class define exactly what the originator is seeking. Allow for discussion and dissension. This will open some eyes to the decisions the composer as well as the conductor must make when creating or recreating a composition. Conduct the class in a rendition of those concepts. Before discussing the outcome, ask each student to write down his or her reaction to the interpretation that was played. This provides an avenue for practicing independent judgment. Any subsequent discussion will have greater meaning when the student can compare her or his own opinion with those of others in the class.

There is a point to having students write their ideas on paper and having the teacher conduct a rendition incorporating some of those ideas. Pencil and paper are not out of place in the music rehearsal class. Students will have ideas, but they may not be well formed until put into words on paper. The writing need not be lengthy or detailed, but it should be thoughtful. Since we are primarily interested in the class's hearing and participating in the sound of the various experiments, the teacher's conducting will serve to focus on the listening rather than the mechanics of the exercise. It will also add credibility to the students' suggestions. Some students may not wish to share all that they have written, but the exercise will still serve as a thought base for them during the analysis and discussion by the class.

An advanced step in experimentation would be for the class to be taught only the notes of a new selection, devoid of any interpretation by the teacher. The student versions can serve as a gauge for the teacher to measure the degree of musical development of the class.

CONDUCTING

Those of us who conduct know that one of the best ways to feel the music is through the act of moving our arms, hands, and bodies when conducting. Our minds have rationally defined our expectations of the music, but our physical movement clarifies and alters those expectations. We say, "This feels right," or "It just does not feel right."

Our students need opportunity to feel the same things we do. Each purchase of band and orchestra music sets could include one or two additional conductor's scores. (Choral music in octavo form already has all the parts printed, so extra purchases are not necessary.) One or two students should be selected each class period to be relieved of their singing or playing responsibility. Conductor's stands could be set up to the right and to the left of the teacher's stand, and the students could be allowed to conduct along with the teacher during the hour. The teacher could stop occasionally and ask them what they have seen and heard. Many instrumentalists will have never seen other players' parts, and their attention should be drawn to the activity of other instruments.

Over time, every student in the class should have multiple opportunities to conduct. As they become more proficient, the teacher might ask one of them to conduct a section and make personal decisions about the music. It would even be appropriate for the student to go counter to the printed expressive markings—for example, perform a forte where a piano is notated—and experiment with the music. In this way each student will have alternative ways of thinking and feeling about the music. The other students will benefit from the varied interpretations of a given section of music.

Being put in command of the ensemble makes the student conductor hear and think critically about the music. How many of us have benefitted from fine educator/conductors who entrusted us with responsibilities at an early age that enabled us to develop our musicianship? There should be more.

ANALYZE THE TEACHER'S INTERPRETATION

This may be the hardest and yet the most rewarding segment of the process of teaching thinking. Should the students challenge the teacher's interpretive decisions?

If the previous parts of this process have been exercised, the students will develop a trustworthy conception of how various types of music should be performed. If there is a degree of difference between the teacher's standard and the student's, there should be a place in our educational setting for those differences to gain credibility. A challenge for the teacher would be to program a student-conceived interpretation on a public concert. Make the audience aware of this teaching and learning technique. Let them participate in the educational experience which goes beyond performance. Such a program would gain high marks from the parents as well as the administration of the school. Parents know little of the education we provide in the classroom and believe we teach only to the performances we present. They enjoy learning about what their sons and daughters are learning in school as much as they enjoy seeing and hearing students perform.

Teaching thinking skills in the music class will serve a dual purpose in the education of the student: to develop independent musicianship through critical thinking, and to teach students to wrestle with ambiguity in subject matter within which there is no single right answer. There are many right answers which must be decided among in music. This practice of confronting equally viable alternatives will serve the student well in making decisions outside of music throughout life.

Music educators often feel pressure to justify music's existence in the curriculum. The best rationale for music in the educational life of every student is this: Music is an expression of reality and is as legitimate as any other expression of reality by human thought, be it in words, numbers, or visual images. If music is an expression of reality by human thought, then we should include the aspect of teaching the thinking process in our music classes.

DEVELOPING HIGHER-ORDER THINKING SKILLS IN HOME ECONOMICS: A LESSON PLAN

by Nancy A. Watts

Nancy A. Watts notes that—contrary to popular assumptions—thinking skills have long been central to home economics instruction. The home economics student is constantly faced with a range of choices in the marketplace that require informed decision making. However, Watts notes that thinking skills instruction may be absent in areas of traditional skill instruction, such as clothing and textiles. Watts maintains that thinking skills instruction should be part of even these areas—that we should "stop 'teaching' Home Economics skills and model thinking in our classrooms." She provides a detailed lesson plan where students apply thinking skills to fabric construction.

The author is a Mentor Teacher for home economics and computer strategies at Lodi Senior Elementary School, California.

Home Economics studies are rarely if ever mentioned or discussed when talking about higher-level thinking in the classroom. Yet critical thinking is not a new concept in Home Economics. In fact, in many of the areas of Home Economics, higher-level thinking is a most integral part of the curriculum.

> If a person is adept at thinking critically, she is adept at gathering, analyzing, synthesizing, and assessing information as well as identifying misinformation, disinformation, prejudice, and one-sidedness. A student with such skills will have the tools of life-long learning. . . (1, p. 1).

For example, in consumer education students learn to gather, analyze, synthesize, and assess information in the marketplace. In interpersonal relationships, we are teaching problem-solving and decision-making techniques. Life is a series of choices and Home Economics teaches choices.

Are we doing as much with a traditional skill area such as clothing and textiles? Or are students becoming bored with discussion in which they are asked to simply identify what teachers already know? The challenge is to stop teaching Home Economics skills and to model thinking in our classrooms. The following lesson plan for an eighth grade Home Economics class takes the learning of fabric construction out of the area of demonstration and memorization, into the area of higher-level thinking.

Background: The students have had no instruction in fabric construction and most have little, if any, background in fabrics.

Objective: Using previous knowledge of categorization and characteristics, students will categorize twelve fabric samples into three methods of fabric construction.

Preparation: Assemble a set of twelve fabric samples for every three or four students. Fabrics mounted on card stock will be easier to handle and more permanent. Samples should include the following:

- woven fabrics, with and without nap
- knit fabrics, with and without nap, sheer
- felt, non-woven interfacing, synthetic suede
- at least three samples in the same color.

A student task sheet, similar to Figure 1, should be given to each student. If possible, a small handheld microscope (2) for each group of students will enable them to gather more information.

The lesson will require a minimum of one day and no more than three days, depending on the class ability and the objectives of the teacher.

After each student has a copy of the task sheet, explain that the assignment is not a test, nor is there just one correct answer. They are not expected to know all about these fabrics, but to look for characteristics that each may have in common with others.

Make certain students understand the terms "characteristics," "categorization," and "fabric construction." Most especially make certain students understand the concept of fabric construction. Perhaps compare the construction of fabric to the many ways a wooden fence may be constructed. When talking about ways of categorizing fabric construction, discuss characteristics briefly, because you want students to identify characteristics already in their knowledge. For example, "Since you have three samples of blue fabric, can you assume that because they are all blue they are all made the same way?"

Explain that you have already given them one piece of new information, in that on the ditto you have said, "Three methods of fabric construction," and have given them three columns in which to record their observations.

They first need to sort the samples into three groups, relying on what they perceive to be common characteristics. Record the numbers of each group, one set in each column. Students are then to record the common characteristics that caused them to think they were made by the same methods. (See Figure 2.)

The final part of the assignment involves students creating a name for each of the three types of construction. Assure them there is no one correct name at this point in the assignment, but that it must be based on the common characteristics. Some of the more interesting, creative types of construction have included "wire" and "chain" to describe pressed and knit construction.

Give each group a set of fabric samples. (Code each set with a letter and each sample with a number for ease in sorting later.) Allow student groups to work at their own pace and in their own way. Monitor each group to make certain they understand the terminology and the task to which they have been assigned.

After groups have had time to complete this portion of the assignment, give them a handheld microscope, briefly demonstrating its use. Ask the groups to see if they can find any additional information to help in correctly categorizing the fabrics. Direct them to add it to their task sheet.

The following day, or as appropriate, conduct a class discussion on their findings. Carefully discuss their findings, possibly charting the information on large sheets of paper. Have students make corrections and additions as necessary on their papers. Through the discussion some conclusions will be drawn by the class as a whole. Use this as a springboard for further discussion of fabrics and fabric construction.

Junior high students need to develop skills in gathering, analyzing, synthesizing, and assessing information. Students need to be taught thinking skills. Give them every opportunity possible to learn.

REFERENCES

1. "Introduction—The Heart and Core of Educational Reform" In *Program and Abstracts*. Sonoma, Calif.: Third International Conference on Critical Thinking and Educational Reform, 1985.
2. Tasco's 30 Power Illuminated Microscope, "The Little Looker." Cost $6.95 (plus shipping and handling) at present writing. Silver Burdett Company, Western Regional Office, 1559 Industrial Road, San Carlos, CA 94070.

LODI SENIOR ELEMENTARY SCHOOL
Home Economics 1

Name _____

Date _____

Period _____

Textiles Unit — Fabric Characteristics*
Identify Method of Construction

ASSIGNMENT: Look at each of the fabric samples in your set, seeing if you can find fabrics that have been constructed by the same method. The three methods of fabric construction are represented by the samples.

Categorize the fabrics; list common characteristics; give each category or group of fabrics a name you feel is appropriate.

Card #'s	Card #'s	Card #'s

Common Characteristics	Common Characteristics	Common Characteristics
Name of this category	Name of this category	Name of this category

*Characteristic — A trait, quality, or property distinguishing an individual, group, or type from every other member of its class or kind.

PLEASE BE CAREFUL WITH THE FABRIC SAMPLES. TRY NOT TO STRETCH OR DAMAGE THEM.

N. Watts   Figure 1.
9/85

LODI SENIOR ELEMENTARY SCHOOL
Home Economics 1

Name _____

Date _____

Period _____

Textiles Unit — Fabric Characteristics*
Identify Method of Construction

ASSIGNMENT: Look at each of the fabric samples in your set, seeing if you can find
fabrics that have been constructed by the same method. The three methods of fabric
construction are represented by the samples.

Categorize the fabrics; list common characteristics; give each category or group of
fabrics a name you feel is appropriate.

Card #'s	Card #'s	Card #'s
1, 9, 10	*3, 4, 6, 7, 8*	*2, 5, 11, 12*
Common Characteristics	Common Characteristics	Common Characteristics
flat *stiff*	*stretches* *soft* *T-shirt*	*loose threads* *not stretch*
wire Name of this category	*chain* Name of this category	*old fashioned* Name of this category

*Characteristic — A trait, quality, or property distinguishing an individual, group, or
type from every other member of its class or kind.

PLEASE BE CAREFUL WITH THE FABRIC SAMPLES. TRY NOT TO STRETCH OR
DAMAGE THEM.

N. Watts   Figure 2.
9/85

245

USING LITERATURE TO DEVELOP CRITICAL THINKING SKILLS*

by Maria Tymoczko

Maria Tymoczko shows how four types of critical thinking—induction, deduction, constructing sound arguments, and model making/theory building—can be used in the study of literature. She provides numerous examples of the development of these thinking skills and suggests that the humanities have certain advantages over science and math for improving these skills in students. In the humanities, unlike those more technical areas, the student can "generate a question that has not yet been answered and that will still be within his or her grasp to answer." Tymoczko finds that critical thinking in literary inquiry results in an open-ended, challenging learning experience for both students and teacher.

The author is Associate Professor of Comparative Literature, University of Massachusetts, Amherst.

Literature is rarely put forward as a vehicle for teaching critical thinking, yet it is as capable of teaching students to think well as the disciplines most often credited with promoting these skills: math, science, logic, and philosophy. After a brief review of various aspects of critical thinking, I will suggest strategies for teaching these skills in literature classes.

Four types of critical thinking are commonly addressed in our educational system. The first is induction: the ability to draw conclusions from data and specific facts. The second is deduction: the ability to reason from premises, to move from the general to the particular, to understand implications of a hypothesis. Both induction and deduction are involved in the construction of sound complex arguments, and in the ability to criticize arguments. Both are also involved in model making and theory building. Model making and theory building, in turn, generally involve a positive feedback loop, whereby known data suggest a theory or model, and that model is tested and refined by further investigation and experiment or data gathering.

Mathematics teaches critical thinking primarily because it exercises stu-

---

dents' powers of deduction: they learn to construct proofs, to move from axioms to theorems. Science teaches critical thinking primarily by teaching students induction—the basis of the scientific method and experimental design—as well as the rudiments of model making and theorizing. Philosophy teaches students both the principles of logic—on what basis deductions and inferences are valid—as well as ways of constructing arguments. Typically in philosophical arguments, students learn to attend to general principles and their implications, as well as to modify assertions so as to accommodate specific examples—that is, students are trained practically in both deduction and induction. Literature is as fine a tool for teaching critical thinking as any of these disciplines. Though literature may not offer opportunities for rigorous proof as mathematics does, or for quantitative experiment as science does, for teaching critical thinking as a whole it is one of the most flexible disciplines in the academy.

The following sections contain four successful strategies for teaching critical thinking using literature. My examples are taken from courses I have taught in Irish Studies and Comparative Literature; analogous types of questions and approaches can be used in any literary field.

INDUCTION

Literature courses can be structured around units of inquiry. That is, readings can be treated as data that will generate general conclusions to questions that have been raised. This is a technique that every literature teacher uses. For example, in secondary schools we use such strategies to get students to delineate the characteristics of short stories as opposed to novels, or to define different sorts of comedy.

It is a technique that comes into its own on the college level, however, when students can be put to work on questions that have no simple answer. The following are examples of questions that have proved successful: What are the distinguishing features of fantasy literature? How does audience affect authors' treatments of form and content? What are the differences between children's literature and adult literature? What folklore exists at a university and what are its functions? In what ways is Yeats indebted to native Irish tradition? Questions aimed at the development of inductive arguments can be posed regarding specific works, genres, periods, and theoretical issues.

Such an inductive approach to literature can be used to structure whole courses, as well as units within courses. It can, for example, be used in a thematics course, such as "The Theme of the Otherworld in Medieval Literature," in which students can be asked to define the typologies and functions of the Otherworld in a specific body of literature.

Students can also be taught induction by being encouraged to do investigative independent projects as final papers. In my classes students have undertaken experiments as diverse as an investigation of oral transmission to see how well people remember various types of stories told to them, and a survey of early Irish literature to determine the role sounds, noise, and music play in the corpus.

Material approached this way will teach students to generate conclusions for themselves about individual works and more general aspects of literature on the basis of texts at their command. That is, students will evolve not only as more critical independent readers, they will also develop metaliterary skills—the basis of theoretical inquiry to be discussed below. Emphasis on induction also encourages students to be specific and precise in their thinking—characteristics as valuable in literary discourse as in other fields.

When students learn that a class has an investigative approach, they begin to generate questions themselves and to answer those questions as well. That is, a learning environment that attends to the critical thinking skill of induction promotes curious and lively habits of mind. In order for such an atmosphere to flourish, however, the teacher has to be ready to listen to and consider carefully the students' assessments of the texts at hand. Indeed such pedagogical openness is essential for teaching and encouraging all critical thinking.

The humanities offer a more satisfying field in which students may undertake inductive inquiries than even the sciences. For in the sciences, it is rare that a student can generate a question that (1) has not yet been answered and that (2) will still be within his or her grasp to answer. For many students, scientific questions in beginning or even middle-level science courses and scientific experiments, particularly those that repeat classic experiments of the past, have something of a contrived nature and seem a repetitive exercise. In humanistic fields, particularly literature, any student on the college level will be able to ask some questions that have not been answered and to generate feasible answers to those questions. This is possible because some of the raw materials of literature (namely, some texts) are more accessible, basic analytic techniques are easier to master, and the experimental designs are generally simpler than the analogous materials, techniques, and experimental designs of scientific fields.

DEDUCTION

Deduction is also a critical thinking skill that can be taught and rein-forced through literature. Again whole courses as well as units can be or-ganized around a deductive investigation. In a literary setting deduction generally takes one of the following forms. In the first form, a course be-gins with an assertion (Proposition A), and ask what follows from this as-sertion. For example, students can be presented with the information "the Celts had a strong belief in the Otherworld," and then asked in what ways this belief appears in and shapes Celtic literature.

A second form that deduction often takes is to ask an if-then ques-tion. If such and such were true (Proposition B), what would then fol-low? The conclusions can then be assessed to see whether they are true or whether they lead to a *reductio ad absurdum*. For example, students might be asked to consider what follows from taking James Joyce serious-ly as an Irishman writing in the Irish tradition. The deductions that fol-low from such a proposition may represent significant new critical depar-tures; indeed, for the example at hand, one can show that the converse, a prominent critical stance regarding Joyce as disconnected from the Irish tradition, does in fact lead to a *reductio*.

Incorporating deductive strategies in the framework of literature classes not only develops students' general critical thinking skills, it makes them better students of literature. It encourages depth of inquiry, and an at-tention to consistency. Teaching deductive strategies of the second sort also teaches students to be open to possible arguments; in short it makes for more creative minds. At the same time, such approaches provide stu-dents with ways of testing arguments so that their creativity is disciplined.

An advantage of using literature as a mode for teaching critical think-ing skills related to deduction is that literature is more concrete than mathematics. Students who have difficulty manipulating mathematical symbols can, thus, still learn these habits of mind. Moreover, by exercis-ing deduction in a concrete domain such as literature, students can more easily learn to apply these critical thinking skills to broader aspects of their lives. They come to understand more readily the implications, for example, of their major life choices on other aspects of their lives.

CONSTRUCTING SOUND ARGUMENTS

Most complex arguments evolve from the interplay of both induction and deduction. In practice, the questions posed to students generally do not depend on either pure induction or pure deduction for their answers. In order for students to construct arguments well, they need to be able to move back and forth between various types of critical processes. The development of this sort of mental flexibility is a particular strength of the discipline of philosophy, but literature classes are also ideal places to learn to construct arguments.

The central aspect of a successful strategy for teaching students to construct sound arguments turns on asking them real questions to which there are no standard answers in the critical literature and to get the class to work collectively on these questions. This is a technique borrowed from philosophy which teaches complex argument by engaging students on real questions that contemporary philosophers debate. Though students may be taught the history of the dialectic on the issue, such history is presented primarily to sharpen students' wits and to increase their awareness of the issues involved. That is, the history of the debate is taught to students in order to facilitate students' own arguments and positions on questions for which no consensus has been reached. Current philosophical topics discussed by students include the relation of names to referents, the nature of translation, the implications of mathematical proofs generated by computers, the logical basis of altruism in moral systems, and so forth. These are also areas on which there is lively debate in the professional journals.

Such questions should be a significant element of every course taught. Examples of questions I have proposed in recent semesters include the following. What are the differences between science fiction and other types of fantasy, and are these differences theoretically significant? Are Celtic poets shaman figures, and if so, how does this affect our understanding of their poetry? Are there signs of thematic coherence in the Welsh *Mabinoqi*? What is the nature of James Joyce's female figures? Is Arthurian romance a form of fantasy literature, and if so, how does this medieval genre relate to and differ from modern fantasy literature? These are questions on which literary critics have no agreement, and yet all are capable of being approached by undergraduates who have read appropriate primary literary texts.

There are several advantages in posing such questions to students. First, if there is no standard critical position on a topic, then students will in fact be thrown onto their own mental resources for a solution. They do not have the easy option of turning to an authority for the Truth; they must puzzle over the question and reason out an answer. Second, asking such questions makes the class an actual forum for inquiry, not a Socratic exercise. As positions evolve, students have a genuine sense of accomplishment—they see that their critical reasoning and arguments have been effective in achieving an increased understanding of the problem at hand. They have become in a small way members of the community of scholars.

Moreover, if open questions are posed, then the instructor also is engaged in the process of argument and investigation. There is nothing so undermining to a student's sense of confidence in his or her growing powers of critical thinking than to believe that the teacher knows it all, that the student's own struggles with the topic are in some way a sham, that the teacher is bored with the students' thoughts because the teacher has heard it all before, that there is only one answer (the teacher's) to be discovered. Such patronizing attitudes are most easily avoided if the teacher also has an investigative attitude toward at least some of the material in a course.

A teacher's openness will also influence the mode of discussion and argumentation. If the teacher is a member of the process of inquiry, then it is not up to the teacher alone to assess students' arguments as they evolve. This facilitates students' talking to each other, learning not only to construct and advance arguments, but to assess and challenge the arguments of others as well. Both are aspects of critical thinking. This sort of discussion provides opportunities for students to practice all aspects of argument formation: making assertions on the basis of evidence (i.e., induction from a close textual reading), offering counterexamples, and so forth. A teacher can also introduce deductive reasoning as a criterion for evaluation of arguments presented in the discussion: if x is the case as is being asserted, what would the implications be? Thus, students can learn to use *reductio* arguments in intellectual discourse.

One advantage literature classes have over philosophy classes as a format for training students to form sound arguments is that the arguments are generally constructed with reference to a closed domain—that is, the literary text or texts under discussion. This is a relative equalizer for class participants; the ability to think critically is foregrounded, and less advantage is given to students on the basis of their general knowledge. Moreover, the basis of evidence and the source of inductive argument are more defined—namely, the literary works under discussion. This sort of structure and framework for argumentation facilitates the process of learning to think critically. It offers security to those students particularly whose educational backgrounds may not be strong or who may be uncertain about the process of constructing arguments, because it presents a limited field of reference which can be mastered by all class participants.

MODEL BUILDING AND THEORY FORMATION

Recently theory has become a topic of great interest to teachers of literature, and literary theory has begun to be incorporated into many courses or to be the primary subject of literature classes. Model making and theory building are major aspects of critical thinking, and literature offers many opportunities to engage in these processes. Students have the opportunity to build such skills in more traditional literature courses as well as in courses directly devoted to discussions of literary theory.

Model making and theory formation are second-order critical thinking skills. That is, they presuppose the ability to handle induction and deduction, to gather and assess data, and to form well-reasoned arguments. This is an advanced critical skill, but one we expect members of our society to understand and master. Model making in the domain of literature is, of course, no different as a process from model making and the search for theoretical formulation in other intellectual disciplines. Theories attempt to coordinate and explain phenomena, as well as to predict. Literary theory addresses many aspects of literature—from genres, to the relation of text and author/teller, to the place of the literary work in its cultural setting.

There are at least two aspects of theory formation that can engage students, even those who are learning basic critical thinking skills. Students can learn to assess existing theories, to test them and modify them. Students can also be engaged in the steps involved in the construction of theory.

An example of the former might be a course such as "The Celtic Basis of Arthurian Romance." In this course, after determining what aspects of medieval romance should be accounted for by a theory of genre development and after deciding what would count as an adequate theory of the origin of romance, students can test the Celtic hypothesis of the origin of romance on the basis of a representative selection of significant romances and Celtic literary texts. Students in this type of framework can discuss theories abstractly, can be presented with a specific theory, and can also be given material for testing the theory in question.

Another approach to stimulate the understanding of theory formation might occur in a course such as "Medieval Lyric." Students can survey the range of non-narrative poetic types in medieval literature. The inadequacies of traditional definitions of lyric to inscribe medieval poetry, as well as the inadequacies of theories that see classical literature and Medieval Latin literature as the fountainhead of medieval vernacular poetry can be presented. The focus in the course would be on developing alternate models for the medieval corpus. This example illustrates one of the practical advantages of theory and model formation: such activities encourage students to develop literary breadth. When students see that counterexamples to theories can often be generated by a broad consideration of texts, students gain enthusiasm for the sort of spade work and research that mastery of any field requires.

A third example of teaching students about theory formation might occur in a freshman-level course such as "Fantasy and Literature." Such a course can present a theory of a particular genre of literature step by step, illustrating the complexity of theory formation, showing how definitions must be established, examples brought forward, evidence incorporated. The theory developed can be related to other theories of the genre, as well as to the wider framework of literary theory as a whole. Such a course, which can teach some of the fundamental elements of critical thinking discussed above (induction, deduction, and construction of complex arguments), can also be a demonstration of the complexity of theory formation. While concentrating pedagogically on the basic critical thinking skills, it can prepare students for more advanced stages. A basic course can thus also serve students whose intellectual development is advanced.

Literature again is an ideal vehicle for teaching model building and theory formation. The basic materials to be organized by theories of literature are often highly accessible, and a sufficient amount of material can be presented so that there is adequate data to build theories around or test theories with. Moreover, students can be engaged on literary projects involving underworked fields, types of literature just being integrated into academic consideration, or old problems that bear reexamination. Thus, they can try their hands at areas that are in need of theoretical formulation or reformulation—a task which is difficult for students to undertake in scientific fields or mathematics.

Teaching critical skills to students is never easy in any field. In literary studies, one must know the substance of a field and the critical debate about a field, without being wedded to a rigid critical stance. It means being vulnerable before students—being engaged as one asks them to be engaged, learning as they learn, being open to having one's own arguments challenged, as well as being prepared to challenge students' arguments. It means giving up the safety of constant dependence on defined positions. It means, in short, being willing to model one's own critical thinking as one asks students to develop their skills. There are obviously great benefits that make these difficulties worthwhile. Students learn thinking skills as well as content, and literary inquiry as a whole also stands to benefit from such approaches. In addition, it makes teaching a tremendous adventure—one opens the door to students' thoughts, and one gets many unexpected and stimulating gifts in return.

On the whole, literature teachers and literary critics consider themselves sharp critical thinkers. Nonetheless, literary studies are generally thought of as one of the least likely disciplines to teach critical thinking, largely because in literature classes we neither conduct physical experiments nor construct proofs. While literature teachers willingly assume the lion's share of teaching students to write well and to express themselves well, they tend to pass on the responsibility for teaching critical thinking to other disciplines. It's time to change these stereotypes.

QUESTIONING IN A WRITING PROGRAM TO DEVELOP THINKING

by Paula K. Flemming

Paula K. Flemming describes using questions to improve primary school students' writing and thinking. She emphasizes the importance of a shift in the teacher's role, from information-giver to facilitator. With numerous examples, including teacher/ student dialogues, Flemming shows how a teacher's questions of student writing can lead to problem solving and improved decision making. The teacher, reading the student's writing in progress, observes the student's intent and asks probing questions. Flemming shows how different questions can have specific effects on students' work: they can help students expand their work when needed, focus on a topic, deepen the students' understanding of their topics, and strengthen their essays' endings. When students externalize their thinking through writing, she finds that they develop as both writers and thinkers.

The author is Reading and Writing Coordinator for the Con Val School District, Peterborough, New Hampshire.

"Should I draw myself in the jacket?" Bridget, a wispy, blonde first grader, asks me as I walk by her desk.

I stop. "What do you think?"

Putting the tip of her thumbnail in her mouth, she looks at the drawing of her jacket. She reads aloud the text written in invented spelling at the bottom of her paper: Where is my denim jacket? She looks at me and asks, "No?"

"Why not?"

"Because it wouldn't make any sense if I was saying, 'Where is my denim jacket?' and I was wearing it."

I touch her lightly on the back. "Good thinking, Bridget." I move on.

Here we see the strategy of questioning within the context of writing to allow the student to develop her/his own thinking process. Bridget rose to the challenge and demonstrated that she could solve the problem at hand through critical thinking.

She needed me at this point in her development as a thinker, not to provide her with the answer, but to provide her with the question to force her into an advantageous position for engagement with her problem.

255

My role as teacher as been "structured away from that of information-giver and into getting the child to develop his own thought processes" (2) through the use of a judicious question at the right time. Studies conducted in the 1960s at the Merrill-Palmer Institute, a private, non-profit educational institution in Detroit, found that parents who were authoritarian did not encourage children to be independent thinkers.

> As a result...these children seemed to have difficulty in handling abstract problems. They had difficulty conceptualizing....So we undertook to train kindergarten teachers to treat children as active learners, to ask questions, to set up tasks in which the child had to solve a problem.
> ....The results... showed that the children became "faster, more effective, reflective and flexible" learners. (2)

Teachers have been asking questions ever since schools began. Most questions asked have stirred the dust of the mind, but have not stripped the outer layers to expose a new surface. Most of the questions have asked for literal, factual information. Questions for which the teacher always has the correct answer. Questions which tap memory only.

> Construed broadly, critical thinking comprises the mental processes, strategies and representations people use to solve problems, make decisions, and learn new concepts. (7, p. 46)

We need to ask questions which force students to solve problems make decisions, learn new concepts. We need to ask questions which help students to understand what they are learning, to apply the learning, to analyze, synthesize, and evaluate. Questions for which we teachers do not always have the one and only correct answer.

The use of questions to develop critical thinking is an integral component of a process-based writing program. Questions are used before writing (What will you write?), during writing (What will you write next?), during revision (Which lead is better?), and during editing (How do you know when to use a period?).

Questions are posed at different times to compel students to think about what they are doing, what they have done, what they will do. The questions oblige students to reflect on and project from their activity and to learn from their intellectual engagement.

Beneath these thought-provoking questions rests the assumption that students are capable of thinking. They can reflect on their actions, words, thoughts. "Birds fly, fish swim; man thinks and learns" (6, p. 189). The power for learning resides with the learner and not the teacher. Once students understand that teachers believe they are capable of thinking critically, students seize their power and soar.

Good questions grow from observations of what the students are trying to do in their writing. The teacher follows the lead of the student and the questions nudge the student forward and prepare the way for instruction and learning. I recall LeeAnn, a third grader who had used a colon in her writing.

"What's this, LeeAnn?" I asked pointing to the colon.

"I don't know. It's two dots."

"How did you happen to use them in your writing?"

"Well, I noticed them when I was reading. Whenever there was a list of things, they used the two dots, so I did."

LeeAnn had written:

> This is what I did during my vacation in Maine: swam, looked for shells, fished, went to the movies, played with my cousin, played miniature golf and slept in a tent.

LeeAnn thought as a writer when she was reading. She observed a convention of print, formed a hypothesis about its use, and filed it for a future need. She experimented with this "new" convention in her writing. The first question probed her knowledge to see if she knew the name for this new convention. (I knew the answer.) The second question probed her understanding of the concept. (I did not know the answer.)

I observed what LeeAnn had done in her writing and asked two questions to probe the depth of understanding LeeAnn had regarding colons. LeeAnn's answers provided the information needed for instruction. LeeAnn had analyzed what she read and applied the new concept in her writing. She needed reinforcement that her hypothesis was correct and she needed the label to apply to the new convention. I also learned a little more about how LeeAnn is thinking about the world of print.

Mike, a first grader, started putting periods in his writing. He knew the label and told me he used periods at the end of a sentence. I then queried, "What's a sentence?"

"It's when you come to the end of a line. See."

He had punctuated his writing just as he said, at the end of each line, not at the end of each sentence:

> This is a Big.
> Foot it is crushing.
> cars I like Big.
> Foots

"What if the sentence doesn't end here but goes on to the middle of the next line?"

"It's like I said, put the period right there, at the end of the line."

I did not push him any further in terms of his definition. I knew his concept of a sentence was too distant from the truth to be tampered with. A teacher should:

> give children opportunities to verify or disprove their own beliefs. When they fail to discern any contradictions between their statements and the evidence

[the teacher] has suggested, she/he does not press further. . . .She recognizes that more experience as well as more maturity will be necessary for more adequate understanding. [The teacher] respects their ideas and does not try to change them with a verbal explanation. (1, p. 73)

Good questions also grow from the teacher. They are real questions he/she has about the writing. What does the teacher want to know about? What does the teacher wonder about? His/her curiosities provide the fertile ground for the growth of questions. I wanted to know what LeeAnn knew about colons and how she had learned about them.

One afternoon Peter, a third grader, and I were talking about his writing. In his story he had built a robot which would do anything he wanted. I wanted to know what kinds of things he had the robot do. His answer was, "Clean my room, take out the garbage, stack wood." He later revised his writing to include these specifics.

Further on in his story, the main character landed on Mars. The Martians "seemed to know him."

My curiosity again caused me to ask, "What did the Martians do which showed that they knew him?"

"Well, if he had been a real stranger, they would have attacked him."

Peter changed this part of his writing from *The Martians seemed to know him* to *The Martians didn't attack him because they remembered him from when he was a baby*.

It is sound practice to look at what the child is trying to do and ask genuine questions, but there are different questions for different purposes. One can form questions based on where the students are in their development as writers and where they are in their pieces of writing.

If the writing needs to be expanded, think, "What do I want to know more about?" And ask those questions. Or ask questions such as these:

- Exactly what happened?
- How did you (or a character) feel?
- Tell me the details so I can picture the whole episode (activity, scene, etc.).
- How did it start?

If the teacher senses a lack of focus in the writing, some questions that may direct the thinking of the writer are these:

- What are you really saying here?
- What's the most important reason you chose this topic? What's important about it to you?
- What do you want your reader to learn?
- Which is the most important part of your story? Why?
- Is there anything that doesn't seem important in your story?

- It seems as if you have two stories here. One is about _____ and the other is about _____. Which one is the more important? (exciting, special, interesting)

If the teacher has trouble visualizing the scene, he/she might ask one or more of these questions:

- Read me the places where you're pleased with your description. What makes it good writing?
- If I had been watching you, how would I have known that you (or a character) felt sad? What exactly would I have seen?

If the lead or ending is weak, ask

- Is your reader going to be hooked into reading right away? Why or why not?
- How else could you start (end) your story?
- Have you told too much at the beginning (ending)?
- Does the reader need to know all that?
- What are ten other ways to begin (end) your story? Which is best? Why?

If the teacher wants information about the student's understanding of a concept or technique, he/she can ask

- Why did you make this change from your first to second draft?
- How did you figure out the spelling for this word?
- This section gives me a good understanding of what was happening. How did you do it?
- How did you decide to write about this topic?
- How do you know when to use quotation marks?
- What do you think of this piece of writing? Why?
- What problems did you have when writing? How did you solve them?
- What did you learn in writing this piece?
- What's the difference between your first and last drafts?

If the teacher wants to know where students are in their development as writers, these questions are helpful:

- How have you changed as a writer?
- What do you have to do to be a good writer?
- If you had more time, what part of your writing would you spend time on? Why?
- What is the best story you have written this year? Why?
- What makes a good lead?
- What is the hardest part of writing for you?
- What is the easiest part?
- What have you tried that is new for you?
- What kinds of response help you most as a writer?

(These questions have been influenced by the research work done by Nancie Atwell (3), Lucy McCormick Calkins (4), Donald Graves (5), and Susan Sowers.)

Students must think to answer these questions. They reflect on their processes, strategies, and representations. They solve problems, make decisions, and learn new concepts. They think about their thinking and decision making. They use language to talk about language. They are thinking critically.

The process of answering questions brings to consciousness what may have been an unconscious action. Melanie, a first grader, had written the final page to her story "Christmas Eve." She ended with the sentence *Kim was happy.* When we were talking about her story, she asked me if I thought *happy* or *glad* was better. Her questions excited me. She was deliberating over a choice of words, unusual for a first grader. I asked my usual question, "What do you think?"

She answered, "I think *glad.*"

"Why?"

"Because *glad* means she was excited and happy all over. And *happy* means. . .just happy, not so exciting, just happy like smiling."

It is less important whether Melanie is correct in her definitions of *happy* and *glad.* It is more important that she is thinking about and analyzing the meanings of words. She knows her message and understands that she must choose the exact word to communicate her message. She thinks about the power of words.

Students who write every day encounter problems. What will I write about? What words will I use to tell my story? What form will I use? What questions will others have about my writing? These self-posed questions cause thinking to occur.

Writing students think after they have written. They think about how they can improve their writing. They think in response to questions posed by teachers and peers.

Through this thinking the students are learning.

Children do not necessarily learn because adults provide opportunities for them to use and explore materials. The children must engage in thinking about what they do. For most children, the intervention by means of questions, whether narrow or broad in focus, numerous or few, is essential to learning. (1, p. 84)

Teachers who use the strategy of questioning within the context of writing help their students to think critically. Students, even the young students, show repeatedly that when the teacher asks good questions, they use them as springboards for the discovery of solutions, for making decisions, and for the creation of new concepts.

REFERENCES

1. Almy, Millie, and Genishi, Celia. *Ways of Studying Children*. New York: Teachers College Press, Columbia University, 1979.
2. Ames, Lynne. "The Need: Teachers Who Can Make Them Think." *New York Times Educational Winter Survey* (January 9, 1983).
3. Atwell, Nancie. "Making the Grade: Evaluating Writing in Conference." In *Understanding Writing*, edited by Thomas Newkirk and Nancie Atwell. Chelmsford, Mass.: The Northeast Regional Exchange, 1982.
4. Calkins, Lucy McCormick. *Lessons from a Child*. Exeter, N.H.: Heinemann Educational Books, 1983.
5. Graves, Donald H. *Writing: Teachers and Children at Work*. Exeter, N. H.: Heinemann Educational Books, 1982.
6. Holt, John. *How Children Learn*. New York: Pitman Publishing, 1967.
7. Sternberg, Robert J. "Critical Thinking: Its Nature, Measurement and Improvement." In *Essays on the Intellect*, edited by Robert J. Sternberg. Alexandria, Va.: Association for Supervision and Curriculum Development, 1985.

SIMULATION AND THINKING

by Ronald Levitsky

Ronald Levitsky shows how simulation exercises can improve high school students'
understanding of and attitude toward history. To clarify his use of the process,
Levitsky describes a Civil War simulation. The simulation, which emphasized the
war's causes, involved students' taking on roles of persons on both sides of the con-
flict. Students spent two or three weeks acquiring background information on the
war's causes before beginning the simulation. In his description of the simulation it-
self, Levitsky discusses students' identification of their allies and opponents in the
conflict, as well as their resistance to voicing unpopular positions. Levitsky discussed
the teacher's role in this process, where the teacher serves as moderator and facilitator.
When the simulation is completed, students return to a discussion of the issues pre-
sented and analyze emotions provided by the simulation. Levitsky finds that the simu-
lation as a whole helps students use new analytic skills: they become involved in the
essential questions raised by historical problems.
The author is Social Studies Chairperson, Sunset Ridge School, Northfield, Illinois.

A loud disturbance broke out against a far wall of the student cafete-
ria. When I arrived, about a dozen eighth graders were shouting at one
another. One boy pointed angrily at a poster illustrated with a white
overseer whipping a kneeling black slave; on it was written, "The South
is cruel, the North will rule!" Students were heatedly discussing the merits of the plantation system vs. the conditions of Northern factory workers, the tariff, and the Biblical justification of slavery with arguments
that might have been heard in Congress one hundred and fifty years
ago. This incident was the result of a Civil War simulation, a spillover
from the classroom, and for the teacher a refreshing example of students
looking beyond the text to analyze the why and how of a historical situation. It points to the intent of this chapter: to show that the use of simulation is particularly suited to the adolescent's thought processes and attitude toward history, and that it is one of the best methods of promoting
thinking that can be used in the history classroom.

Thinking necessitates making a judgment, a type of intellectual exercise requiring an open-ended question and sufficient data for each side
of the question to be defensible. This is precisely the type of thinking
that David Matthews, President of the Kettering Foundation, has called
"civic intelligence" and that he finds necessary for a thriving democracy.
By civic intelligence, he means not only to understand the facts but also

to go beyond them to understand what these facts mean to other people and to oneself, and then to make judgments (1).

Adolescents are particularly suited to engage in this type of thinking, for most have entered what Piaget has called the formal operations stage. No longer are they bound to their own particular world, but now "...the given environment can be treated as one of a number of possible conditions"(2). Students are able to hypothesize about particular situations and then make deductions. Martin Sleeper, Principal of the Runkle School in Brookline, Massachusetts, has applied Piaget's theory of formal operations to the adolescent history student who can now move from abstract principle to concrete example, understand point of view in historical context, and speculate—"...imagine alternatives, construct different possibilities and play out their outcome"(3).

Sleeper goes on to differentiate two distinct categories of historical reality in the minds of adolescents. One has direct relevance upon their own lives and therefore is very meaningful and encourages the greatest use of imagination and hypothesis. He uses as an example the Great Depression, because the historical event helped to shape their parents' values to which they were continually subjected. The other category he calls "formal History" which is less meaningful to students and therefore attracts much less speculative thinking.

All of the above imply difficulties for the teacher seeking to have adolescent students in a history class practice thinking skills. Piaget indicates that adolescents are entering or have entered a stage in thinking which will allow them to hypothesize about what is or, in the case of history, what was possible. Matthews indicates that critical thinking, as much as it strengthens a democratic society, must allow us to "...understand facts as others would understand them for themselves—from perspectives and circumstances quite different from our own"(4). Sleeper cautions the teacher that students will speculate best upon historical situations which are somehow made meaningful to them. Executed properly, a simulation can utilize Piaget's formal operations stage, respect if not incorporate Sleeper's advice, and allow the student ample opportunity to exercise Matthews's call for civic intelligence.

Packaged simulations have been available since the 1960s and have grown in popularity over the years; indeed, the computer revolution has added dozens of such historical activities. However, they have engendered two criticisms. One arises from the essential strength of the simulation—its open-endedness, for why role play a situation if the ending has been preordained? Yet, those who oppose what they term "secular humanism" resent giving a fair hearing to a differing viewpoint. It should suffice here merely to warn those who use simulation as a stimulus for critical thinking to be prepared for such censure.

The second criticism comes from those educators who see a dichotomy between what they regard as real teaching—the 3-R's as instructed by means of lecture, drill, and memorization—as contrasted to a simulation which they regard as merely a game and therefore a time-waster. The recent concern among the general public that American education is somehow failing and needs to get back to basics has no doubt increased the wariness of some teachers to spend several days, or even weeks, allowing their students to role play a particular historical event. This criticism is valid only insofar as a teacher misuses the simulation—for example, not clearly relating the activity to the unit as a whole or not requiring enough student preparation.

The following paragraphs will delineate one simulation that has been used successfully for a number of years in an eighth grade United States History class. It is not meant as a lesson to be duplicated but rather as an example of how such an activity can successfully stimulate critical thinking.

The simulation, entitled "The Union Divides," is published by Olcott Forward Publishers(5). Its major components are a written guide, a record narrating historical background information, and a set of index cards giving biographical sketches of pseudo-governors in charge of the thirty states in the Union in 1850. Although not real personages, these characters have viewpoints which reflect the actual beliefs of ante-bellum governors—the Governor of Massachusetts is an abolitionist; South Carolina, a Southern extremist; and Kentucky, a Southern moderate not wishing to offend the anti-slavery constituency in his state. Students play the roles of these governors and attend a conference in which they attempt to advise Congress regarding a peaceful settlement of the issues that threaten civil war.

In choosing to utilize this simulation, the teacher has consciously shifted emphasis away from the Civil War itself—that is, the study of strategy, military leaders, and battles—to the more difficult but equally fascinating question of causation. Was the Civil War inevitable? If so, why? If not, what could have been done to prevent such a conflict? The ideal recipe for thinking: an open-ended historical situation, ample factual data available for opposing viewpoints, and the opportunity, as Matthews has written, to "...understand facts as others would understand them for themselves..."(1). All these processes are leading to well-reasoned judgment.

Before the simulation is introduced, students need to assimilate as much background information as possible, and therefore spend two to three weeks studying events leading to the Civil War, from the origins of slavery to Lincoln's election. Emphasis is placed on analyzing each side of an issue as well as delving into social history through the use of primary sources—for example, a slaveowner's view of the plantation system vs. Frederick Douglass's. Through classroom discussion and probing by the teacher, students are asked to examine why many Northerners and Southerners viewed certain issues differently, as well as why there were differences of opinion within each region. A common vocabulary is developed, using such specialized terms as "popular sovereignty," "Peculiar Institution," and "Secession." Because the class is studying causation, a concept naturally yielding to analysis and evaluation, the teacher is able to utilize the higher order questions of Bloom's Taxonomy (e.g., "Why did the South defend slavery so strongly?") (6).

Only after having investigated the background of the controversy are students introduced to the simulation. Each is given the role of a governor (two or three students are made officers in charge of running the conference). Roles are generally assigned at random, although the parts of at least a few Northern abolitionists and Southern extremists are given to more vocal students, well suited to live up to their fiery reputations.

Invariably many of the children selected to portray Southern governors voice their dissatisfaction, asserting they have no wish to defend the institution of slavery or to side with traitors. Of course, this is precisely what is needed if the entire class is to appreciate why sectional differences eventually led to secession. These students are told that they are in the position of lawyers who must sometimes defend ideas with which they do not agree. Gradually they reconcile themselves to the luck of the draw, becoming emotionally involved as they are forced in the activity to defend their positions.

After the role selection each student must study his/her governor's biographical card, then demonstrate an understanding of the information by writing in character an election speech. This speech also allows the student to extrapolate upon the governor's imaginary life, engage in campaign rhetoric, and address key issues—all excellent preparation for the upcoming Governors' Conference. For example, a student portraying the abolitionist Governor of New Hampshire wrote,

I feel that slavery has made life in the South shocking and very sickening. I feel that slave trading is the lowest of all human occupations, and slavery should be done away with immediately, even if force is needed to do so, and slave holders should be forced to repent their sin by serving time in jail.

The more moderate student-Governor of Virginia countered,

Our state needs slavery to survive. The crops we plant would never get the proper care needed without slave help. The Northerners don't know the situation we have. If we could educate them to this fact, the states in the Union would work together.

Another purpose of this writing exercise is to help each student clarify his/her governor's position. For example, a girl who portrayed the Governor of Illinois wrote a stirring speech unabashedly in support of abolition. She had assumed, without carefully reading the biography card, that Illinois a Northern state and the Land of Lincoln, would naturally be strongly anti-slavery. Upon closer reading, and questioning by the teacher, she realized that downstate Illinois was strongly Southern in heritage and sentiment, and therefore rewrote her speech in a tone moderate enough to make even a seasoned politician proud.

The last phase of preparation allows the "governors" time to familiarize themselves with their likely allies and opponents and begin to coalesce into voting groups. Through closer analysis students will learn that there are not simply two blocs but four—abolitionists (four governors), Northern moderates (eleven), Southern moderates (eleven), and Southern extremists (four). From the information given as well as through teacher guidance, each student is forced once again to think beyond mere platitudes of anti-slavery and state's rights to analyze just where she/he stands on a particular issue; indeed depending upon the question, governors within the same region might oppose one another. The more clear-sighted soon see, and others discover as the simulation progresses, that Northern and Southern moderates often have more in common with one another—that is, the ultimate preservation of the Union—than they do with their more extreme colleagues. This, of course, is the key issue; will moderation on both sides prevail through compromise to save the Union, or will the result be secession and war? Because the answer is unknown at the activity's initiation, students are forced to respond to each upcoming question as they think the role demands, and because classmates are depending upon everyone's sincere participation, they rarely fail to take their roles seriously.

The Governors' Conference itself comprises four half-hour sessions, each one corresponding to a specific year in which a crucial issue faced the nation, beginning in 1850 with the Compromise of 1850 and ending with the election of Lincoln and the threat of secession. (Based upon but not limited to the packaged simulation, a formal agenda has been developed, a copy of which is included.) Desks are arranged in a horseshoe facing a podium and speaker's table. Within each session students are asked to examine critically one specific issue and then vote either on the original question or an alternative they have formulated.

For example, the first question occurs in 1850—"Shall California be admitted to the Union as a free state?" As with upcoming questions, a guest speaker, usually a teacher, appears to review the background—this time as John C. Calhoun and Daniel Webster (for Lincoln in a later session, the superintendent appears in a beard and stovepipe hat). Next the "governors" are permitted to debate the question. This is usually slow-going at first, but as students begin to feel at ease exchanging opinions with their peers, discussion grows livelier and more and more hands are raised demanding recognition by the harried chairperson (many friendships are temporarily lost that day). Impromptu speeches include emotional outbursts, angry denunciations, and reasoned appeals to logic and compromise. By reacting to one another's remarks, students are achieving much higher level inquiry than in a traditional classroom setting where they merely respond to the teacher(7).

After several minutes of discussion, the chairperson calls time for caucus, in which the "governors" group themselves into blocs, review the question, and attempt to reach a consensus concerning the upcoming vote. Abolitionists and Southern extremists do their part by denouncing the opposition's immorality and any attempt at compromise, while leaders within the ranks of both moderate groups may seek out one another in an attempt to negotiate a deal. When the caucus period has ended, a roll call vote is taken, the teacher noting how each "governor" has voted, and, if the question fails, the floor is opened to compromise measures.

Regarding the admission of California, in a recent playing of the simulation the moderates of both North and South agreed to split the state in two by extending the Missouri Compromise line to the Pacific Ocean, thus concurring that for each side half a loaf was better than none. In previous simulations this question did not always lead to compromise, the extremists on both sides having made the moral issue of slavery paramount. From an educational standpoint there is no wrong answer, only answers well reasoned or not.

During the short recess between sessions, the teacher approaches students who seemingly have not voted in character or have not yet participated actively, and questions them, not to criticize but to help clarify their thinking. Sometimes students who appear to have broken character give good reasons for their actions and have actually engaged in some powerfully original thinking (e.g., a Southern extremist voting for a compromise unfair to the South in order to anger Southern moderates against the North).

The following years (1854, 1859, and 1861) are generally role played far more in earnest, as students grow accustomed to the simulation's format. It is at this point that the line is crossed from what Martin Sleeper has identified as "formal History"—not particularly significant to adolescents—to the more personally relevant history he sees as promoting abstract, speculative, and therefore more truly critical thinking. Students become caught up in their characters. Southerners, goaded by the insults and criticisms of their Northern colleagues, grow more defensive concerning slavery, which more and more of them begin to refer to as their "Peculiar Institution." They boo and walk out in protest when teachers

267

representing abolitionists Harriet Beecher Stowe and William Lloyd Garrison enter to give speeches. They lash out at the Yankees who exploit the factory workers more than slaves are exploited. As those who role played these Southern governors later explained, they never felt that slavery was justifiable but felt trapped into defending an indefensible system, just as Southerners in the ante-bellum era felt trapped.

Whether the Governors' Conference results in a peaceful settlement of the issues or in a civil war is determined solely by how the students have examined and responded to each of the four critical questions. Extremism and conflict win as often as moderation and compromise. What determines the simulation's success is not the outcome but how well students have placed themselves in the hearts and minds of their roles and how effectively their thinking skills have been utilized.

At the simulation's conclusion, students rearrange their seats into rows and return to the present. The activity is not complete, however, until they participate in a closure consisting of two parts. First the teacher leads a discussion examining the questions and attitudes raised by the Governors' Conference. Decisions that individuals and voting blocs made are challenged, as students must reexamine and defend their choices. The emotions that developed are also analyzed to determine what effect they had on the various decisions. One conclusion usually drawn is that feelings tended to grow hotter as the activity progressed, making compromise more difficult. This leads to extrapolation to current events and a discussion of crises in the Middle East, Central America, and South Africa. Students exhibit a deeper understanding of the complexities of these issues after the simulation and in their discussions are less likely to accept superficial explanations. They are generally more cautious and willing to investigate both sides of a question.

The second aspect of closure is a take-home essay briefly summarizing what understandings the simulation helped the student achieve. As one girl wrote,

> I feel that this [simulation] showed me how hard it really is to compromise. When deciding for a whole country it becomes a difficult task, because you're deciding what to do for the present and later on the future. Another thing this taught me was the different sides of the issue. I learned how not only the Southerners felt but also the abolitionists, extremists and the Northerners. It was difficult trying to play a person who was for slavery when you know it is wrong, but in doing so you can better understand the conflict.

As mentioned earlier, *The Union Divides* is but one of a plethora of simulations commercially available. In addition, it certainly is possible to create one to answer a particular need(8). The teacher wishing to utilize a simulation should be certain the activity supports a unit in the existing curriculum, can be tailored to a particular class size or time limitation, and stimulates thinking. Many of the computer simulations currently available appear in the format of an arcade game pitting the individual against the screen. This type of activity yields more satisfactory results if students participate in small groups, where decisions need to be discussed, evaluated, and defended before being made final. Otherwise thinking skills are minimized.

In conclusion, simulation is an excellent means of promoting higher-order thinking in the history classroom. It permits adolescents, having reached what Piaget has termed the formal stage of operations, an opportunity to speculate about the past, analyzing not only what happened but, more importantly, how and why it happened and if it necessarily had to occur. By immersing themselves in the attitudes and emotions of a character from the past—indeed, assuming that personage—students become more engrossed in a historical problem and therefore more willing to investigate it. An intellectual leap occurs as they personalize history and are able to observe and react to events, as Matthews would have them, from a perspective and circumstance very different from their own. Ultimately through analyzing the past in this manner, adolescents prepare themselves for the all important role of citizen in a democratic society with the ability to use their thinking skills in everyday life.

Governors' Conference to Prevent a Civil War—Agenda

Session #1—1850

1. Call to order and roll call.
2. Welcoming speech by Governor of Pennsylvania.
3. Introduction by Chairperson.
4. Background to question.
5. Question: "Shall California be admitted to the Union as a free state?"

   a. Addresses by Sen. John C. Calhoun (introduced by Governor of South Carolina) and Sen. Daniel Webster (introduced by Governor of New Hampshire).
   b. Discussion.
   c. Caucus.
   d. Vote (compromise?).

6. Adjournment.

Session #2—1854

1. Call to order.
2. Address by Harriet Beecher Stowe (Uncle Tom's Cabin) introduced by Governor of Ohio.
3. Background to question.
4. Address by Stephan A. Douglas (introduced by Governor of Illinois): "Popular Sovereignty."
5. Question: "Should the People of Kansas and Nebraska decide for themselves to allow or outlaw slavery?"

    a. Discussion.
    b. Caucus.
    c. Vote.

6. Adjournment.

Session #3—1859

1. Call to order.
2. Raid on Harper's Ferry, Virginia.

    a. Explanation by Governor of Virginia.
    b. Discussion.

3. Question: "Shall the federal government recognize slavery and protect it in states and territories where it now exists?"

    a. Address by William Lloyd Garrison (abolitionist), introduced by Governor of Massachusetts.
    b. Discussion.
    c. Caucus.
    d. Vote.

4. Adjournment.

Session #4—1861

1. Call to order.
2. Review of Election of 1860.
3. Address by President-Elect Abraham Lincoln, introduced by Governor of New York.
4. Background to question.
5. Question: "Can a state legally secede from the Union?"

    a. Discussion.
    b. Caucus.
    c. Vote.

6. Concluding remarks by Chairperson.
7. Adjournment.

REFERENCES

1. David Matthews, "Civic Intelligence," *Social Education* 49, no. 8 (November/December 1985): 680.

2. R. Droz and M. Rahmy, *Understanding Piaget* (New York: International Universities Press, 1976), 58.

3. Martin Sleeper, "How Do Adolescents Use and Understand History?" *Facing History and Ourselves News* (Spring 1985): 6.

4. Matthews, "Civic Intelligence," 680.

5. Eric Rothschild, Joan Platt, and Daniel C. Smith. *The Union Divides—A Simulation of the Causes of the Civil War* (Hartsdale, N. Y.: Olcott Forward Publishers, 1971.)

6. Arthur Carin and Robert B. Sund, *Creative Questioning and Sensitive Listening Techniques* (Columbus, Ohio: Charles E. Merrill Publishing Co., 1978), 16–17.
7. Ibid., 26–27.
8. For example, see Ronald Levitsky and George Steffen, "Supreme Court Simulation," *Social Studies* 74, no. 2 (March April, 1983): 89–92.

THE PRE–CONTACT TIME AMERICAN INDIAN: A STUDY IN THE MEANING AND DEVELOPMENT OF CULTURE— A TEACHING UNIT

by John M. Feeser

John M. Feeser's teaching unit on an aspect of American Indian history/social studies illustrates the integration of thinking skills instruction into the classroom. Students engage in activities that help them examine why and how the culture developed; they learn to hypothesize from evidence, to question aspects of both the Indian and their own culture, and to analyze the criteria they use to evaluate practices from unfamiliar cultures. Teachers can use this teaching unit as a model and guide for constructing similar units from other areas of study.

The author teaches Social Studies at the Salisbury Middle School, Allentown, Pennsylvania.

Teacher Note: This unit is designed to introduce students to the various and unique cultures developed by the aboriginal inhabitants of the Americas prior to European contact. During this process students are introduced to the concept of what culture is and how it develops. Activities are designed specifically to encourage students to examine the whys *as well as the* whats *in regards to the development of culture. The skill of hypothesizing from evidence is stressed and the ability to state and substantiate hypotheses in written form is emphasized. In the process of researching Indian cultures students begin to question and to better understand aspects of their own culture. By role playing students develop the ability to empathize and to more objectively analyze the unconscious criteria they use in the evaluation of unfamiliar cultural characteristics. The range of activities keeps students interested, allows for the exhibition of a variety of skills, and provides flexibility in dealing with various ability levels while at the same time developing the thinking skills we deem essential in the educational process.*

INTRODUCTION

People lived in the Americas many thousands of years before Columbus discovered the New World. This period is known as pre-Columbian or pre-contact time. Some groups of pre-contact time Americans were "uncivilized" hunters who wandered after herds of wild game. Others lived in small villages and tended cornfields. Still others lived in cities as amazingly beautiful as any in the Old World; cities in which the arts, crafts, religious ceremonies, and forms of government were highly developed. The people of pre-Columbian America spoke many languages. Their customs and religious and political systems differed widely. Their story is wonderful and tragic. Much of it has doubtless been lost forever. In this unit you will examine six of the major Indian cultural groups with the goal of understanding what their cultures were like, how they differed, and why each developed in its own particular way.

Filmstrip: American Adventures. New York: Scholastic Magazine, 1973.

Teacher Note: Any appropriate device to spark student interest may be used here.

OBJECTIVES

1. Students will know of the variety of Indian cultural groups existing in pre-contact time America and of the cultural differences between them.
2. Students will know how environment affects cultural development.
3. Students will know how various Indian cultural groups developed divergent systems of status and rank, group personalities, religion, and labor division, and will hypothesize as to the reasons for their development.
4. Students will know how archeological methods are used to discern cultural characteristics.
5. Students will develop a hypothesis as to the origin of man and prove this hypothesis with concrete evidence.
6. Students will develop an attitude by which they evaluate an unfamiliar culture by its success in adapting to environmental conditions rather than by comparison with one's own culture.

UNIT ACTIVITIES

Teacher Note: Activities may be altered, deleted or made optional based on student ability. A grading system may be devised for each activity in order to produce a collective activity grade.

Activity 1

Because there was such a wide variety of American Indian lifestyles, we cannot study just one American Indian culture. Instead we will examine six representative subcultures from throughout the Western Hemisphere. These subcultures are the Eastern Woodland Indians, the Eskimo, the Hopi-Zuni Pueblo culture, the Meso-Americans, the Plains Indians, and the Pacific-Northwest Indians. Although there are more, these will provide us with both a geographical and cultural cross-section of American Indian lifestyles. The class will divide into six groups, each of which will be responsible for researching one of these Indian cultural groups. Using the list provided as a guide, distribute the specific cultural traits to be studied among the members of the group. Each member will then be responsible for researching the topics given his/her group in order to determine how the Indian group practiced these traits and why they developed in this way. For example, Plains Indians lived in *tipis*. That student responsible for the shelter type of the Plains Indians will research that topic in order to determine not only *what* the tipi was like physically but also to discover *why* that unique shelter was developed by this particular Indian group. Each student group will then have opportunity to present the results of their research to the rest of the class. Students are encouraged to use visuals or any other aids that will promote the comprehension of their topics.

Activity I Subtopics:
1. How nomadic was the group and why?
2. Farming (type, crops, domesticated animals)
3. Hunting, fishing, food gathering
4. Food preparation
5. Religion
6. Social structure (e.g., child rearing, marriage, division of labor, status and rank)
7. Shelter, housing architecture
8. Clothing
9. Crafts, art, and music
10. Trade
11. Transportation
12. Government

13. Warfare and weapons
14. Education
15. Personality traits
16. Medicine and healing practices
17. Unusual customs and characteristics

---

*Teacher Note: During these presentations is an ideal time to examine character-
istics of our own culture. For instance, in studying rank among the Plains Indians the student would discover that the accumulation of wealth was not used as
a measure of status. Press students to analyze why it was not used with the
Plains culture and why it is such a significant factor in ours. By so doing students will gain not only an understanding of the role of status and rank in culture, but also the reasons for its development and divergence from culture to
culture.*

Activity II

In this activity you and your group will develop and prove a hypothesis. To accomplish this task you will use a technique which is very similar
to that employed by large think tank organizations such as the RAND
Corporation in developing possible solutions to complex problems. This
technique involves three steps. In the first step you and your group will
brainstorm the question. Brainstorming simply means thinking of all the
possible solutions to the problem. In the second step you will examine
the facts or evidence which you will use to narrow your list of possibilities
down to the one that seems to be the most probable solution to the
problem. Finally, you will develop that solution into a hypothesis and,
in a short essay, show why this possibility is the most likely solution to
the problem. You will be working together with your group but each of
you will develop and prove your own hypothesis and they need not be
the same.

The problem you will consider is this. Anthropologists are fairly certain that people have been living throughout the Eastern Hemisphere for
well over 100,000 years but they have been only living in the Western
Hemisphere for about 20,000 to 40,000 years. This suggests that some
time around 20,000 to 40,000 years ago people (the ancestors of the
American Indian) began migrating from the Eastern to the Western
Hemispheres. Your problem is to determine the route that these original
migrants to America used in getting here. Look at a globe or world map
and along with your group brainstorm as to the possible routes used, listing at least five possibilities. Look for the places where the hemispheres
are the closest to one another, as these would be the most likely routes
utilized.

Now that you have a list of possible solutions, your next task is to examine the evidence in order to narrow that list down to a most probable solution—your hypothesis. Use the following evidence to accomplish this:

1. The American Indian has certain physical racial characteristics which identify him as being of oriental ancestry.
2. The most recent archeological evidence suggests that man first appeared in the Western Hemisphere about 25 to 30 thousand years ago.
3. Thirty thousand years ago the earth was undergoing an ice age. During this period much of the earth's water was locked up in the form of glacial ice. This resulted in lowering the sea level about 300 feet from its present level. (During the ice ages the oceans *did not* freeze.)
4. The cooling of the earth during this period resulted in large scale migrations of the game animals which man depended on for food.
5. According to current data, 30,000 years ago man's ability to build boats was limited, and it is extremely doubtful that he could have built one capable of long ocean voyages.

Now that you have developed your hypothesis you must prove it. In a short essay state what you believe is the most probable solution to the problem and defend it using as much evidence as possible. Remember, the more evidence you can use to support your hypothesis the better it is. You might want to compare your hypothesis with what the experts have theorized occurred using the same data that you did. Read "Search for the First Americans" (*National Geographic*, September 1979), and make this comparison.

Teacher Note: It is helpful to explain that a hypothesis is often disputed and sometimes proven wrong when new evidence is uncovered. The objective here is not to present dogma but to stimulate deductive reasoning. Other sources may be substituted for the National Geographic *article listed in the activity.*

Activity III

There have been a number of people who have suggested that the cultures developed by the American Indian were influenced by outside sources. Speculation as to the origin of these sources has included everything from extraterrestial forces to ancient Eastern civilizations. One of these speculators, Thor Hyerdahl, went to great lengths to prove the validity of one of these theories. He has written a book on the subject, entitled *The Ra Expeditions*. Read the book to determine what Hyerdahl's theory of culture-contact is. In an essay explain the theory he proposes and the evidence he offers. Discuss to what extent you accept his hypotheses and what questions he leaves unanswered that may tend to cast doubt on it. Compare the strength of Hyerdahl's hypothesis with that of the hypothesis discussed in Activity II. Explain why the latter might be more widely accepted than the former.

Teacher Note: This is an excellent activity to enhance critical reading skills. It can be used effectively as an optional activity for more highly motivated students who complete the other activities at a more rapid pace than the majority of the class.

Activity IV

One of the objectives of this unit is to be able to analyze the reasons for the existence of cultural differences between societal groups. This activity will provide you with the opportunity to hone your analytical skills in the comparison of two Native American cultures.

Before you can determine why cultural differences occurred you must first be aware of what differences existed. Accordingly the first step in this activity is to compare two Indian cultural groups using a variety of criteria. Choose any two different Indian groups or two tribes from different cultural groups.

Research the cultures of these two groups to the extent necessary to summarize their cultures in chart form. At the top of the chart indicate the two groups or tribes studied. Along the lefthand side, list the following cultural categories: home, religion, how nomadic, food, warfare, family structure, status and rank, tools, clothing, and transportation. After putting your information into capsule form, fill in the chart. For example, if you were comparing the Plains and Eastern Woodland cultures, the first category on your chart might look like this:

	Plains	Eastern-Woodland
Homes (shelter)	tipi, hides and long poles, portable, one-family dwellings	longhouse, saplings and bark, semi-permanent multi-family

Complete a similar column for each cultural characteristic.

In the second part of this activity you are going to analyze the differences between these cultures and attempt to discern the reasons for the development of these differences. Using your chart, choose five areas where cultural differences occurred between the two groups you have studied. Consider such factors as vegetation patterns, animal life, topography, climate, and the like in order to suggest possible reasons for the development of these differences. For each of the five areas you have chosen to analyze write a paragraph in which you explain what you believe to be the reasons for these differences. For instance, a possible explanation for the differences between the shelters of the Plains and the Eastern Woodland Indians might be as follows:

The environment of the Plains Indians provided them with limited amounts of wood. They did have a plentiful supply of hides and so made use of these as their primary building material. They were nomadic and had nuclear families and so built homes that were relatively small and portable. The Eastern Woodland Indians had a plentiful supply of wood and so used it as their main building material. Since they were farmers they could stay in one place for two or three years and so built their homes to last that long. They lived in extended families and so often built structures to accommodate large numbers of people.

Teacher Note: This activity requires students to analyze and synthesize information in order to develop their own conclusions. Emphasize that the paragraphs in step two of the activity are to concentrate on the question of why differences developed and not what those differences were. The development of these paragraphs is the key to the success of the activity.

Activity V

Teacher Note: This activity is designed to acquaint students with archeological methods and terminology through role playing. While completing this activity students will analyze relatively unfamiliar evidence, synthesize this information, and draw conclusions in the form of substantiated hypotheses. The activity is done in a group setting in order to encourage dialogue which enhances the thinking processes.

In order to set up the activity the teacher must construct two visual aids. The first is a poster upon which pictures of ten to fifteen artifacts (for example, projectile points, awls, bones, broken pots) are glued. Assign a number to each artifact. The second aid is a fictitious archeological site map on which post hole molds, wood ash, bone fragments, tamped areas, and other such finds have been plotted. Use the numbers on your artifact pictures to plot on the site map where the artifacts were found. Add to this some background information in the form of site location, vegetation patterns, rainfall, and occupation date, and your students will do the rest.

In this activity you and the other group members are archeologists. You have just excavated the artifacts pictured on the poster. You have made a map of the site on which the location where each artifact was found has been plotted and other significant data recorded. The map includes a key as well as some helpful background information.

Your job as archeologists is to examine the evidence and to detemine as much as possible about the culture of the people who occupied this site. Ask yourselves questions such as these: What kind of clothing did they wear? What kind of shelters did they use? How long did they stay here? How many of them lived here? These will lead you to conclusions. Sometimes single artifacts may provide clues, but sometimes combinations of artifacts or their locations may prove useful in drawing conclusions. Work together, discuss the evidence and implications, and discover as much as you can about this culture. Use your imaginations but remember that each conclusion must be substantiated by hard evidence.

As your group discovers the various cultural aspects of this Indian group, make a list of all of the characteristics determined. Next to each characteristic explain what evidence can be cited to prove it. For example, if you found the remains of wood ash and charred wood in three areas of two-foot-diameter circles, one statement might look like this:

These people had the use ——————— Remains of charred
of and could control wood and wood ash were
control fire. found only in distinct
 and confined areas.

The more cultural characteristics your group can detemine the better. But remember, each conclusion *must be substantiated.*

Activity VI

When studying a new or unfamiliar culture we have a natural tendency to form judgments or evaluations based on the criteria of our own culture. If the people we are studying have customs and characteristics very different from our own we oftentimes will automatically think of them negatively, using expletives such as "gross" or "horrible" in our descriptions of them. One of the goals of this unit is to learn how to objectively analyze an unfamiliar culture and, if we must evaluate it, to use the criteria of how well that culture serves the physical and psychological needs of the people who have developed it. One way to achieve the goal of objective cultural analysis is to put yourself in the place of the people you are studying and to examine a cultural characteristic from their point of view rather than your own. This process is called role playing and it is what you will be doing in this activity.

The first step in this procedure is to become familiar with several cultural characteristics of various American Indian groups that we would consider rather unusual based on our own culture. Listed below are excerpts from three books that will provide you with information on the practice of three of these cultural traits (self-torture, torturing enemies, and human sacrifice). Read any *two* of them to become familiar with these practices.

After you have familiarized yourself with two of the traits, choose one to concentrate on. Pretend you are one of the Indians who practice this cultural characteristic. You have been asked by an outsider, a person of a different culture who views this practice as wrong, to explain *why* your group does it. In the form of a two- to three-page essay explain why your group has developed and practices this ritual. For example, if you chose the topic *human sacrifice* you would write your essay from the perspective of an Aztec Indian who was explaining the purposes of the large-scale sacrificial killings of humans that occur in his culture. You are, in effect, trying to convince someone who thinks this practice is wrong why you believe it is necessary and right. By doing so you will begin to understand the practice for its actual purpose rather than judging it based on the criteria of what your culture considers right or wrong.

Reading selections for Activity VI:

1. Elizabeth Baity, *Americans Before Columbus* (New York: The Viking Press, 1961), 204–207).
2. Oliver La Farge, *A Pictorial History of the American Indian* (New York: Crown Publishers, 1956), 56–57.
3. Clark Wissler, *Indians of the United States* (Garden City, N.Y.: Doubleday, 1940), 162–63.

Teacher Note: Topics and references for this activity may be substituted so long as they perform the function of presenting what would ordinarily be thought of as negative cultural traits. A good followup for this activity is to select a number of essays for oral presentation during which the teacher asks open-ended questions designed to stimulate thinking into the nature of moral judgments and the philosophical question of whether right and wrong exist naturally or are simply the product of cultural expectations.

Teacher Note: Implementing this unit means taking five or six sections of classes, dividing each class into six groups and having each group working on a different activity all at the same time. On first glance this appears to be a logistical nightmare. It can, however, be effectively done by using the schedule that follows. This schedule assumes that the student groupings for Activity I will be used for the completion of Activity II which will take two class periods and Ac-

tivity V which will take one class period. The teacher will concentrate on these two groups while periodically helping other students individually with their independent work on Activities I, IV, and VI. Activity III is treated as optional.

Unit Activity Schedule
Activity I Groupings

	Plains	Pacific-Northwest	Eskimo	Eastern Woodland	Meso-American	Hopi-Zuni Pueblo
Day 1	Unit Explanations					
Day 2	Act. I					
Day 3	Act. II	Act. I, IV, VI	Act. I, IV, VI	Act. I, IV, VI	Act. I, IV, VI	Act. V
Day 4	Act. II	Act. II	Act. I, IV, VI	Act. I, IV, VI	Act. V	Act. I, IV, VI
Day 5	Act. I, IV, VI	Act. II	Act. II	Act. V	Act. I, IV, VI	Act. I, IV, VI
Day 6	Act. I, IV, VI	Act. I, IV, VI	Act. II	Act. II	Act. I, IV, VI	Act. I, IV, VI
Day 7	Act. I, IV, VI	Act. I, IV, VI	Act. V	Act. II	Act. II	Act. I, IV, VI
Day 8	Act. I, IV, VI	Act. V	Act. I, IV, VI	Act. I, IV, VI	Act. II	Act. II
Day 9	Act. V	Act. I, IV, VI	Act. I, IV, VI	Act. I, IV, VI	Act. I, IV, VI	Act. II
Day 10	Act. I, IV, VI	Act. I, IV, VI	Act. I, IV, VI	Act. I, IV, VI	Act. I, IV, VI	Act. I, IV, VI
Day 11	Act. I Presentation					
Day 12		Act. I Presentation				

Unit Activity Schedule—Continued
Activity I Groupings

	Plains	Pacific-Northwest	Eskimo	Eastern Woodland	Meso-American	Hopi-Zuni Pueblo
Day 13			Act. I Presentation			
Day 14				Act. I Presentation		
Day 15					Act. I Presentation	
Day 16						Act. I Presentation

BIBLIOGRAPHY

Teacher Note: Uncited works are listed specifically for their value in completing the research necessary for Activities I and IV.

1. Ambler, Richard. *The Anasazi.* Flagstaff, Ariz.: Museum of Northern Arizona, 1977.
2. Baity, Elizabeth. *Americans Before Columbus.* New York: Viking Press, 1961.
3. Benson, Elizabeth P. *The Maya World.* New York: Crowell and Co., 1967.
4. Bleeker, Sonia. *The Aztec.* New York: William Morrow and Co., 1967.
5. Bleeker, Sonia. *The Cherokee.* New York: William Morrow and Co., 1952.
6. Bleeker, Sonia. *The Crow Indians.* New York: William Morrow and Co., 1953.
7. Bleeker, Sonia. *The Delaware Indians.* New York: William Morrow and Co., 1953.
8. Bleeker, Sonia. *The Maya.* New York: William Morrow and Co., 1961.
9. Bleeker, Sonia. *The Seminole Indians.* New York: William Morrow and Co., 1954.
10. Bleeker, Sonia. *The Sioux Indians.* New York, William Morrow and Co., 1962.

11. Canby, Thomas Y. "The Search for the First Americans." *National Geographic* 156, no. 3 (September 1979): 330–63.
12. Coy, Harold. *Man Comes to America.* Boston, Mass.: Little, Brown and Co., 1973.
13. Deloria, Vine. *Indians of the Pacific Northwest.* Garden City, N.Y.: Doubleday and Co., 1977.
14. Driver, Harold E. *Indians of North America.* Chicago: University of Chicago Press, 1961.
15. Erdoes, Richard. *Native Americans: The Pueblos.* New York: Sterling Publishing Co., 1983.
16. "First Americans." *American Adventures, Unit II.* New York: Scholastic Magazine, 1973. Filmstrip.
17. Heyerdahl, Thor. *The Ra Expeditions.* Garden City, N.Y.: Doubleday and Co., 1971.
18. Josephy, Sophia, and Josephy, Alvin. *The Indian Heritage of America.* New York: Knopf, 1968.
19. La Farge, Oliver. *A Pictorial History of the American Indian.* New York: Crown Publishers, 1956.
20. Rachlis, Eugene. *Indians of the Plains.* New York: American Heritage Publishing Co., 1960.
21. Stuart, Gene S. *The Mighty Aztecs.* Washington, D.C.: National Geographic Society, 1981.
22. Turner, Geoffrey. *Indians of North America.* Poole, U.K.: Blandford Press, 1979.
23. Wissler, Clark. *Indians of the United States.* Garden City, N.Y.: Doubleday and Co., 1940.

Teacher Note: This unit was developed approximately five years ago and has been used successfully by high school students of all ability levels. If used as the initial unit in a school year it results in several added benefits. Students newly placed in sections must work cooperatively in order to complete several of the activities and so quickly get acquainted. The teacher must work with students both individually and in small groups and in so doing rapidly learns about the personalities and skill levels of his students. Both research and writing skills are necessary in several activities and the teacher has the opportunity to determine early the students' assets and liabilities in these areas. The open-ended discussions produced by the activities establish an open classroom atmosphere which is non-threatening to students. The initial creation of such a classroom atmosphere enables it to be more easily maintained throughout the school year.

THINK METRIC

by Delores Gallo

In this chapter Delores Gallo demonstrates a method for teaching content knowledge (in this case, a unit on the metric system) by having students practice and develop imaginative problem-solving skills. Gallo notes that intellectual tasks must exercise students' skills in such areas as classifying, sequencing, identifying, and evaluating assumptions, and clarifying problems. Improved creative thinking, on the other hand, requires divergent thinking skills, such as sensitivity to problems, and perceptual and cognitive flexibility. Further, Gallo believes that by requiring students to relate new knowledge to past experience, and to transfer new knowledge to different contexts, teachers can help students integrate information in a meaningful way.

The author is Co-founder of the Critical and Creative Thinking Master of Arts Program, University of Massachusetts, Boston.

THE NEED FOR IMPROVED PROBLEM-SOLVING SKILLS

The most recent National Assessment of Educational Progress (1982) again documented the lack of conceptual understanding and problem-solving skills among students of mathematics in the United States. For example, only one-fifth of thirteen-year-olds and two-fifths of seventeen-year-olds correctly answered this question requiring estimation in a multiplication problem with decimals: "Estimate the answer: 3.04×5.3" (1). Often the memorization of mathematics procedures and formulas is substituted for logical problem solving, permitting successful computation skills to obscure the reasoning deficiency. For example, when students were asked to compute the exact answer to a similar decimal multiplication problem, almost three-fifths of thirteen-year-olds and more than four-fifths of seventeen-year-olds computed correctly. The pattern is consistent across the NAEP mathematics assessment: students compute accurately following given rules but fail to reason with numbers. In a recent issue of *Educational Leadership*, Marilyn Burns reports that "Elementary grade children spend an estimated ninety percent of their school mathematics time on paper-and-pencil computation practice, most often learning computation skills by rote"(2).

This chapter suggests a way of introducing the study of the metric system to students in the upper elementary school grades that develops and practices logical and imaginative problem-solving processes and the attendant personal attitudes and traits, while developing content knowledge and practicing computational skills. It outlines the teacher's role, the unit plan, and guides, and offers a detailed analysis of the way in which the unit develops critical and creative thinking. I begin by defining terms, identifying the components of teaching for thinking—cognitive processes, traits and attitudes, and social context. I list specific recommendations for practice related to each component and identify an exemplary feature of the metric unit.

Inspired and inspiring teachers have long cultivated in their students both reason and imagination along with content knowledge. For such teachers, much of the material here will seem familiar; for them, I hope it will provide a supportive example and a clarification of the structure and principles of such practice. For those who are newly embracing the goal of teaching for critical and creative thinking, I hope to provide a convincing rationale for such effort and a clear example to adopt for implementation or use as structural guidelines for developing other curriculum projects.

EDUCATING FOR CRITICAL AND CREATIVE THINKING

Cognition occurs in an intrapersonal and interpersonal context by which it is influenced in appearance and meaning. The consistent demonstration of complex cognitive processes requires the support and/or contribution of appropriate personal attitudes and traits. The cultivation of attitudes and traits is, of course, much influenced by classroom climate and general procedures (3). A discussion of each set of factors follows, with specific recommendations for practice.

Cognitive Processes

Improved critical thinking requires a focus on the development of refined discrimination in the convergent processes of observation, analysis, inference, and evaluation. Tasks exercising these processes call for the following:

- idea evaluation
- observing
- defining
- analyzing
- classifying, categorizing
- comparing, contrasting
- sequencing
- summarizing, generalizing
- pattern-proving

285

- inferring, interpreting
- elaborating, detailing a plan
- evaluating, assessing against articulated criteria
- identifying assumptions
- evaluating assumptions
- problem clarification.

Questions beginning with "How" and "Why" most often elicit reflective thinking.

Improved creative problem solving requires a focus on the development of divergent thinking skills: sensitivity to problems, fluency, flexibility (perceptual and cognitive), and originality. Tasks exercising these processes call for the following:

- question-generating
- idea, problem, design generating
- observing through all the senses
- hypothesizing
- predicting
- estimating
- synthesizing, combining
- problem-finding
- pattern-finding.

Questions asking "What if" elicit creative or imaginative thinking.

Several recommendations for practice are implied by this conceptualization; they appear in the list that follows. Other recommendations based on relevant principles of learning are also noted. In each case, a specific aspect of the Think Metric unit (which appears later in this chapter) is referred to as demonstrating the principle or strategy.

1. *Facilitate conceptual preparation.* Studies of comprehension, and memory indicate that new information is perceived as most meaningful and is best retained when it is related to prior learning. It is essential to ask students to recall, articulate, and focus relevant prior knowledge in order to enhance the meaningful acquisition and retention of new knowledge. In the Unit Motivation, students recall and describe ways in which they have measured with and without tools in order to identify and articulate general measurement procedures known and used.

2. *Facilitate purposive learning.* Learning proceeds most effectively in relation to a consciously held and ascribed-to goal. In the Unit Motivation, students measure with nonstandard tools in order to evaluate the utility and limitations of these tools, and to identify problems as well as the need for standard tools and their skilled use.

3. *Invite and model the organization of information.* Facilitate the development of concepts and relationships. First, avoid instruction of isolated facts; provide opportunities for connection-finding and association-building. Think Metric's interdisciplinary approach facilitates this. Second, structure information. Develop cognitive maps. When students have completed Acquaint Yourself activities, they generate and evaluate a cognitive map with teacher direction, such as the following:

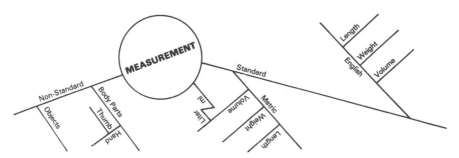

Third, organize information that is not hierarchical. Develop charts, graphs, and reference tools. See the Learn the Code chart. Fourth, have students put concepts into their own words, orally or in writing. See Develop Your Skill activities B, C, and D.

4. *Facilitate image-building* through visualization, drawing, developing models, and movements. See My Personal Metric Reference Sheet and art objectives of the Unit Overview.

5. *Facilitate the explicit use of critical evaluation procedures.* Generate, select, and prioritize criteria and principles. Impartially and systematically assess items against these procedures. Draw conclusions and generalizations. Assess assumptions. Use critical writing after such oral activities. See Develop Your Skill activities B2, B4, and D.

6. *Facilitate the development of executive processes and metacognition.* These processes produce awareness and conscious control over one's thought processes and over one's understanding or lack of it. First, use "think out loud" activities (4). See Develop Your Skill B2. Second, use double-entry journal writing with information from texts, films, and other sources (5). (See reference for sample form.) See Unit Motivation for example. Third, eventually, students can monitor their thought processes to be aware of when they are beginning to lose comprehension of a problem procedure or reading. (See Develop Your Skill C.)

7. *Accommodate learning style differences.* Develop, apply, and practice concepts in all four learning modes (see, say/hear, move/write, touch). See the variety in the learning center activities.

8. *Focus on questions.* First, use student-generated questions to structure inquiry and research, and discussion. See Unit Motivation and Inquiry Structuring. Second, use student-generated questions to promote student-led discussions of quality. Here students use study skills (*preview, question, read, study, test*) when they read on the history of measurement or other topics. See Science and Social Studies objectives. Students write three questions on the reading, beginning with How, Why, and What if. They write the answer to each question, consulting the text, and circle the preferred question. In a small group, each student takes a turn at leading the discussion, using the preferred question. Compare, contrast, and evaluate answers. Combine several answers into one fully elaborated answer after practice with this procedure.

9. *Facilitate transfer of learning to new contexts.* First, request the bridging of concepts and procedures to other subjects and settings. (For example, How can you use what you have learned about measurement procedures to improve your work in English? Your life at home?) Second, assign tasks that require the application of information and the invention of new information. See Spread the Word activities.

Social Context

Requesting and probing for complex ideation and independent risk-taking action requires the support of a psychologically safe environment with respect for persons, ideas, differences, and provocative questions (6). Several specific recommendations are as follows:

1. *Be sensitive to the threat and difficulty of the task. See failure as part of the learning process.* Reward honest effort, as well as success in students and in yourself. With humor, build a sense of community among students and for yourself with colleagues. Invite peer coaching for both. The Unit includes extensive pairing and cooperative work.

2. *Alternate error tolerances.* First, divergent thinking requires deferred judgment or a high tolerance for error; elicit a quantity of ideas including wild and silly ones. Apply and Invent activities as well as Spread the Word activities practice divergent thinking. Second, convergent thinking requires systematic and careful work. Be precise when evaluating ideas against criteria; be consistent in ap-

plying principles. Develop Your Skill B2, B4, C, and D focus on convergent processes.

3. *Have reasonable, high, positive expectations for all learners.* Teaching for thinking submits to the same influences as teaching for other goals.

4. *Invite active learning and varied responses to meaningful problems to elicit and sustain motivation.* For example, vary tone (playful/purposeful), structure (teacher-directed/student-led), tasks (question-generating/research), effort (short-range projects/projects requiring sustained, immersive inquiry and invention), and outcomes (evaluation of concepts/applications, invention with concepts). The unit as a whole attempts to demonstrate this recommendation.

Teaching for critical and creative thinking, along with content knowledge and skills, is demanding work. But it is also joyful and energizing to watch students grow in competence, self-governance, and commitment to complex problem solving. A growing body of empirical evidence supports the belief that test score gains are produced by such instruction (7). One recent example: Sadler and Whimbey report that in their holistic, remedial mathematics program, founded on six strategies included in this chapter's recommendations (teaching active learning, articulating thinking, promoting intuitive understanding, structuring courses developmentally, motivating learning, and establishing a positive social climate for learning), students improve. In fact, their students, who initially score at about the seventh grade level on standardized math tests, show an average improvement of about three years after only one semester's work (8). Take as a hypothesis, then, that teaching for critical and creative thinking in the recommended ways produces joy and achievement, and test it with your class now.

The following section of this chapter presents a specific application of incorporating thinking skills into a content area. I have chosen a unit on the metric system to show how problem-solving skills can be enhanced with appropriate instruction.

THINK METRIC

Unit Overview

Think Metric is an interdisciplinary unit focusing on the development of metric system content knowledge, skill in metric measurement, applications and invention with metric system information, and, importantly, enhanced reason and imagination.

It begins with a whole-class, teacher-directed lesson to facilitate conceptual preparation, to identify needs and goals, and to clarify the procedures (9). Most of the work is done by students working in pairs, in small groups, or independently at learning centers; it uses author-developed and commercial materials. The time required for implementation depends on students' age, ability, motivation, and skill in self-directed and contract-guided work (10).

The Learning Center work is organized into three general categories to be approached sequentially: Acquaint Yourself, Develop Your Skill, Spread the Word (11). Acquaint Yourself activities are designed to develop intuitive knowledge, or personal body referents for metric measures of length, weight, and volume. Here students also make measuring tools and assemble a recordkeeping book. In Develop Your Skill students do extensive work in estimating and then measuring items in each category, both in and out of class.

Mid-unit, working with a partner, each student does a content and procedure self-assessment and plan for improvement. Students develop and trade problems using metric measures, which require estimation before computation, thus producing their own practice problems (and answer keys), while developing idea and problem-generation skills. (Text problems can augment this practice if the teacher chooses.) Finally, with Spread the Word activities, students apply and invent with their information and skills. They develop imaginative ways to inform and educate others through writing, drama, music, and visual responses. The unit culminates with a whole-class, teacher-directed lesson in which students practice and summarize sound estimation and measurement procedures. They also share their new knowledge and skills, and imaginative products (problems, riddles, skits, writing, visual products, and work done with other classes or out of class).

The Teacher's Role

Planning. In teaching for thinking, the structuring of information and procedures to be learned is crucial, as is fostering motivated, self-directed work. This role requires the teacher to—

1. Identify and prioritize content and process goals and objectives. Be specific.
2. Identify the purpose of knowing these goals and objectives.
3. Distinguish between fact, concept, and procedure goals. Organize hierarchically. Develop cognitive maps.
4. Develop diagnostic procedures or devices.
5. Identify and sequence reasonable clusters of goals.

6. Develop or modify activities to stimulate the development of concepts, procedures.
7. Identify places where metacognitive, application, and invention activities are appropriate. (Think Metric was planned using these procedures.)

Implementation. While students are working in learning centers, the teacher has several important functions as facilitator and model. This role requires the teacher to—

1. Raise questions and encourage students to raise questions about the content and process of the work (for example, How might the way you are holding the tool be affecting your outcome?).
2. Use "wait time," several seconds of deliberate silence to encourage reflection and discourage hasty responses.
3. Encourage students to verbalize and reflect on their thought processes. Model discriminating listening and reflection.
4. Invite self-evaluation, and provide constructive evaluative feedback. Where needed, augment planned work with additional individual tasks, or subtasks.
5. Promote cooperation and commitment; support a purposive or playful tone, as appropriate to the task.

Learning Center Activities: Specific Guides

The Learning Center guides and worksheets are based on the unit objectives overview, or curriculum web.

Curriculum Web/Objectives Overview

Unit Motivation

Conceptual Preparation

Students *recall*, *articulate*, and *assess* prior successful and unsuccessful experiences with measurements using both standard and nonstandard tools in teacher-led discussion. *Problem-Finding, Problem Clarification* (See Nonstandard Measurement Recordkeeping Tool)

Students—

- *measure* the length of items using nonstandard tools.
- *compare* and *contrast* their results with those of a partner.
- *analyze* procedures needed for precise measurement.
- *evaluate* the utility and limitations of nonstandard tools; give *reasons*.

- *predict* problems and causes of problems.
- *self-assess* thought processes and procedures.
- *design a plan* for improvement.
- *analyze* the need for standard measurement devices and their own needs.
- *generate questions* about currently used tools and their development.

Information Gathering

Students—

- *view and analyze* a filmstrip on the history of measurement, including the development of the English and metric systems.
- *summarize* the development in a journal.

Inquiry Structuring

Students—

- *generate and categorize questions* under the headings:
  — What I Know About the Metric System
  — What I Think I Know
  — What I Need to Know.
- *combine questions* and use them as the basis of Learning Center activities, and to structure independent research and projects, and final evaluation.

Math

1. *Develop, compare*, and *contrast* nonstandard systems of measurement.
2. *Assess* utility, limitations of nonstandard tools.
3. *Develop intuitive knowledge of identified units* of metric measurement through direct sensory experience with measurements of *length* (millimeter, centimeter, meter), *weight* (gram, kilogram), and *volume* (milliLiter, Liter).
4. *Generate and evaluate cognitive map* to show the relationship of measurement concepts.
5. *Estimate* the length, weight, volume, and temperature of items, accurately using metric tools to *measure and compare* with *estimates*; identify problems, and revise procedures.
6. *Estimate* the solutions to metric number and word problems, *compute* solutions, *compare*, draw conclusions about personal skill growth in estimation or math reasoning.
7. *Generate number and word problems* using metric measures, *estimate* solutions, *compute*, *compare*, develop answer key for other students.
8. *Self-assess* math thinking and procedures after extended work.

9. *Record* accurately all estimates, measurements, procedures, and evaluations.
10. *Evaluate* math problems against articulated criteria.
11. *Categorize* items by length, weight, and volume through estimation and prediction.
12. *Make* and use two metric measuring devices.

Language Arts

Idea generating, evaluating, detailing a plan

Select two of the following activities:

1. *Develop* a maxim, slogan, riddle, rhyme, or joke and write it on the Metric Graffiti Wall.
2. *Write* a poem, verse, limerick, lyric to a song, or prose piece (dialogue, story, vignette).
3. *Develop a mime*, improvisation, or skit (Metricmatics) to inform or instruct about a fact or concept.
4. *Invent* or develop some new *words* to describe new concepts (Metricmatics) or some fanciful definitions for existing words.
5. *Read, analyze*, and *discuss biographies* of persons who developed or helped develop these and other measurement systems (Celsius, Fahrenheit).
6. *Identify* and use the prefixes *milli, centi*, and *kilo*.
7. *Role-taking*—develop a dialogue or skit that—
   a. presents at least three points of view on learning metrics.
   b. presents some information on the metric system from the point of view of an object (a meter stick, a calibrated beaker, a tree).
   c. presents problem solving or the life of someone who has contributed to the history of measurement.
8. *Assess* the characteristics of a good math problem; *generate criteria* and *assess* against criteria. Write a paragraph taking and *defending a position* using evidence.

Science-Health

1. *Measure* height, weight, and body temperature in metrics.
2. *Measure* and record the temperature of the room, the hall, etc.; *analyze* and *predict* the temperatures of other places.
3. *Read* and *analyze* an article on the use of the metric system in weather prediction and relate it to the above. (Optional)
4. *Identify* and gather articles and cartoons on measurement, and the metric system and its use; place in class scrapbook.

Social Studies (History)

1. *View, analyze*, and *summarize* a filmstrip on the history of measurement.
2. *Generate questions, read*, and *discuss* the origins of the different "standard" measurement systems around the world.
3. *Predict* future measurement needs and tools. (Optional)
4. *Work cooperatively* with classmates in pairs, small groups, and whole group.
5. *Inform* others outside the class about the metric system by wearing an advertisement (performing a social service).
6. *Problem finding*—develop and implement a survey to assess parents' knowledge of the metric system; *summarize* the results; *generate ideas* (brainstorm) for possible graphs, graph results. (Optional)

Art-Music*
Idea generating, evaluating, detailing a plan

1. *Design* and make a cover for the Metric Recordkeeping Book using printing, collage, tempera, or paper cutting.
2. *Design* and make one *"adornment"* (bracelet, headband, hat, vest, pendant) or *"advertisement"* (poster, bumper sticker, pennant) to inform and motivate others to learn metrics.
3. *Design* a cartoon and draw it on the Metric Graffiti Wall.
4. *Listen* to a record. *Develop* a nonstandard musical notation using metric measures to describe the lengths of the different sounds in the music.
5. *Sing* into a tape recorder the song whose lyrics or music you have developed.
6. *Design* an informative musical display of metric products, locate a site outside school (such as a library or hardware store) and display the products.

Unit Culmination

Content Review

Each student—

- *identifies* an item that serves as a personal reference point for the identified goal measures (mm, cm, m, gr, kgm, mL, L)
- *recalls* own height, weight, and temperature.

---

*Items 1 and 2 are required.

Problem-Solving ("Measuring Off" Contest)

Students—

- *estimate* measurements and *categorize* items into one of three categories such as the following:

< .5 m	.5 m	> .5 m
< 2 kg	2 kg	> 2 kg
< 11.	11.	> 11.

(Students can *generate the categories*.)

- observe individual students *measuring* each item *using the appropriate tool*.
- *summarize* sound estimation procedures and accurate measurement procedures.

Observation/Evaluation of Product Presentations

Students—

- *present* their imaginative products.
- *observe* and *evaluate* presentations.
- *self-assess* their own presentation, work, learning throughout the unit by reviewing, evaluating their folders of work, and writing a journal entry requiring assessment against criteria and planning for future work.

Learning Center Guides and Worksheets (12)

Acquaint Yourself—Introductory activities of metric measurement

A. Introduce yourself to the metric system by doing activities E, F, and G below using the materials provided.

B. Make *two* metric measuring devices: and (1) a 20-cm ruler, and (2) any other, on Making a Tool Sheet.

C. Complete My Personal Metric Reference Sheet.

D. Assemble your recordkeeping book. Record all Develop Your Skill measurements there.

E. *Length*
   1. Hold a centimeter cube between your thumb and index finger. Measure the first digit of your thumb and the nail on one finger, using the cube. How long is a cm? What part of your body is 1 cm long?
   2. Hold a decimeter, 10-cm rod, the orange rod, between your thumb and index finger. Place the rod on different parts of

your body to find an equivalent you can remember. How long is a decimeter?

3. Close your eyes and estimate the length of something placed in your hand. Measure it. Do this three times.

4. Using a meter stick, cut a piece of string 1 meter long. How long is it in relation to your arm, leg, torso? How long is 1 meter?

5. Estimate your height in meters and centimeters. Measure yourself with a wall chart. How tall are you? Record.

6. On a sheet of paper outline your shoe. Cut it out; fold lengthwise. Estimate the length of the fold or shoe in centimeters. Measure the fold. Write the length in centimeters on the back of the "foot." Place "foot" in the Metric Problems Box for future use. (Optional)

F. *Weight*

1. "Weigh" a paper clip (approximately 1 gram) in your palm. Weigh 10 more the same way.

2. To get a sense of weight in metric terms, weigh in your hands the items of stated weight in the Metric Center (soup, breadsticks, crackers). Close your eyes. Be able to distinguish new items placed in your hands weighing 1 g, 100 g, 500 g, and 1 kg.

3. Estimate your weight in kilograms; weigh yourself.

G. *Volume*

1. Pour 10 mL of water. Drink. How much is 10 mL? In the calibrated beakers, *look at*, *pour out*, and *fill up* 50 mL, 100 mL, 500 mL (1/2 L), and 1 L of water.

2. Estimate the volume of the teacher's coffee cup, your drink can, and three other items in mL. Measure the cup's volume using the beakers. How much is 10 mL, 50 mL, 500 mL, and 1 L?

Develop Your Skill

A. *Estimate* and then measure these self-selected items:

1. The *length* of five items—include something very large such as the height of the room, the length of the hall, or the perimeter of the elevator.

2. The *weight* of five items—include some pumpkins.

3. The *volume* of five items—how much water does our watering can, urn, or soft drink can hold?

4. *Record* your results in your record book as you work. Reduce to state in simplest terms (for example, 1,002 cm = 10 m, 2 cm or 500 mL = 1/2 L).

B. *Develop your own metric problems* working with a partner.

1. *Develop* five number problems (algorithms) using metric measures. *Estimate* the answers. *Discuss* your estimates, how you got them, and why you think they are correct. *Compute* the answers. See the teacher if you need help.

2. *Compare* your estimates and computations. *Analyze* why you were correct. Analyze where, if anywhere, you went wrong. How can you avoid making that error again? Record your plan.

3. *Develop* two metric word problems. *Estimate, discuss* (analyze), and *compute* as in #1. See the teacher if you need help.

4. *Analyze* and *evaluate* your work here by following the procedures listed in #1.

5. Place your problems in the Metric Problems Box. File the answer key.

C. *Estimate and compute* five problems from the Metric Problems Box working alone; self-assess your progress in estimating. Record. Place in the teacher's "Today's Work" box.

D. *Critique* problems from the Metric Problems Box with a partner.

1. Develop a *list* of characteristics of "good" math problems. These are criteria.

2. Assess each of three problems from the Metric Problems Box against this list of criteria. Which is the best/worst problem?

3. Write a paragraph on the characteristics of a good or bad math problem. *Explain* (justify) the *reasons* you chose these characteristics. Use examples of the problems you assessed.

E. *Apply and invent*—Do at least one of the items below.

1. *Metric Montage*—Estimate the dimensions and check your assessments of three items on the self-correcting montage. Add one or two items.

2. *Metric Graffiti*—Adapt or invent a maxim, riddle, slogan, or joke using metric measurements. Record it on the papered graffiti wall.

3. *Metric Music*—Listen to a record or recall a song you know well. Develop a nonstandard musical notation using metric measures to describe the *lengths* of the different sounds in the music. Develop new lyrics.

4. *Metric Poetry or Prose*—Using some of your experiences with metrics as starting points (combined with the titles or first lines posted if you like), write a poem, story, dialogue, or song.
5. *Metricmatics*—Develop a mime, improvisation, dialogue, or skit using one of your metric experiences as a starting point.

Spread the Word—Make one item in order to encourage the people you encounter to Think Metric, or to learn one metric fact or measurement.

A. *Adorn Yourself*—Design and make a bracelet, headband, armband, hat, vest, pennant, pin, ankle bracelet, or earring. Use any procedure you know (sew, braid, weave, model clay) or want to learn. See books in the art corner.
B. *Advertise*—Design and make a bumper sticker, window sign, poster, pennant, banner, or transparency. Use any materials in the art corner. See the teacher if you need help.
C. Wear A or advertise B for at least three days.
D. *Present* your products and projects after the "Metric Measure Off" contest.

THINK METRIC!   HAVE FUN!

Recordkeeping Tools and Worksheets

Nonstandard Measurement Recordkeeping Tool (diagnostic)
- Select a nonstandard measuring device for length.
- Identify six items in the room to measure. Include something very large and something very small.
- Measure each one carefully, using the device selected.
- Record the information requested below.
- Do the above tasks with a partner using his/her own device and recordkeeping sheet.

	Item	Part Measured	Tool Used	Dimension
1.				
2.				
3.				
4.				
5.				
6.				

Reflect on Your Work—With your partner, discuss and record your answers to the questions that follow.

1. Are your measurements precise? Why? Why not?
2. What procedures are needed to measure precisely? List. Be prepared to explain.
3. Compare your measurement of one or more of the same items.
4. What problems arose in the measuring activity? List. Why? Discuss.
5. What problems do you predict might arise from continued work with this device? List. Why? Discuss.
6. What other problems do you predict? List. Why? Discuss.
7. *Assess your measurement work.*

    *   List some ways in which you worked well in this activity.
    *   List some ways you want to improve in doing similar activities.
    *   How can you help yourself to make these improvements? How can your partner help you? Make a plan listing three things you can do. Circle the one you will do today.

My Personal Metric Reference Sheet

After doing the introductory activities, review your personal metric references by writing and drawing below.

Length	*Write or Trace*	*Visualize and Draw*

How long is a centimeter?
How long is a decimeter?
How long is a meter?
(You may attach something to the page here.)

My height is _____ m and _____ cm tall.

Weight

Visualize and draw a picture of an item to help you remember the weight of

1 gram
1 kilogram

My weight is _____ kg.

Volume   *Write or Trace*   *Visualize and Draw*

Visualize and draw a picture of an item to help you remember the volume of

10 milliLiters

A standard one-portion can or carton of my favorite drink is _____ mL. Draw and label in milliLiters.

Other

My normal body temperature is _____ Celsius.

The room temperature is _____ Celsius. It feels _____ (warm, tepid, chilly).

Sample Recordkeeping Book

LINEAR MEASUREMENTS*   MEASUREMENTS OF LENGTH

1. Record in this section all linear measurements as follows:
   A. Write down the *name* of the item you are measuring.
   B. *Estimate* the length. Record the estimate.
   C. *Measure* the item. Record the results.
   D. Express as meters. (Optional)

Example 1.   *The hall* outside Room 116, from double door outer frame to door frame of Room 116.

   Estimate: 12 m
   Measurement: 9 m,   50 cm   =9.5 m

---

*Develop a correlate for measures of weight and measures of volume with a logo for each. Color code (13).

LEARN THE CODE

The Code

milli	= 1/1,000		kilo	= 1,000
centi	= 1/100		*hecto	= 100
*deci	= 1/10		*deca	= 10

*The three important prefixes are *milli, centi,* and *kilo.* The other prefixes—deci, deca, and hecto—are used infrequently.

LENGTH: Fundamental Unit = *meter*

1 millimeter = 1/1000 of a meter
1 centimeter = 1/100 of a meter
1 kilometer = 1,000 meters

1 meter = 1,000
    millimeters
1 meter = 100 centimeters
1 meter = 1/1,000
    of a kilometer

WEIGHT: Fundamental Unit = *gram*

1 milligram = 1/1,000 of a gram
1 kilogram   = 1,000 grams
1 metric ton = 1,000,000 grams
(1 metric ton = 1,000 kilograms)

1 gram = 1,000 milligrams
1 gram = 1/1,000
    of a kilogram
1 gram = 1/1,000,000
    of a metric ton
(1 kilo = 1/1,000
    of a metric ton)

VOLUME: Fundamental Unit = *Liter*

1 milliLiter = 1/1,000 of a Liter
1 kiloLiter = 1,000 Liters

1 Liter = 1,000 milliLiters
1 Liter = 1/100
    of a kiloLiter

REFERENCES

1. Marilyn Burns, "Teaching 'What to Do' in Arithmetic vs. Teaching 'What to Do and Why'," *Educational Leadership* (April 1986): 34.

2. Ibid.

3. For a more comprehensive discussion of the concepts of critical and creative thinking and their relationship, see J. Passmore, "On Teaching to Be Critical," in *The Philosophy of Teaching* (Harvard University Press, 1980), and D. Gallo, "Empathy, Imagination and Reasoned Judgment," in *Thinking*, edited by J. Bishop, J. Lochhead, and D. Perkins (Hillsdale, N.J.: Lawrence Erlbaum Associates, 1986).

4. One thinking out loud procedure: one partner listens, identifies, describes, and records partner's strategies. Together they evaluate strategies, identify patterns of strength and need, and make a plan. Reverse roles.

5. A double entry journal might look like this:

Observations on Item Quotations, précis Interpretations	*Evaluations, Questions, Responses* Questions raised about text or one's understanding of text; address of questions, indentification of structure of work

6. For a fuller discussion of personal traits and attitudes, see D. Gallo, "Educating for Creativity," in *Thinking: The Expanding Frontier*, edited by William Maxwell (Hillsdale, N.J.: Lawrence Erlbaum Associates, 1983).

7. William A. Sadler, Jr., and Arthur Whimbey, "Teaching Cognitive Skills: An Objective of Higher Education," *National Forum* (Fall 1980): 43–46. See also a series of articles by Lillian C. McDermott, "Helping Minority Students Succeed in Science" *Journal of College Science* (January, March, May, 1980).

8. William A. Sadler, Jr., and Arthur Whimbey, "A Holistic Approach to Improving Thinking Skills, "*Phi Delta Kappan* (November 1985): 202.

9. Students not practiced at learning center work should participate in a second whole-class lesson designed to develop specific procedures for center work. A problem-solving approach should be used: "How can we help ourselves to learn well using learning centers and concrete materials? What procedures and techniques will be useful? Why? What should be avoided? Why?" Develop lists. Evaluate and prioritize items. Predict problems that might still occur. Generate and select solutions. Develop final, revised lists: "Working alone, I will...; working with a partner, I will... (I will avoid...—optional). Students copy procedures into math notebook and/or make a class chart for reference.

10. For able, independent learners, the unit may take as little as two weeks of daily classwork, with some activities done at home. For less skilled or less independent learners, for whom in-class work and teacher guidance are indispensable, the unit may take four to six weeks to implement in its entirety.

Modification is, of course, expected. Please be alert to retain all categories of activity (e.g., intuitive knowledge, estimation, measurement, application, and invention). See S. Kaplan and others, *Change for Children* (Glenview, Ill.: Scott Foresman, 1980), 22–24 for a "Step-by-Step Approach to Creating Learning Centers."

11. Martin Simon, "The Teacher's Role in Increasing Student Understanding of Mathematics," *Educational Leadership* (April 1986): 40–43.

12. (a) A Metric Learning Center Contract should be added as a cover sheet to guides and worksheets that are not included in the recordkeeping book. (b) To assist students to work accurately at centers (Linear Measurement, Measurement of Weight, Measurement of Volume), I suggest that center guides, etc., be color coded. Use one color for each kind of item; guides or direction sheets (white), personal reference sheet (green), linear measurement recordkeeping sheets (blue), weight recordkeeping sheets (yellow), volume recordkeeping sheets (pink). (c) Learning Center materials needed: standard metric tools of length (Cuisenaire rods, meter sticks, and tapes); weight (scales with 1 gr to 10 kg weights, metric body scale); volume (calibrated beakers, Liter bottles); temperature (Celsius body and room thermometers); lots of realia (here I use 1-gr metal paper clips, styrofoam cups, and soft drink cans; Liter soft drink and wine bottles; and apples, potatoes, and pumpkins of various weights); a commercial or teacher-made box of metric problem cards for evaluation.

13. See Note 12(b).

THE ART OF SOCRATIC REASONING

by Erling Skorpen

Erling Skorpen illustrates the process of instruction in dialectical reasoning. He provides a step-by-step analysis outlining the argument of Socrates' dialogue, Euthyphro, *in contemporary terms. As he proceeds through the analysis, the reader is presented with a series of definitions that are crucial to the argument: real, essential, and qualitative definitions. In each section, he explicates the text through a definition, a rationale, and questions for the student. By the end of the exercise, students will begin to reason both for and against a definition—they will understand the use of dialectical reasoning from both philosophical and pragmatic perspectives.*
The author is Professor of Philosophy, University of Maine, Orono.

INTRODUCTION

A Socratic *dialogue* is a philosophical conversation between two or more participants. It is related to *dialectic* defined as "the art of critical examination into the truth of an opinion." *Definitions* mark the key turns and transitions of such examination, and are prompted by the use of the *elenchus* or cross-examination. For even good definitions require refutation to promote the search for better ones.

Definitions vary in kind and purpose. Dictionary definitions are called *lexical*, and record ordinary word usage. But they also preserve the outcomes of critical inquiries termed *theoretical* definitions. The art of Socratic reasoning gathers ordinary into theoretical definitions of great insight each step of the way.

Like most ancient philosophers Socrates favored *real definitions* of natural objects and human activities, not *verbal definitions* of words we use or *nominal definitions* of our ideas about the world. Real definition is therefore the search also for *essential definitions* of the indispensable features of things we are defining. If church-going more than arm-wrestling illustrates religious conduct, for example, is it essential to religion? If not, what defines its essence?

These distinctions bring us to the difference between *qualitative* and *quantitative definitions*. $F=MA$ and $E=mc^2$ are quantitative but also theoretical definitions of a formal or abstract nature, and no one doubts that such definitions are crucial to modern science.

Not all definitions, however, need be numerical to have power. The qualitative we seek through Socratic reasoning also have power. Again, if

304

it should turn out to be more essential to religion's definition to treat others justly than it is to go to church, temple, or mosque, this could change the way we live. Qualitative definitions can also be *precising definitions*, leaving the demand for exactness to quantitative formulas.

We use the example of defining religion because that is the question of the Socratic dialogue called the *Euthyphro*. To exhibit the art of Socratic reasoning we shall outline the argument of this dialogue using modern terms and illustrations and taking other appropriate liberties. Yet we shall follow its pattern of definition faithfully throughout. The pattern begins a *definition by example*, proceeds to a *general definition*, and ends with a *definition by genus and difference*. It remains a classic pattern of real, essential, and qualitative definition for students and teachers alike. Professional philosophers still use it effectively.

For easy reference, in any definition what is to be defined is termed the *definiendum*, and what does the defining the *definiens*. The symbol "=df." is shorthand for "equals by definition." It differs from "=" in numerical equations.

THE ARGUMENT

FIRST STEP: This is to raise the question or to state the problem for critical examination.

The Question: WHAT IS RELIGION?

Note: Traditional religious practices include a host of related activities from church, temple, or mosque attendance and ceremony to holy day observances, parochial instruction, and political expression. The opening question invites investigation of what is crucial to religion itself.

Questions for the Student

1. What does it say about us that we ask questions about the nature of such things as religion?
2. Why do proper names like our own not lend themselves to questions of definition like "What is religion?"
3. If computers can be programmed to ask "What is religion?" would they ask it with the intent we do?
4. Is there any mystery why religious terms like "piety" can correspond to religious practices like prayer?

SECOND STEP: We begin with a *definition of piety by example(s)*. The examples we choose should be familiar and not so remote from the sphere of religion as to mislead us. We do not need many to put us on track. If some do

305

not come to mind right way, don't worry; it is part of critical thinking.

Definition: RELIGION =df. WORSHIP AND PRAYER

Rationale: Worship and prayer are widespread practices in the history of religious adoration and atonement for wrong-doing the world over. Taking walks or seeing films would not be obvious examples of religion—unless it turned out that the walks were prayerful and the films religious. Whatever else, it is hard to imagine that religion could be religion without some form of worship and prayer.

Refutation: Problems with the definition show up when we recall that worship and prayer can be practiced by racketeers whose criminal activities include extortion, drug-trafficking, even murder. Not everyone who worships or prays, therefore, may be truly religious. Another problem with this definition, however, is that it does not explain what worship and prayer have in common. Further, how do we tell them apart from such non-religious activities as playing the horses or the stock market?

Questions for the Student

1. Are ancient acts such as Abraham's willingness to sacrifice his son Isaac religious?
2. Why can't regular worship at a church, temple, or mosque make a mobster religious?
3. Is someone who sings in a church or temple choir out of sheer love of singing necessarily religious?
4. If someone goes to church, temple, or mosque services from habit or fear, is he or she truly religious?

THIRD STEP: A *general definition* should hit upon what it is that all religious practices have in common. Since all have historical roots, this might be thought to be religious tradition or custom. However, roots go back to divinely inspired founders and scriptures like Moses and the Old Testament. Should a general definition of religion mention this particular source? What, then, of Christian, Muslim, Hindu, or some other source? To escape

306

from such a predicament, we may assume that the divine speaks with one logically consistent voice, not many conflicting tongues, and that the various religious traditions are fallible. Just the same, we may have to explore more than one general definition.

Definition: RELIGION =df. ALL HUMAN PRACTICES PRIZED BY DIVINE REASON

Rationale: "Prized by divine reason" should be a common denominator of any religious practice we can rationally conceive of. It postulates very strong interest by the divine in at least some human affairs. In other words, the divine may be neutral about our race, color, or sex, but not about whether our different creeds cause hostility, harm, or death to one another. Religion, therefore, favors practices that enjoy the approval of divine (and human) reason.

Refutation: But are practices prized by divine reason because they are already religious, or do they become religious because they are prized by the divine? How does a friend you prize become prized by you? Don't you find in him or her qualities worth prizing such as humor, patience, loyalty, and other prizable traits? And isn't it only because of them that you prize your friend? Similarly, the divine must find in our religious practices yet-to-be-defined qualities that make them worth prizing.

Questions for the Student:

1. How do practices like infant baptisms, bar mitzvahs, and alms givings tell different religions apart?

2. Why do prayers for divine forgiveness arouse more human emotion than do studies of algebraic equations?

3. Does loving someone make him or her lovable, or is he or she lovable because of his or her traits?

4. If you think the divine prizes you, does it follow that the divine is concerned about the way you live?

FOURTH STEP: Religious prohibitions from murder and adultery to stealing and lying are very long-standing and make up a sizable list of actions not prized at all by the divine.

So there is no question that religion is concerned with justice and injustice or that this should now be taken into account.

Definition: RELIGION = df. ALL HUMAN PRACTICES THAT ARE JUST

Rationale: A religious practice like worship is quite unlike murder which is defined as unjustifiable homicide. If we fault someone's worship it may be that we take him or her to be a hypocrite or some other insincere person, not that worship itself is wrong. The same logic holds for other religious practices such as good samaritanism. Religious behavior always implies right conduct or just behavior even if misguided, as with earlier human sacrifices or religious crusades.

Refutation: The problem is not relating religion to justice, but that the class of just actions is larger than that of religious actions. Stopping for red lights and paying one's bills are right things to do but not necessarily religious obligations. How should they be distinguished from just obligations of a religious nature like good samaritanism? Religious actions are all meant to be just, but surely not all just actions are meant to be religious.

Questions for the Student:

1. Is someone who obeys all traffic laws to avoid fines or jail terms nevertheless justly motivated?
2. Can you be a good samaritan if you are helpful to others but still do not pay back your student loans?
3. As a law-abiding citizen are you still able to approve of abortion or euthanasia?
4. Can church schools consistently desire to be free of state school laws?

FIFTH STEP: Defining the essence of religious practices must proceed beyond *general definition* to *definition by genus and difference*. A genus (or class) contains more than one species (or sub-class). What distinguishes the members of these species (or sub-classes) from one another are their *differentiae* (or differences). (What, for example, distinguishes canines that are wolves from canines that are chihuahuas?) For religious actions that are just, there may be more than one likely *differentia(e)*.

Definition:	RELIGION =df. JUST PRACTICES THAT FEATURE SERVICE TO THE DIVINE
Rationale:	Church, synagogue, or mosque services pay homage to the divine through readings of tribute, prayers of gratitude, hymns of praise, offerings of thanks, and the like. These all show that worshippers care about the divine. They also place worshippers in a subservient position relative to the higher status of the divine. Our *precising definition* of religion in terms of service to the divine acknowledges all this.
Refutation:	This *differentia* implies that the divine served by human worshippers is needy, as are employers who hire servants or nations that draft their young. Does the divine benefit from human service, or can religious service transcend the idea that the divine has an ego in need of tribute, gratitude, praise, or thanks from lesser mortals?

Questions for the Student:

1. What kind of service is it if a male who can wash his own clothes asks his girlfriend or wife to do it?
2. Is there an analogy between entering a nation's service and becoming a servant of God?
3. What kind of need do you have if you must surround yourself with flatterers or yes-people?
4. Do church or temple services bear any analogy to the "service charges" on a bank loan?

LAST STEP (continued):	If not demeaning to religion or the divine, should the essential *differentia* explore the contractual nature of this relationship further?
Definition:	RELIGION =df. JUST PRACTICES THAT FEATURE AN EXCHANGE BETWEEN HUMAN BEINGS AND THE DIVINE
Rationale:	From time immemorial, religious practices depict the divine as responsive to human petitions and offerings. Devout prayers invoke blessings from the divine, and

309

	penitent wrong-doers are forgiven, redeemed, or in other ways saved from their injustices or trespasses. Such transactions between religious people and the divine make them different from just people who ignore the divine and face only human judges and judgments.
Refutation:	Religious exchanges between just human beings and the divine are often crass. Examples include not only pious people who think their wealth is reward for their righteousness, but even those who expect paradise in return for their pious existence. This does little justice to the human beings involved, and casts discredit upon divine intent. It also directs reason away from the rewards inherent in human lives well spent.

Questions for the Student:

1. Should good fortune in life be taken as a sign that one is on the good side of the divine?
2. Should the divine feel any obligation to reciprocate the good intentions of ordinary mortals?
3. If someone is just but not particularly religious, should he or she expect harsh judgment from the divine?
4. Why might a relationship to the divine enrich the life of an otherwise decent human being?

THE NEXT STEP:	We have learned a lot about being religious, but still miss the *precise differentia* that distinguishes just people who are religious from just people who are not. Plato who wrote the *Euthyphro* means for us to study Socrates' life to find the answer. When we ponder the *Apology, Crito, and Phaedo*, we discover that Socrates devoted himself to a just life by refusing, for example, to take part in any political wrong-doing. But he also devoted himself to the pursuit of self-knowledge by living an examined life at what he could do best. This was to encourage his fellow citizens to engage with him in dialectical inquiry into the truth of everyday opinions such as what religion really means. This got him into trouble, of course, but Socrates believed that he was following a divine imperative, and that if he did so justly, no real harm would come to him.

So if we define religion in the following genus and difference terms:

Definition: RELIGION =df. LIVING JUSTLY IN PURSUIT OF SELF-KNOWLEDGE

we perhaps arrive at a *precise and essential definition* of what we started out to define. For any thinking person can agree that the divine would prize people who fit the definition, and that those who fit do serve divine reason in a rational exchange. Anyone who lives justly in pursuit of self-knowledge, whether as a philosopher, as a plumber, or as something else, knows that this is all that the divine can ask of him or her, and that in return divine reason reassures that the only real harm that can befall him or her is his or her own injustice. Thus does our beginning attempt to define religion end in a theory of what life may be all about.

Questions for the Student:

1. Why may someone who steals money from you be hurting himself or herself more than you?
2. If you live honestly as a skilled worker always trying to become better at what you do, can the divine ask more of you?
3. Do you have to attend church in order to live with integrity and explore the talents you have?
4. Can Jews, Christians, Moslems, and others agree on the definition of religion as the just pursuit of self-knowledge?

AN EXERCISE

To help a student overcome his or her stage-fright in using the pattern of definition illustrated above, the following is offered.

The Question: WHAT IS LOVE?

Definition: LOVE =df. PUPPY LOVE AND PARENTAL LOVE

Rationale: Puppy love and parental love are recognized examples of love. The affection of puppies for one another originated in instinct and is reinforced by playfulness. Analogies allow the extension of "puppy love" to human adolescents. Parental love is also rooted in paternal and maternal protectiveness of progeny for most species. Among human beings, it is reinforced by mutual pleasure and long years of dependency until children are ready to "leave the nest."

311

Refutation: A disanalogy exists between the shorter-term puppy love and the longer-term parental love. However, it can be admitted that even brief romantic involvements can be intense, intimate, and genuine. More relevant is that the two examples may not illuminate other sorts of love such as marriage, friendship, or even the love human beings have for their gods, relatives, teachers, fellow men and women, pets, and their homes. What do all such examples have in common?

Definition: LOVE =df. AN ATTACHMENT OF SOME DURATION BETWEEN LIVING BEINGS FOR ONE ANOTHER AND THEIR THINGS

Rationale: Here the student may begin to reason both for and against the definition. Perhaps a different and more suggestive general definition will occur to him or her for scrutiny. The dialectic may then proceed to definitions by genus and difference, perhaps to distinguish loving from non-loving bonds—e.g., mercenary or conspiratorial—so that the essential difference can be identified.

Refutation: (The student should remember that dialectical reasoning is an art, not a rote. Many hypotheses may therefore be considered and rejected before hitting on the most promising ones. Quite possibly several sessions may be necessary to make further progress, as befits any art.)